PUERTO RICAN
VOICES
IN ENGLISH

The "Barrio" or Spanish Harlem is as much a spiritual enclave as an actual location. Far from Puerto Rico, and equally distant in spirit from mainstream American Culture, Puerto Ricans have tried to recreate the sounds and tastes of home in the middle of Manhattan. Photograph by Miguel Trelles.

PUERTO RICAN *VOICES* IN ENGLISH

Interviews with Writers

CARMEN DOLORES HERNÁNDEZ

Westport, Connecticut
London

Library of Congress Cataloging-in-Publication Data

Hernández, Carmen Dolores, 1942–
     Puerto Rican voices in English : interviews with writers / Carmen
Dolores Hernández.
          p.   cm.
     Includes bibliographical references and index.
     ISBN 0–275–95809–4 (alk. paper)   —   ISBN 0–275–95810–8 (pbk.)
     1. American literature—New York (State)—New York—History and
criticism—Theory, etc.   2. American literature—20th century—
History and criticism—Theory, etc.   3. Authors, Puerto Rican—
United States—Interviews.   4. Authors, Puerto Rican—20th century—
Interviews.   5. Puerto Ricans—United States—Intellectual life.
6. Puerto Ricans in literature.   I. Title.
PS153.P83H47   1997
810.9′8687295—dc21   96–53924

British Library Cataloguing in Publication Data is available.

Library of Congress Catalog Card Number: 96–53924
ISBN: 0–275–95809–4
          0–275–95810–8 (pbk.)

First published in 1997

Praeger Publishers, 88 Post Road West, Westport, CT 06881
An imprint of Greenwood Publishing Group, Inc.

Printed in the United States of America

Copyright Acknowledgments

All of the interviews in this book are published with the permission of the writers.

El Nuevo Día newspaper in San Juan and Miguel Trelles have given permission to use several of the
photographs in this book.

Extract from "An Essay on William Carlos Williams" (chapter 4) is reprinted from *Red Beans* by Victor
Hernández Cruz, Coffee House Press, 1991. Reprinted by permission of publisher and author. Copyright © 1991 by Victor Hernández Cruz.

"A man's gotta learn to respect a woman's dreams" (chapter 12) by Piri Thomas, *No Mo' Barrio Blues*,
reprinted courtesy of Piri Thomas.

Translation of the Ed Vega interview (chapter 14) is courtesy of Mercedes Trelles.

Dedicated to all those
who have felt the pain
of exile in any way

To my mother, Carmen Badillo Vda. de Hernández Usera,
whose courage, intelligence, and sensibility
have always been an example

CONTENTS

CONTENTS

ACKNOWLEDGMENTS

This book could never have been written without the generous and constant help of Antonio Luis Ferré, owner and publisher of *El Nuevo Día* newspaper in Puerto Rico. His understanding of the need for a book of interviews like this evidences the breadth of his interests and his vision of the cultural role of journalism in our society.

Many other persons at the newspaper were also helpful, among them José Luis Díaz de Villegas, editor of the Sunday magazine, and Benjamín Pastrana, Brenda Pérez, Rebeca Carrión, and Asunción Cantres Correa, who helped me with the computer.

I am also indebted to writers Ed Vega and Miguel Algarín. Vega was the first person to alert me to the importance of Puerto Rican writers in the United States, and Algarín helped me to get in touch with many of them.

Professor Marithelma Costa's help and suggestions were extremely valuable in organizing my material. She generously shared with me her experience with scholarly interviews and revised part of my manuscript. Professor Juan Flores, who directs the Center for Puerto Rican Studies at Hunter College, helped me to adjust my outlook and breadth. Writer Zoe Anglesey and Professor Arcadio Díaz Quiñones gave me useful suggestions in regard to publishing, and Professor Juan Gelpí helped me to define some concepts with more accuracy. I am also indebted to Professors Luce López Baralt and Yanice Gordils of the University of Puerto Rico for bringing to my attention pertinent material on, respectively, exiles and migrations.

Editor Nina Pearlstein made me very happy with her enthusiasm for my book.

Alexandra Vega and Ada Nurie Pagán, both students, were able assistants in transcribing some of the interviews.

Benjamín Bernier, Teddy and David Soto, computer experts, helped out when I thought I would never be able to get the manuscript ready.

Last, but certainly not least, my three oldest children, Miguel, Mercedes, and Carmen María Trelles, proved to be perceptive first readers of my manuscript, making me focus more clearly on my goals. To Miguel I am especially indebted for the photographs; Mercedes translated an interview from Spanish to English and gave me extremely useful suggestions; and Carmen María gave me a hand with the computer.

My husband, Luis Trelles, and my two youngest children, Luis Rafael and María Dolores, tolerated with humor and understanding the long hours I spent on this project and my absences from home.

All the writers interviewed were exceptionally gracious, helpful, and patient with my persistent questions.

INTRODUCTION

ABSENCE DOES NOT MAKE THE HEART GROW FONDER

Like so many other islanders, I was only peripherally aware of the English-language literary production of my fellow Puerto Ricans living in the United States. I had received part of my education in the mainland, and some members of my extended family were among the several thousand who migrated after World War II, settling primarily in cities of the Northeast, especially New York.[1] Nevertheless, neither in my readings nor as an assiduous student of Puerto Rican literature had I followed the writing of a sector of our population that had been forgotten, for all practical purposes, on the island and that was mostly known in the States through negative attention. Puerto Ricans were frequently mentioned there in relation to crime, violence, inner-city strife, and drug use. The image projected by *West Side Story* seemed to have become a standard.

Some names, however, began to crop up sporadically in my readings: Pedro Pietri, Miguel Algarín, Piri Thomas. Some books claimed my attention as a regular reviewer for San Juan's *El Nuevo Día* newspaper, especially Nicholasa Mohr's *Rituals of Survival* and Judith Ortiz Cofer's *The Line of the Sun*. At first I ignored them, not knowing where I was to place a hybrid kind of writing that did not belong (according to the traditionally accepted canon) to Puerto Rican literature, because it was not in Spanish. Nor did literature written by Puerto Ricans in English seem to have found a place in American literary tradition, being intimately connected in themes to a displaced sector of the Caribbean population. This writing also made liberal use of Spanish forms of expression: words, idioms, and whole sentences. Indeed, it did not seem to fit anywhere.

The writer I first read with some attention was Pedro Pietri. I was struck by the strength of his irony and the dynamic quality of his poetic images. I went on to Miguel Piñero's plays, their playful but savage bite, their strange perspectives. His and Miguel Algarín's anthology, *Nuyorican Poetry: An Anthology of Puerto Rican Words and Feelings* (New York: William Morrow, 1975), introduced me to the work of the poets, as did Efraín Barradas and Rafael Rodríguez's *Herejes y mitificadores: muestra de poesía puertorriqueña en los Estados Unidos* (San Juan: Huracán, 1980).

Soon afterward Ed Vega, a Puerto Rican novelist living in New York, called my attention to the quantity and quality of Puerto Rican writing in the United States. It was the beginning of a literary friendship that would encompass, with time, many more writers. In Vega's books I found fantasy and humor. His realism, in fact, became magic because of his works' incongruous settings and unexpected contrasts in cultural perceptions, as well as his depiction of the pathos of lives that were striving to become ordinary but were marked by an unrecognized, unresolved loss.

Those first readings were the thread that, when pulled, unraveled for me the fabric of U.S. Puerto Rican writing. With my curiosity piqued and my interest aroused by what I was reading, I kept on looking and found what could be described as a tradition: a notable body of work written by Puerto Ricans in the mainland. It helped document a migration that had gone from a trickle to a flood in the course of the century.[2] Names such as Arturo Alfonso Schomburg,[3] Jesús Colón,[4] Bernardo Vega,[5] and Clemente Soto Vélez,[6] among others, gave me a trail to follow up on the abundant production of the sixties, seventies, and beyond.

(BEST) SELLING A PUERTO RICAN STORY

In 1967 Knopf published a "shocking" book, full of four-letter words. It was narrated in the first person and was a novelized memoir depicting the life of a young black Puerto Rican delinquent who had grown up in the streets of Harlem, ending up in jail after attempting an armed robbery. Reviewed in many newspapers and periodicals, it was hailed as a major work and became a best-seller.

Piri Thomas's *Down These Mean Streets* was a narrative of fall and redemption. In a manner somewhat akin to Claude Brown's *Manchild in the Promised Land* (1965), which documents the lives of African Americans in an urban community, it revealed the feelings of a young boy besieged in the streets by prejudiced gangs, troubled at home because of poverty and racial distinctions (he was the blackest of five children), and displaced later within the white Long Island neighborhood where his parents had relocated, looking for a better life. Like *The Autobiography of Malcolm X as Told to Alex Haley* (1964) and Eldridge Cleaver's *Soul on Ice* (1968), in both of which rage against society is turned into a life of commitment to a cause after a stint in prison, Piri Thomas's book tells about the time served in Sing Sing and Comstock prisons. There he turned to both religion and a writing career. His story, told with both anger and grace, in a strangely poetic gutter English interspersed with Spanish, was compelling[7]: "The daytime pain fades alongside the feeling of belonging and just being in swing with all the humming kicks going on around. I'd stand on a corner and close my eyes and look at everything through my nose. I'd sniff deep and see the *cuchifritos* and hot dogs, stale sweat and dried urine. I'd smell the worn-out mothers with six or seven kids, and the nonpatient fathers beating the hell out of them. My nose would go a high-pitch tingling from the gritty wailing and bouncing red light of a squad car passing the scene like a bat out of Harlem, going to cool some trouble, or maybe cause some."[8]

His book established the parameters for a genre of novels set in the New York ghettos (Spanish Harlem, the Lower East Side) where most Puerto Ricans lived, spawning a tradition whose latest offshoot is Abraham Rodríguez, Jr.'s *Spidertown*. These novels document, narrate, and dramatize the life conditions of a marginalized sector of society that has had serious problems adjusting to an English-speaking white majority of Anglo-Saxon background. This sector has not only remained in relative poverty, but has also had to deal on a daily basis (having remained in great numbers in the inner cities), with crime, violence, and temptation in the streets. Its young people tend to suffer from a confusion between two conflicting codes of behavior: a Puerto Rican ethos that puts loyalty to the family before everything else and that also encompasses a male code of "machismo,"[9] versus American individualism and energetic enterprise (often subverted in the ghetto into criminal enterprise).

CROSSOVER GENRES

Within this genre of adventure and violence in the ghetto, certain variations have appeared, such as the ones contained in Judge Edwin Torres's novels, especially *Carlito's Way*. This writer, who is a judge of the Supreme Court of the State of New York and who has also written *Q & A* and *After Hours*, combines the Puerto Rican cum gangster novel formula with another kind of street delinquency from a far different time and place: sixteenth-century Spain. It was there and then that the picaresque novel developed. It is a curious type of narrative told directly, under an autobiographical guise, by a small-time delinquent whose aimless life (within a society of dramatic contrasts between rich and poor, whose imperialist schemes contrasted with the decaying conditions of its cities) takes him from master to master and often from licentious freedom to prison.

Suggestive parallels could be made between two hegemonic nations whose politics shaped a certain age (Spain was the dominant country in Europe during the sixteenth and seventeenth centuries, with a huge overseas empire that brought it immense riches, while the United States has become the major world power during our century), but whose economic policies gave rise to a floating population of unemployed drifters. There are also certain similarities regarding the respective situations of marginalized sectors of each society. They can be seen in such apparently diverse works as *Carlito's Way* and *El Lazarillo de Tormes* (generally thought to be the first picaresque novel, published shortly before 1554; author unknown). Whereas *El Lazarillo* reflects a sort of philosophical resignation to a life eschewing accepted conventions, in other novels of the genre—*Guzmán de Alfarache,* by Mateo Alemán (1599), and *El Buscón* (written between 1603 and 1604 by Francisco de Quevedo but published in 1620)—the tone gets progressively more disenchanted and cynical. That same tone permeates *Carlito's Way.* The first-person narration in this novel underscores a likeness that is also emphasized in the way the protagonist moves from one patron to another (in the form of gangs with diverse ethnic bosses). Savagely realistic—even naturalistic—in its portrayal of atmosphere, the picaresque novel seems a mirror in which the urban Puerto Rican novel of America in the twentieth-century can recognize itself.

Much as Edwin Torres grafts a different literary tradition from the American one onto his gangster novels, the young writer Abraham Rodríguez creates in *Spidertown* a Dickensian atmosphere, especially close to that of *Oliver Twist,* with its vivid portrayal of Fagin's school for crime. By giving us the world of present-day Puerto Rican junkies and pushers in the South Bronx, this author describes a highly structured community in which the young are instructed by a master (a small-time drug lord nicknamed Spider for his building-climbing abilities and who, not so coincidentally, loves to read *Oliver Twist*) and live according to his rules. Their society is a mirror image of the legitimate one in terms of hierarchies, differentiated tasks, progress, and rewards. It is just as exacting, competitive, and stressful as that other one, prompting Miguel, the main character, to wish for a less pressured life.

The picaresque novel and the Victorian one are not the only genres that "cross over" into Puerto Rican literature written in English in the United

States. Curiously enough, the *auto sacramental*[10] has exerted a fascination for Jack Agüeros. A poet and short-story writer, he is also a playwright who feels drawn to the moral implications of that medieval dramatic genre ultimately developed by Calderón de la Barca in the seventeenth century, although the meaning of morality and its scope is different for him from what it was in that century. Using allegorical allusions, he expresses moral and spiritual positions regarding tolerance, racial relations, and the interpretation of past historical events.

These "crossover genres" and others that may develop in the future may prove to be an enriching stimulus within American literature. There is a long tradition of such combinations within Spanish literature, where the first known literary works have turned out to be lyrical verses arranged in short stanzas tagged on at the end of Arabic or Hebrew poems called "moaxajas." Moreover, the famed Spanish mystical poets from that country's Golden Age of literature have been found to have more than a few points of contact with Islamic medieval mystics, whose works may have come to their attention through various channels, among them their transmission through the Arab minorities who remained in Spain after the conquest of Granada.[11]

POETS IN THE CITY

At about the time that Piri Thomas was publishing *Down These Mean Streets*, some New York Puerto Rican poets were expressing—in a different literary idiom—the incongruities between the myth of the American Dream and the harsh realities encountered by their families upon migrating. Drawing on a long, centuries-spanning oral tradition of poetry common in the rural parts of the island—where troubadours can still be counted on to improvise verses at a moment's notice in order to liven up a party, singing them to the strains of a cuatro (a guitar-like instrument) or a guitar—the poetic movement that was later to be called Nuyorican began as a performance. A poet like Jorge Brandon, who could be seen in the streets of the Lower East Side pushing along a shopping cart full of discarded odds and ends, made up verse—some very patriotic—as he walked through the streets. Another "foreign" tradition was thus made part of the New York City scene, which took to it with the fervor accorded to similar manifestations that originated from Southern black song and oral literature. The impromptu audiences responded enthusiastically, and the resonance of their poetry quickly expanded beyond specific neighborhoods as the poets—among them Miguel Algarín, Pedro Pietri, Miguel Piñero, Lucky Cienfuegos, Sandra María Esteves, Bimbo Rivas, and Jesús Papoleto Meléndez—wrote down and published their work.

These poets were in the right place at the right time. New York during the late sixties and the seventies was a hotbed of protest against the Vietnam War and of activism for civil, racial, and feminist rights.[12] It had also just been through the literary commotion occasioned by a group of writers who exhibited a contempt for conventions—including those in the sexual sphere—and a profound dissent in relation to established society—which they dubbed materialistic and conformist—and who denounced the dominance of the military-industrial complex which seemed to have driven the country into the Korean War. They also exhibited considerable enthusiasm for altered mind-states provoked by drugs.

They were the writers known as the Beat Generation (so-called because of the connotations of the word *beat* (down and out, beat up).[13] Among them were Allen Ginsberg, Jack Kerouac, William Burroughs, Gregory Corso, and John Clellon Holmes. They were committed to a "New Vision" in art, especially literature. They drew on their experiences of bohemian city life, writing about jazz musicians and Times Square junkies. In various genres, they projected a mood that could be described as one of cultural disaffection with the prevailing, central currents of thought and the presumed moral values of the United States. Many experiences that had until then been alien to American literature became part of this movement: homosexual sex, drugs, the low street life of a sector of society.[14]

In introducing these themes in literature, the Beats had set the stage in which the young Puerto Rican–New York poets would appear. The fact that they lived in New York was, then, central to their poetry, and they fittingly adopted the name *Nuyorican* that referred both to that city and the Puerto Rican origins that gave them their particular perspective.[15] The city had opened the way for them to develop their own expression: they could relate directly to the Beats' literary scene. But unlike Burroughs (who was a Harvard graduate), Ginsberg, or Kerouac (who attended Columbia), the Puerto Ricans were "the real thing." They were literally as well as figuratively "beat up" by their place in the city's lowest socioeconomic rungs as the children of poor, uneducated immigrants who knew no English. Their protests took a literary turn, but they referred to a concrete situation. They also found America's established values wanting, but not because of surfeit or exhaustion, but because of privation. It was a time of solidarity against the perceived "enemy." Of the group, Pietri was sent to the Vietnam War and Miguel Piñero landed in prison. Besides being a poet, Piñero was also a playwright who won an Obie and the New York Drama Critics Best American Play Award for the 1973–1974 theater season for his prison drama, *Short Eyes*.

Nuyorican poetry used the words of everyday speech among Puerto Ricans in New York, writing down what was popularly known as "Spanglish" but can be more aptly described as "code-switching." It is the back and forth shift between English and Spanish, using words and phrases of one and the other within a framework that is predominantly English. It also entails the juxtaposition of two distinct cultural sets of references implicit in the respective languages, both of them highly developed and of European origin. They used it to their poetic advantage, "playing" one language against the other in plentiful puns and metaphors. Their themes were also commonplace for Puerto Ricans: the frustrations of daily life, the sting of prejudice, the incomprehension of bureaucrats, the inadaptation to life in the city. Like the Beats, they also wrote highly erotic poetry, either heterosexual or homosexual, and dealt with the culture of drugs in their poems.

And just as Spanish Harlem—*El Barrio*—had become identified with the group of Puerto Rican novelists already mentioned, the Lower East Side (dubbed *Loisaida* by Puerto Ricans, loosely following the Spanish pronunciation of the name) became the place where *Nuyorican Poetry* was born. In 1972 the poets had begun to meet in Miguel Algarín's apartment on the Lower East Side to read their work. Soon that space was too small. The Nuyorican Poets Café opened in a small locale on East 6th Street. It quickly became a gathering place for the poets and their ever larger audiences. The popularity of the place was helped, of course, by the fact that writers like Allen Ginsberg and William Burroughs were often to be seen at the Café, as was also the black playwright Amiri Baraka.

Plays began to be performed there on a regular basis besides poetry readings. In 1980 the Café moved to 3rd Street but closed three years later to reopen in 1989. Since then, it has become a cultural haven not only for Latino poets but for those from all ethnicities and persuasions. The well-attended weekly poetic competitions (called "poetry slams"), are broadcast on the last Saturday of every month to Tokyo, Chicago, and San Francisco. Miguel Algarín has widened both his aesthetics and his audiences, becoming ever more universal.[16]

Other poets who were not among the original Nuyorican group share some aspects of their aesthetics in terms of language and poetic rhythm. Most of them speak Spanish at home; it is the language of feelings and affection. In contrast, English has been learned at school and in the streets. Many of them claim, however, not to have sufficient command of literary Spanish to write in it. For some, to write in English seemed to signal a surrender of their cultural personality. Thus, *Spanglish* seemed the solution because it was the language of the Puerto Rican community, both in the

Lower East Side and in El Barrio. They also strove to express through it a resistance to a norm or standard imposed by the two "uncontaminated" groups: the Spanish-speaking island writers, seen as an elite who defended that language as a symbol of the nation, and the English-speaking writers of mainstream United States literature. Neither of those languages by itself could transmit the experience of the Puerto Rican migrant in New York. Code-switching thus became a response to a sociocultural situation.[17] In the introduction to his first anthology, Miguel Algarín writes: "The poet is responsible for inventing the newness. The newness needs words, words never heard before or used before. The poet has to invent a new language, a new tradition of communication."[18]

STAYING ALIVE

Tato Laviera has emphasized the role of the poet as a recorder of a community's experience. In his book, *La Carreta Made a U-Turn*, he writes that as a poet, his purpose is to document the life of his people: *I am nothing but a historian. . . .* His poetry is an affirmation of Puerto Ricans in the United States as neither wholly American nor Puerto Rican—nor even Nuyorican—but AmeRícan, as reads the title of another of his books.

Based on an intuition born out of a cultural substratum, this is a role assumed by Puerto Ricans who, like the narrator of the stories in the *Arabian Nights*, write "to forestall death."[19] Their writing is an affirmation of individual and collective survival. It is born of the pressure to keep on being distinct, to record the life of a forgotten community, marginalized within a host country that has refused to take into account its particular experience within its accepted repertory of images. It is a community that has also been forgotten in its society of origin, which has obliterated their memory in the context of daily life. In a way, this situation has literally driven them into writing. Paradoxically, their American experience, in effect—the *American Dream* gone awry—may have helped them become the important writers they have come to be, relevant both to the multicultural experience in the United States and to the exemplary expressions of distinctiveness within a Metropolis that has not swallowed them, as opposed to the isolated culture of the island itself.

It is fascinating here to posit a historical reverse parallel that may be found in the literature of the last Muslims in Spain, also called "moriscos." Rejected in the place where they had been born and raised and unable to adapt to the Arab world to which they did not fully belong because of their hybrid experiences, some also turned to writing as a way of surviving. Luce López Baralt has written: "precisely out of the cryptomuslim's troubled identity came an unexpected literary creativity. The underground moriscos took to the task of urgently trying to preserve from oblivion their rich cultural heritage, and, in the very process of rewriting their classical literature 'del arabi en aljamí'—from Arabic to Spanish in the Arabic script—they ended up re-inventing themselves as authors and readers."[20]

Their rapidly changing new environment was another important stimulus for Puerto Rican writers in the United States. "Nobody was writing down these experiences," says Judge Edwin Torres. Silence, in this case, could be equivalent to nonexistence, oblivion, and forgetfulness because there would be no other record of the impact of their lives and feelings and of the identity that they were collectively forging. Their writing gives a widespread voice to a people at the fringes not only of U.S. but also of island society. Historically, in Puerto Rico writers as a rule had until then belonged to the bourgeoisie with access to the means of intellectual and artistic production (universities, libraries, learned societies, some amount of leisure, editorial possibilities). Most of the Puerto Ricans who began writing in the States during the sixties and seventies (and all those interviewed in this book) have a working-class background with little or no academic tradition in their families. The overwhelming majority have been the first generation to be college-educated. Some are self-taught.

Many of their experiences were unique. When Victor Hernández Cruz writes about a journey in time as well as in place, he is aptly describing what it must have been like to go from a backwater little town in the center of the island of Puerto Rico in the 1940s and 1950s to the center of New York, a city at the height of its power and influence. The shock of such a change could be devastating, especially when we consider that it was compounded by language difficulties and by enormous differences in climate, landscape, and social mores. The documentation that some of this writing provides about the encounter between two such different stages of development is invaluable, since the experience may never be repeated again in quite the same terms. No matter how many Puerto Ricans migrate now to the mainland and no matter where they come from, the island's industrial development during the last fifty years and its wealth of communications have turned it into a country aware of what is happening in the rest of the world, and particularly in the United States.

WOMEN, WOMEN EVERYWHERE

One aspect that was not amply "documented" at first in the New York–Puerto Ricans' creative literature of the sixties and seventies was the women's perspective. Whereas young males were constantly exposed to violence in the streets of the ghetto, women's lives were subject to another kind of oppression. They were doubly invisible, both because they came from a segment of society that had been marginalized by poverty and ignorance and also because their roles were circumscribed to the home by male dominance within their community. Even when they were heads of families and worked outside the home, their need to support and care for their children kept them from taking part in artistic and social projects. Therefore, their range of both experience and action has been different from that of men. Rather than being the direct subjects or objects of street violence (although they have been victims of the domestic variety), they have often suffered its after-effects.

Sandra María Esteves in her poetry and Nicholasa Mohr in her novels and short stories were among the first Puerto Rican women to become successful writers. Esteves was the most visible—if not the only—woman among the Nuyorican poets. Using the Nuyorican emphasis on colloquialism and its continuous references to a specific context, she explores the conflicting identities of a Latino woman within both the marginalized Puerto Rican community and North American society as a whole. Poems like her *María Christina* express that conflict (and its resolution: found wanting by another Puerto Rican woman poet, Luz María Umpierre, who replied to what she thought was the expression of a subservient role in another poem titled *My Name Is Not María Christina*). Other Esteves poems, such as *From the Commonwealth*, express a greater resistance to being subservient to the prevailing Latino concept of culture.

Today, however, a numerous group of women poets—the aforementioned Luz María Umpierre, Giannina Braschi, Gloria Vando, Magdalena Gómez, Rosario Morales, Aurora Levins Morales, and Judith Ortiz Cofer, among others—are creating a strong body of poetry in different styles, themes, and emphases. Their works mirror the complex issues involving race, gender, nationality, and migration.

Other women who write prose have striven to overcome their invisibility. Many seem to prefer the autobiographical novel, or *bildungsroman*, which places the feminine subject at the center of the action, thus overcoming its marginality.

Nicholasa Mohr was the first to document immigrant Puerto Rican women's lives in a semiautobiographical mode in *Nilda* (1973), a novel about a girl who grows up in the Barrio within a hard-working lower middle-class family. The gently developing story line follows Nilda's growing consciousness of family economic hardships and the disruption of traditional ties. A different street culture is seen encroaching within the atmosphere of the home. She becomes conscious of that difference while being kept somewhat shielded from the turbulence of the first line of confrontation taking place outside the apartment, the school, the summer camp.

Recent novelized memoirs or semiautobiographical novels by Puerto Rican women in the States have established a continuity of sorts with Mohr's *Nilda.* In *The Line of the Sun,* Judith Ortiz Cofer—who lives in Georgia—develops two parallel stories. On the one hand, there is a somewhat mythical Puerto Rico constructed out of family tales and folklore, with a family black sheep at its center. On the other, there is the young girl growing up between a Latino household and a typical American education in Paterson, New Jersey. The book reclaims the unusual past of the first part for an American girl who is in the process of being acculturated to a different way of life than that of her forebears.

Another narrative, avowedly autobiographical, also has a young feminine protagonist, this time in a rags-to-riches story. Negi, in Esmeralda Santiago's *When I Was Puerto Rican* starts out her life on the island in a rural community. The deteriorating relationship between her parents determines her mother's move, with all her brood, to the States. There they all have to come to grips with the wider social issue of discrimination before attaining one of the biggest rewards the United States has to offer: a college education at prestigious Harvard University.

All is not unconditionally well after that goal is reached, however, in a reversal of the usual trajectory of the American Dream narrative. Scholastic achievement and financial independence, American-style, may seem to pave the road to fame and fortune, or at least to full integration within American society, but they also exact a price. Negi's goal is only achieved, it seems, at the expense of a profound uprooting and an implied break from her origins as indicated by the past tense used in the title and the nostalgic tone of the prologue.

Esmeralda Santiago's latest novel, *América's Dream,* though not a memoir or an autobiography, recreates circumstances that often affect women's lives. América is isolated in her job as a maid with a Westchester County family, where she has gone after fleeing from an abusive lover. In a sense, the action mirrors the wider Puerto Rican experience. While seeking escape from an oppressive situation, a person or a group may find a life of isolation that may cripple them emotionally if they are unable to come to terms with it.

OF RACE AND RACISM

One important aspect of Puerto Rican writing in the States has to do with racial considerations. Present in Piri Thomas's and in Tato Laviera's works (they are both black men), race and its implications are also central in Louis Reyes Rivera's poetry. In his works he emphasizes the common historical, cultural, and literary roots of Antillean and American people, with African ascendancy as the source of similar experiences, rhythms, and aesthetic considerations. Rivera is also aware of the nuances of racism, from the Caribbean variety (which appears to be subtler and less aggressive, but is nevertheless present and limiting in the social and professional fields) to the North American one. If it is all part of the same situation of injustice and oppression, then "black" poetry comes from the same tradition, be it written in English or in Spanish. Louis Reyes Rivera points to similar word rhythms and themes in Caribbean and in North American black poetry. It was the Harlem Renaissance which first seemed to point along this way. Writers Claude McKay, whose book of poetry, *Harlem Shadows,* was one of the first literary successes of the Harlem Renaissance, and Wilfred Adolphus Domingo were born in Jamaica, as was also Marcus Garvey. During the early twenties, Garvey galvanized African-American political sentiment in the United States, thus setting the stage for an increased racial cultural consciousness that was simultaneous with a burst of literary production. Langston Hughes, on the other hand, went to Cuba in 1931 and became acquainted with Afro-Caribbean poetry. He translated many of Nicolás Guillén's writings into English. [21]

Both Louis Reyes Rivera's and Tato Laviera's poetry is indebted not only to Afro-Caribbean poetry and to the Négritude movement[22] but also to African-American poets like Ishmael Reed and Imamu Amiri Baraka (LeRoi Jones). Baraka used his writing as a political instrument and founded the Black Repertory Theater of Harlem, with which Sandra María Esteves was closely associated. In this way, Baraka brought together the *Nuyorican* and "black" aspects of Puerto Rican poetry in the States, both of which were entirely open to include different ethnic responses to the challenge posed by the New York type of North American experience.

Not all Puerto Rican writers in the United States focus on race or gender. The experience some of them mirror in their writings can also be seen as a variant of a wider North American experience by shifting the emphasis from the particular ethnic concerns of Puerto Ricans to the way this experience relates to those of other groups. Jack Agüeros' stories in *Dominoes* strive to portray the Puerto Ricans within the wider panorama of the city and its racial and ethnic multiplicity. His characters are not so much typical as common, in the sense of men and women who are well adjusted within an already established sector of society that may not be central but is never-theless accepted. They sometimes shun—as Max Vázquez does in the wonderful story, *Horologist*—any protagonism that may single them out as spokespersons or representatives of their particular group, taking them out of their settled routine of work. Yet their difference is always there, lurking in the background and beneath the surface, waiting to erupt at a provocation (as in the title story) or a temptation (as in *Horologist*). Normality may not be as normal for Puerto Ricans in the States as for other, more established groups.

Many of those who appear in Ed Vega's short stories (especially in *Casualty Reports*) have also subdued their differences and appear to have fully adapted to the society in which they live and work. In this case, however, the differences do not so much erupt as implode inside of them in the form of a sudden consciousness of irreplaceable loss.

On an aesthetic plane the difference is played up in the stories of Vega's book, *Mendoza's Dreams*. In some of these stories, New York turns into a surreal city in the process of trying to deal with people who have another cultural frame of reference from that which is the organizing principle of a society. The space between stereotype and expectation becomes the characters' field of action. They are thus able to subvert and turn to their advantage the blind spot society has toward their distinctness. Mercury Gómez, in the story that bears his name, creates a flourishing messenger business by using to his advantage the physical stereotyping of his ethnic group. Vega's work examines prejudices and conventions on both sides of the cultural divide and plays each side against the other.

BETWEEN REALITY AND MYTH

Where did these writers find their models? What stimulated them to resort to the written word as a form of expression and communication?

The pervasive influence in their work is that of the oral tradition, which may have been received by direct means, such as the telling of family stories and traditional lore or through the influence of the radio, which many refer to as crucial in their artistic development.[23]

Music—popular Puerto Rican music, which was recorded to a significant extent in New York during the thirties and forties[24]—is also an influence (and not only Puerto Rican music, but all kinds of Latino and North American music).

Some of these writers are the sons and daughters of people uprooted in Puerto Rico's "Industrial Revolution," whose parents had strong country roots and were thus familiar with the troubadour tradition of improvised verse.[25]

This literature, therefore, was born from varying stimuli within the context of a Puerto Rican immigrant community that seemingly provided no models for the written word. When Abraham Rodríguez was young, a teacher told him: "There's no such thing as a Puerto Rican writer." Pedro Pietri thought that blacks and Hispanics didn't write books. (He discovered otherwise when he came across García Lorca while working in the Columbia University library reshelving books.) Nevertheless, they did come into contact with books and learning in many ways which had to do with the educational opportunites they found in the States. Moreover, a city such as New York, with its multiethnic, multiracial population, made differences in culture and in levels of technological advancement much more palpable than they had been on an island which, until the fifties, was mostly agrarian and had a fairly homogeneous population. Literature was a venue that seemed apt to express their contradictions and frustrations (especially, as we have seen, after the Beats turned to it in protest). Their situation also suggested themes that seemed to be begging to be put into writing: the contrasts between present reality and past memories (or myths).

For all of them, the island is a problem both in itself and in relation to the society in which they find themselves. Some (like Abraham Rodríguez) have a love-hate relationship with Puerto Rico and look back in anger and disappointment; others (Esmeralda Santiago, Judith Ortiz Cofer) look back with some degree of sadness; and still others (Ed Vega and Victor Hernández Cruz) mythologize the island as a lost paradise from which many were forcibly ejected.

Some coined the term *Nuyorican* to describe Puerto Ricans *in* and *of* New York. They embraced their present situation but kept alive the memory of where they had come from. Not all of them favor being called *Nuyoricans,* nor are they all now in and of New York. With increasing frequency, Puerto Ricans have moved out of that city and into others, settling in sizable communities.[26] They have thus constituted a kind of "floating island," a culture that does not depend so much on a geographic location as on a shared horizon of references. This culture deals not only with common origins but also with perceived differences that come to the fore only when they are far from the original "home" and put into direct contact with a reality perceived as alien. This phenomenon, of course, is not exclusively Puerto Rican or even Latino. Migratory groups worldwide are conforming geo-cultures that, more than geo-nations, define them.[27] North Africans in France; Indians and West Indians in Great Britain; Turks in Germany; even the Dominicans who flock illegally to Puerto Rico; and, of course, the Chinese in a great many places are coexisting without melting, and their artistic productions (literary or otherwise) are generally distinct from a main, internationalized, Westernized current of canonic art and literature.

Yet second-generation Puerto Ricans in the States (or even these of the first generation), are already different from those who live on the island. Even the term *Puerto Rican* can have another meaning in the mainland. It may simply be an expression of a distinctness within the United States with no specific reference to the island, or a sociopolitical position, which in the past has been equated with radicalism (as exemplified, for instance, in the organization of the Young Lords, active during the seventies).

Writers become especially relevant in such a situation. They must help the nascent community to re-imagine itself through new perspectives. Having reclaimed a distinctive past through their texts, they must define, in imaginary terms, their present and project the future. Their position is two-edged. It often applies to the island of origin the critical stance to which those who have championed a cause through thick and thin are entitled. They may see more clearly than those who are immersed in Puerto Rican society the changes that have occurred and the transformations that are taking place. The close contact with other cultures has given them a breadth of experience difficult to attain within insular confines. They are able to take from many and to give back. This could be a step toward the *mestizaje*[28] which in nations with a Hispanic heritage has seen the fusion of races, cultures, and traditions (with plenty of problems, to be sure) or a broader comprehension of a hybrid kind of society where contact and conflict result in a dynamic culture. The United States' Puerto Ricans are at the cutting edge of a linguistic and cultural frontier between the island and the mainland, crossing over it continuously. Their experience may be immensely valuable for all involved. As Homi Bhabha has written:

a range of contemporary critical theories suggest that it is from those who have suffered the sentence of history—subjugation, domination, Diaspora, displacement—that we learn our most enduring lessons for living and thinking. There is even a growing conviction that the affective experience of social marginality—as it emerges in non-canonical cultural forms—transforms our critical strategies. It forces us to confront the concept of culture outside *objets d'art* or beyond the canonization of the "idea" of aesthetics, to engage with culture as an uneven, incomplete production of meaning and value, often composed of incommensurable demands and practices, produced in the act of social survival."[29]

WHATEVER HAPPENED TO THE MELTING POT?

Some of the writers interviewed for this work were taken by their families as children to the States (e.g., Miguel Algarín, Pedro Pietri, Victor Hernández Cruz, Ed Vega, and Esmeralda Santiago). A fairly equal number (Piri Thomas, Edwin Torres, Abraham Rodríguez, Sandra María Esteves, Nicholasa Mohr, Jack Agüeros, and Louis Reyes Rivera) were born in New York, to one or both Puerto Rican parents. This circumstance entails a further interest. What makes that second generation retain a distinctive—an affirmative—Puerto Rican identification? Why the resistance to melting away in the famous pot?

Some writers, like Ed Vega, allude to race as the reason why the Puerto Ricans will not assimilate fully into the American mainstream. (They would have to identify themselves as black or white. Since many of them are not, in fact, white and since to be identified as black would entail a considerable amount of prejudice, they prefer to remain Puerto Rican.)

According to Esmeralda Santiago, since Puerto Ricans are already U.S. citizens, there is no need to make any further effort to blend in. The cake can be had and eaten at the same time.

A generalized view is that the frequency and ease with which Puerto Ricans go to and from the island to the mainland constantly renews their contacts with their "roots" and keeps alive the hope of returning. (Many do, in fact, return: among those interviewed, Victor Hernández Cruz has returned to his native town of Aguas Buenas.)[30]

There is yet another aspect of this situation. Far from "melting," Puerto Ricans—and, indeed, Latinos in general—have made of the United States a place of encounter, an equivalent of a nationally unaffiliated *locus* (amoenus?) where they can recognize each other as more equal among themselves than they are with their "hosts." Moreover, for Caribbean writers, the United States has become an equivalent of what Europe (especially Paris and Barcelona) was in the sixties for the Latin American ones who initiated the so-called "boom."[31]

THE ISLAND STRIKES BACK

How does Puerto Rico relate to these writers? It has, for the most part, ignored them. Save for a few scholars who have studied and anthologized their writings (mostly their poetry), a void has surrounded their texts, the immense majority of which are not even translated.

The main reason for this is that they write in English. Spanish is not only the language commonly used in Puerto Rico, but it has also become a symbol of the island's national identity, in conflict with what is traditionally considered—especially by an important intellectual and artistic elite—the United States' encroaching cultural imperialism. As Nancy Morris has written: "In the early twentieth century, as the United States overhauled Puerto Rican institutions by fiat, Puerto Ricans' sense of difference was reinforced, and so were their opposition to U.S. domination and their attachment to symbols felt to be under attack. Language is paramount here. . . . Throughout the century, language has both engendered opposition and provided an excuse for it."[32] Within this context, which directly affected the class from which most writers emerged, literature has traditionally been assigned the mission to preserve linguistic integrity and purity. Thus there is little room for English-speaking and -writing Puerto Ricans in the traditional cultural circles, no matter how passionately they also might resist assimilation into the North American reality.[33]

Their language represents a problem that not many people know how to face. The easiest way out is simply to ignore their existence, developing a blind spot toward this literary production . Although this attitude is changing, especially among the younger intellectuals, many of whom have been educated in the United States, the consensus is still against an English-language Puerto Rican literature. There is, however, a growing perception that although the preservation of an endangered language is important for a colonized people, there is also danger in "the fixity and fetishism of identities within the calcification of colonial cultures."[34] Stateside developments in politics and the arts are now being seen as crucial for Puerto Rico's future. Responses are required, not just the apparent indifference or passive resistance to colonial pressures.

The influence of stateside Puerto Ricans must be acknowledged on both island and mainland as part of the continuous transactions that culture must engage in if it is to endure as a living, dynamic force that inflames and inspires a society. To be closed to new experiences is a neoconservative stance "associated with a past that is no longer recoverable except by denying or somehow downgrading the lived experience of those who, in Aimé Césaire's great phrase, want a place at the rendezvous of victory."[35] This goes for both sides of the cultural frontier which the Puerto Ricans are straddling.

The literature written by Puerto Ricans in the United States may contribute strongly to the island's cultural atmosphere by defusing the kind of stifling oppositional discourse traditionally associated with island letters.[36] It may also prove to be innovative and refreshing within U.S. literary contexts in ways that the following interviews will reveal.

Photograph of Jack Agüeros taken by Miguel Trelles.

1

JACK AGÜEROS

Puerto Rican poet, playwright, fiction writer, and scriptwriter, Jack Agüeros has the appearance of the U.S. Army veteran that he is. With closely cropped hair and serious mien, he looks tough, a man of action. Unlike most Latinos, he is tight-lipped and measures his words.

His background, however, belies those appearances. He grew up Latino in New York City, having been born of Puerto Rican parents in Spanish Harlem. His social work among Latinos further steeped him in the hybrid culture of Hispanic immigrants to the United States whose productions in the fields of literature, art, theater, dance, music, and film are becoming an important part of American cultural life. He is particularly familiar not only with Latino literature but also with Latino art, having directed the Museo del Barrio from 1976 to 1986.

Agüeros was born in East Harlem in 1934 and studied in the public schools of the neighborhood. In 1964 he obtained a B.A. with a major in Literature and a minor in Speech and Theater from Brooklyn College. He began graduate studies in Theater History at Hunter College but left when he was one course short of his M.A. He has an M.A. in Urban Studies from Occidental College in Los Angeles.

He has published a collection of short stories, *Dominoes and Other Stories* (Willimantic, Conn.: Curbstone Press, 1993) and a book of poems, *Correspondence Between the Stonehaulers* (New York: Hanging Loose Press, 1991). He is also compiler and translator of the complete poems of Julia de Burgos (published in a bilingual edition, *Song of the Simple Truth* [Willimantic, Conn.: Curbstone Press, 1997]). Another book of his own poems, *Sonnets from the Puerto Rican*, will be coming out shortly. His poetry has appeared in *Poetry Newsletter, Bardic Echoes, The Goliards, Revista Chicano-Riqueña, The Portable Lower East Side, Common Ground, The Rican, Agni Review, Parnassus*, and

Boston Review among other publications. His stories have appeared in *Nuestro, Sombra, Callaloo,* and *African Voices.*

Agüeros has several unpublished plays, some of which have been produced. *Kari & the Ice Cream Cone,* co-authored with David W. Smith, was produced at Monroe Community College Theater in Rochester (1988) and at Eastern Connecticut State University Theater (1994); *Awoke One* was produced at the Ensemble Studio Theater of New York (1992); and *Love Thy Neighbor* was produced at HERE Theater in New York (1994).

Among the scripts Agüeros has written for film and television are *No Matter What Your Language,* a half-hour training film for "Sesame Street"; *He Can't Even Read Spanish,* a half-hour drama broadcast over Channel 4, NBC, on May 8, 1971; *Usa tu voto,* segments of which were aired on Channel 41, in 1989; *Makers of the Night Sun,* a fifteen-minute drama broadcast over Manhattan Cable TV in January 1990, and *Who Killed Freddy Fulano?,* a fifteen-minute drama in Spanish and English versions, broadcast in August 1990 on Manhattan Cable TV.

Agüeros has written articles for *The Village Voice, El Diario-La Prensa, Soho News* and *New York Newsday.* His work has appeared in the following anthologies: *Borinquen, An Anthology of Puerto Rican Literature,* edited by María Teresa Babín and Stan Steiner (New York: Knopf, 1974); *The Immigrant Experience,* edited by Thomas C. Wheeler (New York: Dial Press, 1971); *Daily Fare: Essays from the Multicultural Experience,* edited by Kathleen Aguero (Athens, Ga.: University of Georgia Press, 1992); *Men of Our Time: An Anthology of Male Poetry in Contemporary America,* edited by Fred Moramarco and Al Zolynas (Athens, Ga.: University of Georgia Press, 1992); *Currents from the Dancing River: Contemporary Latino Writing,* edited by Ray González (New York: Harcourt Brace Jovanovich, 1994); and *Boricuas: Influential Puerto Rican Writings,* edited by Roberto Santiago (New York: Ballantine Books, 1995).

"I FEEL LIKE ONE OF THE LUCKIEST GUYS IN THE WORLD TO HAVE BEEN BORN IN NEW YORK"

CDH: Were you born in New York?

JA: I was born in New York, but my parents are from Puerto Rico. My mother is from Quebradillas and my father from Naranjito. They came over to live in El Barrio, where I was born.

CDH: Were they seeking the American Dream in any way? The so-called American Dream.

JA: I think they were running away from poverty, especially at that time, which was the Depression.

CDH: Do your parents still live here?

JA: My mother lives in Puerto Rico, in the same place where she was born: *barrio*[1] San José in Quebradillas. She turned a full circle. My father died there.

CDH: Did anyone in your family write or have defined cultural interests?

JA: My mother used to read; she still reads a lot. My father liked sports, he liked to play sports, to watch them on TV. He liked to read about politics and that type of thing in the paper, but he didn't like literature or poetry, he didn't go to the theater, and he didn't like the movies that much. He hated ballet. My mother loved the movies, she liked to read, she used to take my books and read them.

CDH: El Barrio overlaps with Harlem, right?

JA: It is East Harlem. It goes from 96th Street North to 127th Street or so and from Fifth Avenue East. That is generally accepted as El Barrio. However, the Puerto Rican community actually began in Harlem at St. Nicholas Avenue from 110th Street up to 135th Street. Every year it grew more to the East. This I know because I was doing research for a film, and when I read old newspapers I saw the ads that indicated where the commercial enclaves were. The first Puerto Rican barber shop, for example, was on 135th Street and Seventh Avenue. There's another interesting thing: Schomburg[2] thought that the Puerto Rican community would settle down within Harlem. That's why his books are in that library right in the middle of Harlem. He wanted his books to be in the community of which he formed part, but the community slowly moved. The first Puerto Rican church, where everybody was baptized and married, was La Milagrosa. It was on 114th Street and St. Nicholas. That's where I was baptized.

CDH: Were there other minorities living in El Barrio then?

JA: Oh yes, there were plenty of other minorities: Chinese, in large numbers, Jews, Irish, Russians, Italians, and some blacks.

CDH: What was it like, to grow up in such a multiethnic atmosphere?

JA: It was a beautiful experience. I was in school with all of them. At home, it was mostly Puerto Ricans who lived on the block. When I was about 12 or so, we moved to a different block, and the Jews and the Italians began to disappear and everyone was Puerto Rican. Those are the years that coincide with the Great Migration.[3]

CDH: This is the kind of experience you would never have had had you lived in Puerto Rico.

JA: Not in numbers and not in that same diversity.

CDH: Did you feel different from the other groups?

JA: Every group had its own characteristics, but I began to feel Hispanic with the Great Migration. When all those people began to arrive, racism increased and turned against them [against the Puerto Ricans]. They had their own kind of racism too, as an answer. At that time I began to feel the difference and to identify myself more as Hispanic.

CDH: What do you mean they had their own kind of racism?

JA: It was sort of a reaction to the African Americans. At first, we thought they would be like allies, but they rejected us and then we rejected them back.

I think the trouble was that they felt we could pass as white so they've always had mixed feelings about that.

CDH: You yourself, however, cannot have been the object of much racial prejudice because you're not dark.

JA: I'm pretty dark, for whites, that is. There are many distinctions here. Even in Harlem itself black people make distinctions and have a lot of words to tell apart the colors. There's such a vocabulary! For example, I used to have an office in a lower floor of a church in Harlem during one summer that I was working as a member of the Youth Corps. My secretary was very black, very, very dark-skinned. She fell in love with the minister's son. He was light-skinned. There was a big uproar in the family. They all were mad at me because they thought I was helping the romance between the two young people. And his family was opposed because she was so black. But they were all black. I had heard of those things, but it was the first time I had lived the experience at first hand. I was in the middle. The minister was a bishop of the Church, and he gave us that space without charging us for it so that we would work with the kids. It was awful. I was rooting for the kids, you know, saying "you love each other, you get married, don't worry about it!"

CDH: But were *you* ever the object of prejudice?

JA: I don't know, if somebody walks up to you and calls you a *Spik* and smacks you, you call that an object of prejudice? This was common if you tried to get out of the neighborhood; the neighborhoods became more solidified, more highly defined, and if you crossed those boundaries you had problems. The Italians didn't want us to cross Third Avenue, the blacks didn't want us to go into Fifth. We didn't want for them to come where we were. The Irish were more or less at 103rd Street, what we called The Hill, they didn't want us over there. When I was in elementary school, that was not so strong. But there weren't so many Puerto Ricans then.

CDH: When did you realize that you wanted to become a writer?

JA: Ever since I was in elementary school. That's when I realized I liked to write. But I did it more as an avocation than a vocation. I write, but I also do other things. Now I'm thinking that what I should really do is write; that the other things are minor things in my life. I'm trying to write every day and to publish one book a year if it is possible.

CDH: Is it difficult to publish?

JA: I've had a lot of luck in that sense. Right now I have a second book of poetry already finished, and I don't know if I'll be able to publish it. It hasn't been rejected yet, but if this publishing house isn't interested, I'll look for another one.

CDH: Do you think that the fact that you are a writer has to do with your life here, in the United States, that in some way you want to document that experience?

JA: Definitely. That interests me. I try to write more every day from the point of view of a person who was raised within what is called a minority here. In much of my poetry I try to speak about people I have met here and of landscapes. And in my stories I always try to have a Puerto Rican as the center, although I try to put him in situations that are not the usual ones because I think that point of view is necessary too. I'm not denying the other point of view, but I want to affirm some things.

CDH: What do you want to affirm?

JA: I'm sick of certain Puerto Rican characters that are stereotypes. I try to reject that even as a playwright. Everyone writes about mothers who are sweet and sit in rocking chairs and say *Ay bendito!*[4] all the time. I wrote a play about a Puerto Rican mother who was practically a murderess because there are those kinds of women too. If we write within stereotypes, we ourselves are perpetuating them even more than the other side because the other side doesn't write about them at all. In all my life I have been like that. I'm not a typical Puerto Rican, I've traveled all over, I've done lots of things "typical" Puerto Ricans have not done. In another way I am a typical Puerto Rican. And thinking of stereotypes, we could immediately identify two kinds. One could be defined in visual terms as a man wearing rolled up white pants, a straw hat and with a machete[5] in his hand. That would be the island stereotype of the *jíbaro*[6] But there is also another stereotype, that of the *Ghetto-Rican*, the ghetto kid, tough and with a gun in his hand.

I wanted to stop that ridiculous thinking they do, that people have to be a certain way, of a certain height and a certain color if they are Puerto Rican.

CDH: That watchmaker, Max Vázquez, in your story *Horologist*, is an extraordinary character; he is certainly not the typical Puerto Rican character.

JA: Some people have told me that they would like to know more about those characters, about Max and Livrehomme and Gary García; they tell me I should turn that story into a novel in order to make known their lives outside the watch repair shop.

But I wouldn't want to go back, I'd like to leave it alone. I've thought about writing a whole cycle of stories from the characters in *Dominoes*. When I was speaking at a high school in Willimantic, Connecticut, the kids asked me, "Why are your stories so sad? Why do they end so abruptly?" I don't believe they are sad. I like abrupt things because life is like that. In life one does not finish things, signed, sealed, and delivered. But the truth is that I left Ebarito [from the title story of *Dominoes*] in a hospital, and nobody knows if he's going to talk or what he's going to do when he gets out. And there are the dead man's two friends, there's a possibility of a vengeance. What is going to happen with Alma, who's left without her favorite uncle? But I felt like that's artificial, I got to move on, you know?

CDH: Leave it to the imagination.

JA: That's what I think too. Go on to other ones. I've written another story that's not in the book. It's called *The Man on the Landing*. It's different because it's written in the first person. Somebody also observed, "You don't use the first person." I hadn't noticed. I don't like the first person too much. In this story there's a man who goes down to the subway every day and begins to see a guy lying always in a corner, and every day he sort of wants to see but doesn't want to see. He sees more details every day. I like that story.

CDH: There's a phrase in *Horologist* where someone speaks of the "Puerto Rican burden." Do you feel that as a writer?

JA: Yes, absolutely. But not as a burden but as a privilege. Gary doesn't mean it in the sense of burden, either. He wants to explore; he feels frustrated because he says that there are so many Puerto Ricans here. We are building this country, and nobody gives us credit because we are so shy and unassuming that we don't want to get up front and say, "Yes, I'm a wonderful watchmaker." There's this part of Max Vázquez that doesn't want to be on TV. He is a retiring man. So that's what Gary means. He would want the man to be willing, right away, to make a video. But people are not like that.

CDH: Maybe he feels an obligation.

JA: There is an obligation.

CDH: Do you feel it?

JA: Yes.

CDH: To what?

JA: To present our people as we know them, from the inside, from the heart, with all the details. It's not a question of a headline which says a Puerto Rican killed a woman in the Bronx and that's the end of the story. Or that two Puerto Ricans got into a fight and knifed each other during a game of dominoes and that's the end of the story. That is not the end of the story. The story is to find out why these things happen to these people.

CDH: That's the beginning of the story, right? So in a way your writing is an advocacy, would you call it that?

JA: Yes, I think so. In my poetry I think I do a lot of denunciation, but in my stories I don't think I do. In the stories I try to imply rather than explain. I don't know if I achieve it, but that's what I try to do.

CDH: I found that in the collection of stories titled *Dominoes* there is an evident stylistic intention, particularly in regard to the form of the story, and there is an economy of the narrative elements. Do you think maybe that has to do with the fact that you also write poetry and for the theater? Your stories go straight to the point and you build up the structure carefully. They are very poetic in that way.

JA: I have to tell you two things. First of all, it took me seven years to finish *Dominoes,* the title story. I wrote the first draft of it on an airplane flight. I took out a piece of paper and began the story called *Dominoes.* When I got off the plane, I had it written. But I didn't like it. I spent seven years, off and on, working and reworking it. I felt I had to explain how the game works because you can't take for granted that everybody knows what dominoes are, so you have to explain the game at the same time that you are developing the story. That gave me a lot of trouble.

My other problem is that my plays are always very short. People ask me: "Well, why don't you make this longer?" I don't feel it long, I feel it short. So I like things that are brief or more concise.

CDH: Isn't that better for the short story form?

JA: It's given me a problem with writing a novel, though. There I have to go on, and on, I don't like that.

CDH: Well, don't write novels.

JA: I don't know if I can. That's right. I don't have to.

CDH: Would you define yourself as a Nuyorican writer? I have found that some Puerto Rican writers in New York don't like to be labeled *Nuyorican.*

JA: I don't like it either. I'm a New York Puerto Rican. Algarín [Miguel Algarín, a poet] can call himself Nuyorican if he wants to because he has a sort of schizophrenic formation. He was born over there, and he is totally conversant in Spanish when he comes over. And then he turns to the other culture, trying, at the same time, to not let go of the first one. That doesn't happen to me. I begin within this culture, and the other one is the one that is less a part of me. I'm lucky that because I am old, I come from a time when I had access to Spanish through the radio and because it was spoken at home, but I never learned it in formal terms. I resent that part a little bit. But I can't feel like a Nuyorican because I identify with many Puerto Rican things and I'm interested in the island's culture, but I would be a liar if I said that culture has been an influence over me. It has been an influence, but not that big a one. It has enriched me and it is a source of pride, but right now I couldn't even tell you what Puerto Rican authors I have read, not even how many Spanish-speaking authors I have read. They are very few. When I went to college, there were no Puerto Rican Studies Departments. There were not even many Spanish Literature, or Spanish American Literature

Departments. My parents couldn't talk to me about literature so I read a little Cervantes and that's about it. I can't identify with all that about having a leg here and a leg there; that's not my case. Both my legs are here. And you know when I notice that most? When I try to write in Spanish. I can't. I don't control Spanish, I can't manipulate it; I can't make it go this way and that. So for me Spanish is like a dog whom I can't discipline. I love it a lot, but it doesn't obey me.

CDH: Have you tried it?

JA: Well, I've written a poem in Spanish. I've never written a story in Spanish because I begin and then I find it flabby. I don't have the vocabulary, I can't control my vocabulary.

CDH: So you resent not to have had the opportunity to be proficient in Spanish?

JA: Yes, they took it from me when I was young. Now we have bilingual education; before, nobody talked about that.

CDH: Do you feel that Puerto Rican writers in the United States form a community? Are you conscious of a special solidarity, or is it every man for himself?

JA: Well, I would say there is no group consciousness. It's not like the Round Table.

CDH: You don't have a space, a place where you can meet with other Puerto Rican writers and establish communication with them?

JA: Well, I don't know if the others have it, but I'm not part of it. The Nuyorican Poets Café[7] is now more American than Puerto Rican. I don't want you to misunderstand me; it's an interesting place, but it's not Puerto Rican, it's American. But you see, there's also the fact that writers have such big egos that it's hard for them to come together in groups. They are anarchists. Every one of them is an anarchist.

CDH: Do you have contacts with literary life in Puerto Rico?

JA: No.

CDH: And with Anglo writers or with the literary establishment here?

JA: Writing is a very lonely and solitary activity. And the thing is that you also have to work. So between the solitude of the writing and the need to work, well, for me it's almost impossible to have an active life. For example, the Pen Club; if I were to go to the meetings and to be active in it, when could I write?

I belong to a playwright workshop. We meet once a week, we read our texts, we discuss our scripts, we criticize each other strongly, we give each other suggestions, and then we go home. But that stuff of meeting once a week to philosophize and argue about whether we are Puerto Ricans. . . . I wouldn't be a part of it. I can't be a part of it. I gotta go and write a story.

It takes so much time to write for me anyway, because I am very slow. I can't afford to be held up in those conversations.

CDH: Did you have any models, literary models, when you started writing? People that you admired as writers?

JA: Oh yes. Charles Dickens. Unbelievable writer. And of course a lot of the Americans. And I loved a lot of the English poets. I majored in English Literature in college. So I loved everybody down from the Brontë sisters and Jane Austen, George Eliot—*Middlemarch*—Thomas Hardy, all those people. There's a strange period in American Literature that I like a lot and had an influence over me in college. It's a period in the United States around the turn of the century; it's called the local colorists, a group of writers who invented names for themselves like Petroleum V. Nasby. And there's another one named Lafcadio Hearn.

It was an interesting thing. You know, for a time the United States culture was a poor imitation of English culture. Same thing, more or less as happened with Puerto Rico and the United States. It's a colonial relationship: the United States was a colony of England. High culture was always an imitation of English culture. Around 1850, or maybe a little later, the American thinker Ralph Waldo Emerson, wrote an essay, *The American Scholar,* and in it he more or less says, 'To hell with English things. Let's see what is happening in the United States. What's the matter with us that we look down on what is ours?' From that point on a lot of writers began to be known. He was one of the first who accepted Walt Whitman. There was also Thoreau. And these other writers I was talking about, they come a little later. They start to look around, to see what is happening and many of them write trying to sound just like people talking. There are some stories that are almost impossible to read now because those accents and those rhythms are a thing of the past. In a way sometimes I think some of our writers now are trying to do the same for the Puerto Ricans, to give that sound, to mix in those words, that Spanglish. I think it's a continuity with that kind of literature. They are writing the way their people speak, like what happened with the Negro dialect at the time of the Harlem Renaissance.

The local colorists were an influence on me. I've thought: "While everybody is trying to find these magnificent world themes to write about, why don't I go down to the bar in 110th Street and listen to what they are saying and write about that?" That was what Mark Twain did. He was the next step from those local colorists. Then of course I like Edgar Allan Poe, and among the poets I love e.e. cummings and Edna St. Vincent Millay. My next book of poems, by the way, is going to be all sonnets.

CDH: You are a poet, playwright, and fiction writer and you also worked on "Sesame Street," right?

JA: I wrote a film script that they still use. It's called "No matter what your language." I think you can still get it in videotape. It was to encourage parents to speak Spanish to their kids. But I never wrote for their episodes or anything like that. However, I believe I was the first Puerto Rican in the United States to have a prime time program aired on a major studio, NBC.

CDH: What program?

JA: My show was called "He can't even read Spanish." That was back in the seventies. The subject matter was some kids who picket the local library because it doesn't have books in Spanish. And the title refers to the father of one of them, who's a shopkeeper and who can't understand why his son is doing this because he doesn't even read Spanish. He sees it as a contradiction, but it isn't so for the son, because the son says, "If they don't give me books in Spanish I'll never be able to read them." It was a half-hour melodrama.

CDH: Was it successful?

JA: I don't know because it was aired on a Saturday night at 7:30 or something like that, and it was one of four programs that NBC did and then they never renewed the series. We had a lot of fights with NBC about rights. It was a long time after that before any Puerto Rican started to write for television again. And I had such a negative experience with those rights that I never wanted to write for them again.

CDH: What about your work as a playwright?

JA: My work as a playwright has been a little less frustrating. I've won a couple of prizes with my plays, starting in college. I won a big prize for a play called *The News from Puerto Rico.*

CDH: Has it been published?

JA: No, unfortunately. None of my plays has been published.

CDH: Have they been produced?

JA: Produced, yes. The Puerto Rican Traveling Theater made a one-night production of *The News from Puerto Rico* as part of the awards ceremony. I've had a one-act play produced at the Ensemble Studio Theater and another one-act play produced not so long ago at an off Broadway theater, *Here.*

CDH: Have you written more plays?

JA: Oh yes. I have a series of long plays, about three of them; short plays I have a dozen. I have been working on a cycle that I call *The New York Cycle.* They are one-act plays where I try to combine modern things with classical things like the *autos sacramentales*[8] and medieval plays. It was one of those that they produced at the Ensemble Studio, a play written in blank verse.

CDH: How do you work with the *autos sacramentales* in a contemporary context?

JA: I work with them on a moral plane, although I may do perverse things with what comes out of that morality. I also combine characters from different periods, like, for example, some that belong to Greek mythology with people on the street.

I have a play, for example, about a man who falls in love with a bird, with a pelican. The pelican is sitting on a huge stone and the man is willing to lose his life, if he has to, just to catch the pelican. (I work this play showing slides that are like symbols.) The bird doesn't want to be caught. I mean to signify the encounter between Christianity and the New World and what happens to people in that process. The play ends with the man getting hold of one of the pelican's legs while the tide is coming in. The bird says to the man: "You're going to die because of your stupidity." "Maybe yes, maybe no," says the man, "but I'm not going to let you go." In that meeting between two cultures nobody knows what is going to really happen. That's the kind of thing I like to do in my plays.

CDH: In the poems of the book *Correspondence Between the Stone-haulers*, you present a certain simultaneity between what happened in Egypt and in Peru in ancient times, how each civilization was building up its great monuments and how the common people fared about the same in both places in spite of their different cultures. Does that say something about two cultures like the Latino culture and the Anglo one and the way they could establish a dialogue?

JA: It says something about the way we look at history. The conventional wisdom is that Christopher Columbus came over 500 years ago and wrecked our civilization, the civilization that was flourishing in this continent. But the fact is that we still have not fully understood the effect of Columbus's arrival. That effect is still with us. The process of hispanizing the United States of America is still going on. It's not clear what is going to happen in the future. Christopher Columbus helped to spread Spanish culture, and that same impulse is still expanding. The process is not over yet.

The reason why more and more Americans freak out over the issue of bilingualism is because they feel it as a very pressing issue and more so every day. They feel threatened because it's a phenomenon that is growing.

Another thing, take the Indians. It was said they were all exterminated. But I still see the Indians. They are coming over every day. I see the Mexican Indians who arrive in the United States. They are small and sometimes weak because they have still not been absorbed by the culture of good nutrition. Maybe in one or two generations their sons and grandsons, their daughters and granddaughters will be tall and strong, but they will still be Indians. The concept of frontier is not as absolute as the great China Wall. The Indians still cross and come up and go back down, and they go in and out as they did before Columbus set foot in America, it's just that they come in planes or cars (although some still come on foot).

CDH: Another one of your interests is art, right?

JA: I had a gallery called *Cayman* for two years. It was a nonprofit gallery. I was the first in Soho to show Puerto Rican and Latin American works of art. After that I started at the Museo del Barrio.

CDH: What was that experience like?

JA: I directed it for nearly ten years, from around the middle of the seventies. It was a wonderful experience. I think I took the museum and put it through one of its biggest changes ever. It was also a murderous experience because in those ten years I wrote very little. I didn't have much time to myself. I put in a lot of hours working in the museum. Too many. But it was important so I don't regret it. Though I doubt I would ever do that again in a job, get so crazy with the job that I forget the rest of my life. I got to know a lot of artists in New York and in Puerto Rico.

CDH: What niche does the Museo del Barrio fill in the New York art scene?

JA: The Museo del Barrio absolutely had to exist as a Puerto Rican museum. We had the culture to fill it, and we needed it. When I was director I also included Latin American art, but it was primarily Puerto Rican art. Now they don't stress Puerto Rican art.

The trouble with the move toward homogenizing it is that somewhere in our community we have to preserve the strange things that have happened to us. At first, when I presented young artists and their *avant garde* concepts, Puerto Ricans who came to the museum would be disappointed. They wanted to see nostalgic recreations of the Puerto Rican landscape. They wanted to see pictures of cows and *flamboyanes*.[9]

That's when I realized that to reach the variety of tastes and needs among the New York Puerto Ricans we needed to have pre-Columbian exhibits, folk art and historical paintings, as well as modern art. That's why I had a permanent exhibition of *santos*.[10]

CDH: Do you think the Latin art movement in the United States is as strong as the literary movement?

JA: I would say yes; maybe even stronger. I would say there are more painters than writers.

CDH: Really? Do you think the American experience is also crucial for those painters?

JA: Sure, because one is inserted within one's culture at home, but at the same time one gets on a subway and has five of the greatest museums in the world within the space of one mile. So nobody can stay closed in within his own culture in the United States. Maybe that is good and maybe it isn't, I don't know. What I do know is that it is impossible to stay isolated within one culture. This situation also gives everybody the opportunity of intro-spection, of thinking about one's own culture at the same time that you can go out and get into contact with others. People used to say to me: "How do you feel, having been born in New York, a city that has so many problems?" I feel like one of the luckiest guys in the world. If I had been born in Puerto Rico under the same circumstances, I doubt I would have made it to a university. I studied at night while working during the daytime and while holding down several jobs. That doesn't exist, it didn't used to exist, in Puerto Rico. I don't know if it exists now. It doesn't exist in Paris. One doesn't have access to night classes at a university. The military also helped because I was in the Air Force. I had a small scholarship that wasn't enough to live and have fun on, but it helped pay for the courses and the books. That didn't exist either in Puerto Rico or in France. Maybe it did in Puerto Rico because it is the same military.

So, I have to admit that I was lucky in those aspects.

CDH: Do you think there is a real interest in Latino art and literature right now in the States?

JA: I definitely think so. Nicholas Kanellos, a professor at the University of Texas, who heads Arte Público Press, has a big project going. It's called *Recovering the U.S. Hispanic Literary Heritage*. He's looking for lost, old, and unknown texts, and he's translating them to English in order to publish them. Sometimes he publishes them in the original Spanish. He has a project dealing with newspapers that were written in Spanish in the United States. We had newspapers in Spanish in the United States by the 1850s. I think the first one was published in Louisiana.

CDH: Besides art and literature, you have also studied urban problems, right?

JA: I've always been interested in cities, how they are made, how they work, the way they decay, but I am out of that now. That little change there from that to literature, it's an interesting thing that happened in my life. I was studying my Master's in theater history at about the time things began to get tough in Harlem. A friend of mine comes up to me and says—he is now the president of Boricua College—he says to me, "Jack, the Barrio is on fire, What are you doing? Let's go over there and get in there again and see what we can do." So I said: "OK, let's go." And I started to work in Harlem and sort of got distanced from my studies. I began to feel that it was stupid and boring to be studying when so many things were happening in society and I also felt I should be part of that movement. I didn't return to school for five or six years. I was organizing in the Barrio, I was working with the federal government, with the city . . . those were very turbulent years. And I kept on trying to write at that time. I was already publishing poetry when I was at the university; and I had won two prizes.

So all that took me away from writing because it's more interesting to be active than to be holed up somewhere writing. I left a budding career as a poet. I had published, up to then, in American magazines, but I didn't have a Puerto Rican consciousness or anything like that until then.

CDH: You have done translations. What have you translated?

JA: Mostly theater, but now I just finished the translation of all of Julia de Burgos's[11] work to English.

CDH: Do you go down to Puerto Rico often?

JA: I was there last July, visiting. I went with my daughter. I have two sons and a daughter. She is 16 years old, and I took her down so that she would see her grandmother and get to know Puerto Rico.

CDH: How do you feel when you go to Puerto Rico?

JA: I feel anonymous but happy. I go to Quebradillas and go all over the island. Among my cousins—of whom I have a lot—the word is that I know more of Puerto Rico than they do, that I know the history better and that I have gone to more places. I find that very funny and strange too. I ask them, "Have you gone to the Caves at Camuy?" The answer is "No." And I say, "But that's right over there, very near, just a couple of hours away." They are not even interested.

I think Puerto Ricans don't appreciate what they have. They have this complex that everything is better outside the island. That is strange because it's not true.

CDH: Do you feel accepted there? Have you ever felt a prejudice against you in the island because you were born and raised in the States?

JA: Yes. I think that prejudice has a certain validity in the sense that if a Puerto Rican from here goes back throwing his achievements in the face of everyone, and begins to pride himself on his English and says Spanish is not important, well, nobody likes such an attitude.

CDH: Do you think that if you had been born and raised in Puerto Rico in circumstances similar to those you had here you would still have been a writer?

JA: I don't know. I think my parents would have pushed me into the university because they both saw that I could be a good student. They were interested in having me get ahead, they tried to help me to study. But maybe I'm wrong because in Puerto Rico I doubt that they would have had the means to pay for my study, so maybe I am a writer because I have lived in the United States.

2

MIGUEL ALGARÍN

Miguel Algarín's voice is strong and resonant; it's a voice often used to charm roomfuls of people. His laugh is contagious. But his eyes—shrewd, sharp, always observant—speak of an analytic mind. Miguel knows who he is and where he came from. Because of that, he is not afraid of words or of the barriers they erect between people. For a long time now he has worked at tearing down those barriers. In his Nuyorican Poets Café, the theater *cum* nightclub he has established in the Lower East Side, he comes close to having achieved it.

Born in Santurce, Puerto Rico, in 1941, Algarín moved to New York with his family when he was 9. They settled in the city's Lower East Side, where a growing community of Puerto Ricans gave that neighborhood a decidedly Latin flavor. Attracted since childhood to literature, he obtained a B.A. in Romance Languages from the University of Wisconsin. He has an M.A. in English Literature from Pennsylvania State University and did his doctoral studies in Comparative Literature at Rutgers University, where he teaches courses on Shakespeare, ethnic literature, and creative writing.

Together with other Puerto Rican poets and playwrights like Miguel Piñero and "Lucky" Cienfuegos, Algarín was active in a poetic movement that flour-ished in the Lower East Side during the late sixties and the seventies. This movement sought to reach the common people by means of the poetic word recited and performed—often on the streets. They wrote poetry in a language that often combined English and Spanish and their themes revolved around their daily lives. It was a poetry born of the new frontier established between immigrant Puerto Ricans and the society that both received them as citizens and rejected them as aliens because of their color, their language, and their different culture.

In 1975 Algarín established the Nuyorican Poets Café in order to provide a space for that poetry. It has undergone various changes of locale and admini-

Photograph of Miguel Algarín, *El Nuevo Día* newspaper.

stration since then and is now managed by a group of five people, one of whom is Algarín. It is located at 236 East 3rd Street in Manhattan. Open at nights, from Tuesdays to Sundays, the Café offers poetry readings, stages plays, and on Fridays holds poetry competitions called *slams*. During the last few years the Café has become multicultural, welcoming poets from every nationality and race. "Our movement could not get ahead if it excluded non-Puerto Ricans," Algarín has said. "We Puerto Ricans are living in this society in global company."

Algarín's poetry has been published in several books: *Mongo Affair* (New York: Nuyorican Press, 1978); *On Call* (Houston: Arte Público Press, 1980); *Body Bee Calling from the XXI Century* (Houston: Arte Público Press, 1982); and *Time's Now/Ya es tiempo* (Houston: Arte Público Press, 1984; in 1992 there was a trilingual edition made in Japan, which included the poems in English, Spanish, and Japanese). In 1976 William Morrow published his translation of Nobel Prize winner Pablo Neruda's poem *Canción de Gesta* with the title *Song of Protest*. Algarín has edited two anthologies: *Nuyorican Poetry: An Anthology of Puerto Rican Words and Feelings* (with Miguel Piñero, New York: William Morrow and Co., 1975) and *Aloud: Voices from the Nuyorican Poets Café* (with Bob Holman, New York: Henry Holt and Co., 1994). *Aloud* won the American Book Award for that year. He has two more books in print, to be published by Scribners: *Action: The Nuyorican Theater Festival,* a collection of all the plays that have been produced during the last twenty-five years in the Nuyorican Poets Café and a book of poems, *Love Is Hard Work.*

He has written several collaborative plays, some of which have been staged in New York: *Olu Clemente* (Delacorte Theater, 1973), *Apartment 6-D* (Lincoln Center, 1974), *The Murder of Pito* (Nuyorican Poets Café, 1976), and *Blue Heaven.*

Algarín's poems can be found in anthologies such as *Herejes y mitificadores: muestra de poesía puertorriqueña en los Estados Unidos*, edited by Efraín Barradas (San Juan: Huracán, 1980); *Papiros de Babel: Antología de la poesía puertorriqueña en Nueva York*, edited by Pedro López Adorno (San Juan: University of Puerto Rico Press, 1991); *Puerto Rican Writers at Home in the USA*, edited by Faythe Turner (Seattle: Open Hand Publishing, 1991); *Currents from the Dancing River: Contemporary Latino Fiction, Nonfiction and Poetry*, edited by Ray González (New York: Harcourt, Brace and Co., 1994); and *Boricuas: Influential Puerto Rican Writings*, edited by Roberto Santiago (New York: Ballantine Books, 1995).

"I WAS BORN IN PUERTO RICO, RAISED IN NEW YORK, AND I AM 400 YEARS OLD"

CDH: Where were you born and where did you spend your childhood?

MA: I was born in Santurce. My childhood was a very protected one. My mother was a very cautious woman and took good care of us. I can recall a Catholic school where the nuns were extremely methodical in their teaching.

It was near 15th Street, two or three blocks from a small square in the middle of Barrio Obrero. It was there where I learned to read and write, even though my parents had already introduced me to those skills.

My aunt, Carmen Ana Figueras, used to live with us and took care of us while my mother worked. She made lunches for working people and sold jewelry. She was a great businesswoman; she had a lot of initiative. She is also a writer and published a book of her poems. And my aunt used to sing in Quiñones Vidal's radio program, "Tribuna del Arte."[1]

CDH: When did your family move to the United States?

MA: My aunt had moved to the United States and lived at Pleasant Avenue and 121st Street. We went to live with her. I was 9 years old, and what I remember most was that when we arrived in New York it was still light even though it was 8:45 at night. It was July 13, 1951.

My father found a friend at the airport who took us to my aunt's house for $15. He left us—with all our bags—to wait on the sidewalk for my aunt, who wasn't at home. When she came back she found us all there. Those first three months we were in New York we spent cramped up in tiny rooms.

CDH: When did you decide you wanted to be a writer?

MA: There are two answers for that. One is the atmosphere at our home. My mother, María Socorro Algarín, published a book of poems titled *Lluvias de otoño* (that means Autumn Showers). But that was after I had published my first book. She said, "Well, if Michel can do it, I can too." She's still living in New York, she is still writing, and she also writes songs. She has published poems in magazines, and her music has been recorded by Gloria Mirabal.

I was a very docile boy, I was always inside the house. Sometimes I was naughty, but I was generally inside the house. In my family everybody thought that I had inherited my mother's literary vocation. They all saw in me an extension of her cultural impulse.

Sometimes I try to determine the moment in which poetry and literature entered into my life. My aunt tells me that when I was very small I used to take part in all the school plays. I also liked to read a lot.

But there is one thing that I believe was essential to my decision to become a writer, to turn words into poetry. I remember that when there was a birthday, my mother used to insist that we say something meaningful to the person whose birthday it was. That was my mother's idea, to communicate the emotions that you had toward a person. It was a commemorative act and it taught me a lot. It is something I still do because in the Cafe,[2] we give a turn to all the poets who have a birthday.

My mother not only respected the Word, she also liked to use it; she always sought to express herself with elegance. It is possible that it may have something to do with our family's history, which is extremely complicated.

CDH: Could you tell me about it?

MA: My mother's mother was a black woman named Julia who bore the children of a white man. She was a leper. When I met her she had already lost her toes. I was terrified of going to visit her, especially because Mami always wanted me to kiss her. She insisted I kiss her.

My father and mother were first cousins.

My grandmother was black, but my mother is light-skinned. My grandmother worked all her life and wanted her children to have a better life than hers. She insisted that her daughters not greet her or speak directly to her when they were in public because she did not want them to be associated with her. It might limit their possibilities, she thought. That hurt my mother. She had to cross the street or go on the other side of the plaza if she saw Julia coming around the corner. Puerto Rican racism is something terrible. My grandmother was afraid that if people associated her daughters with her, they would not be able to get married to acceptable men. We are talking of the thirties and forties. She wanted to protect her daughters' futures and demanded that they ignore her in public. When I think about that now, I find it is extremely painful.

My grandmother committed suicide: she slashed her veins, then drank a bottle of denaturalized alcohol and finally threw herself out a window. She never wanted to go to live with my mother or my aunt. She never wanted to leave Juncos to go to Barrio Obrero or to New York.

CDH: How do you interpret all this?

MA: All that is a product of Puerto Rican racism. When my aunt fell in love with the man who was to be her husband, my mother was against him. He was a black Dominican. We are talking about Puerto Rico, not about New York. That was how my character was formed. I am a Puerto Rican man; I was raised by a woman like that.

I am very conscious of all this, but I never understood it. This interview has become an encounter of important dimensions. All this is similar to what is happening now in New York with the Dominicans.

CDH: What was your family's life in New York like?

MA: My father worked in gas stations here and there. I remember one at 138th Street. Afterward he and my uncle moved to Queens and became managers of some parking lots.

When we lived in the projects, my mother, my father, and my uncle took part in all the cultural and social activities of St. Bridget's. They organized dances; they dressed up during Holy Week and organized processions. My mother was always the leader of these two men: my father and my uncle. My father used to type my mother's poems; my uncle took the tapes of her songs to Astoria. There was a Colombian there who put them to music so they could be recorded. Then she went to the shows to hear her songs being sung. New York's mayors used to send her greetings on her birthdays. That was María Socorro Algarín.

CDH: How would you describe life among the Puerto Ricans in New York at that moment?

MA: When we arrived we had to look for work and shelter. We were not used to the cold. It was terrible. It wasn't a question of looking for *Wilfredo* (that was what we called the Welfare Office). It didn't exist. Those who came looked for work to get ahead. It wasn't a question of sitting in a corner waiting for a gift from heaven.

Puerto Ricans have a very special position among other immigrants because of their citizenship. The Puerto Rican doesn't feel the need to adapt; he does not have to reject his Spanish language or his way of eating or his culture. He can keep them because he does not have to renounce his flag or his citizenship. He does not have to become another person, like the Dominicans do.

Puerto Ricans who arrived in New York in the thirties and forties were not usually professionals or businesspeople; they were usually unskilled workers. It wasn't the shoemakers who left the island. My uncle and my father were mechanics; my aunt's husband was a carpenter. That made a difference because we could adapt better. But one part of our family arrived without having any skills, and just as soon as they arrived they became idle. Their possibilities were very limited, and they have not been able to get ahead.

There is a difference between making an atmosphere for yourself and being adapted by the general atmosphere.

CDH: Did your adaptation to American life have anything to do with your becoming an artist, a writer?

MA: I have to go back to my family again. Without my father I never would have known what an opera was. He loved classical music. We used to go to Queens to wash cars in the gasoline station. Papi used to play his classical music the whole night while I helped him. He taught me to listen to the opera. He taught me who Renata Tebaldi and Carlos Bergonzzi were. He took me to see them in *La forza del destino*. He took me to my first piano recital and to Carnegie Hall to hear a violin recital. He also gave me my first violin lessons.

Nothing I have ever done has been born spontaneously; I had a lot going for me. I am the end result of very strong people with a great respect for life, people who had a lot of love in them. I think all artists get ahead like that. Now some speak of an abstract spirituality. I never had to go to prison to learn; I did not get an education behind bars like so many Nuyorican poets. That is not my experience.

CDH: But did life in the United States help you to become a writer?

MA: Of course. Do you know what it was to be 12 or 13 years old and to go out of my apartment—6D—at 725 FDR Drive, to turn toward the West, and go through where the Jewish people lived and through where the Polish people and the Hungarians and the Ukrainians lived? I heard those languages: I had to deal with Yiddish, with Polish; I had friends all over. All that is North American reality. That would not have been the same in Puerto Rico.

The New York experience gave me a lot. The island of Manhattan is much smaller than Puerto Rico, but the cultures of all the world can be found in it. There are magnificent opportunities in its high schools. I was a member of the choir in my high school. We used to give concerts in Carnegie Hall, and we traveled all over the world. When I decided to leave New York, it was to go to college. It would have been very difficult to leave New York if I had not been going to a university.

I remember that when I went to study in Wisconsin, Papi asked Mami, "Socorro, do you think we ought to let him go?" I didn't say anything, but I thought, "Who's going to stop me?"

CDH: What is your relation, as an artist, with Puerto Rico?

MA: Here in Puerto Rico there is still a sort of inferiority complex in relation to Europe, especially in the case of the white Puerto Rican, who is the leader, on this island, of all intellectual endeavors. The Puerto Rican bourgeoisie still sends its children to study in the States or in Europe, not here. University of Puerto Rico is for middle- and low-class Puerto Ricans.

I was discovered in Puerto Rico not because I wrote in English or in Spanish but because they discovered me in French translations. The first time that any Puerto Rican intellectual came into contact with me, it did not have anything to do with my profession as a professor of Shakespeare; it was when a group of young Puerto Rican intellectuals discovered me in Paris. They read my poems in French translations at the beginning of the seventies. And I was born in Barrio Obrero.

Nobody invited me to come and read my poetry here. Miguel Algarín was translated from French into Spanish, and that was how they came to know my poetry on the island. That is why I tell you that Puerto Ricans from the island can't go to New York to talk with New York Puerto Ricans. They have to go all the way to Europe to come back with the writings of a Puerto Rican.

CDH: Where did the word "Nuyorican" come from?

MA: I came to Puerto Rico once with Miguel Piñero[3] and when we came out of the plane we were talking away. We had had some drinks and kept talking, and then I heard the word *newyorican* but I did not know they were talking about Piñero and me. I did not understand. Finally, when we were waiting for our bags I paid attention: *new-yo-rican,* that is, New York and Puerto Rican. They were looking down on us, as if we were nothing. We were Puerto Ricans talking in English, and that to them was contemptuous.

I thought, "Well, here they are on this island, under a master who speaks English. We come speaking perfect English." Not only did we speak good English, but we were presenting a play on Broadway, we were writing for TV, and we were famous in Europe, but for them, we were just *newyoricans.* They were passing judgment on us, looking down on us.

Then, when we got back to New York, I found that William Morrow had sent me a contract for an anthology that was published in 1975 and that they wanted to call *Puerto Rican Poets in English.* And I said to Piñero: "Why don't we give the title of *newyorican* to this anthology?" Piñero said: "But I am not new anything, I am not *neo,* that is an intellectualism." So I asked him, "What are we then?" And we both said, "We are *nuyoricans.*" We spelled it like that, and we said it like that and in less than six months after the anthology was published the word connected and has currency now all over.

What I did was to take the insult that the islander threw at me and take away its sting by making it the title of a book. Puerto Rican intellectuals were left dumbfounded, and they tried to get me to come here and to engage in a discussion about whether that *nuyorican* business was a way of dividing the Puerto Rican people, of weakening their political positions, but I refused to get into that. It was not worth my while to come here and enter into an argument if I had already used the word that they used with contempt as the title to my book. I turned the tables on them and they had to keep silent.

CDH: Do you feel Puerto Rican or North American?

MA: I was born on this island, I was raised in New York, and I feel I have 400 years experience. I don't have to hide anything from anybody. I earn my money teaching the white man from the North his own culture. My classes are cultural classes given in English, and they are about Shakespeare.

There is no reason for the insecurity that I find in Puerto Ricans from the island who want to insist on the purity of Spanish over English, especially when I see that in Puerto Rico today, almost as much English is spoken as Spanish.

CDH: When did you become interested in Shakespeare?

MA: I studied Romance Languages in my B.A. and have a Master's degree in English Literature, and then I studied my doctorate in Comparative Literature. But Shakespeare was my favorite author and I enjoyed reading him a lot. I began to teach Shakespeare when I was 19 years old. And when it became fashionable to teach Puerto Rican Studies and Black Studies, I thought that if I knew anything at all about the white man, this was not going to last for long. He was going to get tired, and all those departments were going to shut down. Now there are no more than two or three departments of Puerto Rican Studies. I also wanted to have a profession that had nothing to do with the fact that I was Puerto Rican. To teach English to 275 white students, to teach Shakespeare, has nothing to do with being Puerto Rican but with being prepared as a man to teach the culture of those people.

CDH: Does Shakespeare enter into your poetry?

MA: What I learn from the Master is the way he lets us into his characters' inner lives by his use of words. He uses metaphors, for example, to illuminate what is inside.

I obviously don't write like him because you can say that no one knows and understands what Shakespeare knew by intuition when he lived centuries ago, but I feel comfortable using English because the Master of English verse is my friend. When he writes historic plays, he uses rhetoric, he uses the concerns of his day to explain the turbulence that affects people in power. He entertained people with stories from the past. He dared to enter into the human psyche. When I teach *Othello* and I see how he dealt with that character, I can appreciate how he makes evil stand out, how he presents those types of people who are out to destroy another person.

In a way, I think Shakespeare was a Nuyorican.

CDH: Together with Piñero, you initiated what is called Nuyorican Poetry, the first affirmative literary Puerto Rican movement, and now you say Shakespeare is a Nuyorican. Could you explain that combination?

MA: We never had to reject our Puerto Ricanness to affirm what is North American in us; that is important. To reject what is North American and to insist on being Puerto Rican while one is over there is absurd.

In the Café I have North American theater, white theater, Chinese theater. Some people come up and say, "Miguel, I would like to see more Latin theater" and I answer, "Why?" When the time comes to produce Latin theater I will produce it. But I do not have to do it now because I never based my work on pro-Puerto Rican affirmations where the white man, the black man, or the Chinese man could not enter. I will publish a book with all the plays that I produced during the last twenty-five years in the Nuyorican Poets Café. It will come out shortly. There are Asian, African-American, ethnic white plays and also Puerto Rican and Cuban plays. Our theater has reflected the international mentality of the Nuyorican.

CDH: How did the performance aspect of Puerto Rican—Nuyorican— poetry in the United States become so important?

MA: For Puerto Ricans, the figure of the "trovador" is very important. In Puerto Rico *la trova*—the desire to compete by improvising poetry—is something that is alive. The point is to see who uses the language best, to see who pleases the public more. That performance value is part of our history, and I think that we have never forgotten it. I think that Cienfuegos[4] and Piñero were profoundly involved in that Puerto Rican feeling. We all loved to recite, to say our poetry out loud. We also had a teacher, Jorge Brandon.

Brandon[5] is a Puerto Rican who had recited poetry in Puerto Rico during the thirties and forties. He was always an eccentric, but he taught us in the parks of lower Manhattan how to work with air so as to keep it in our lungs and to let it out so that we could speak out loud. That is very important.

CDH: There is a noticeable change in themes and style from *Mongo Affair* and *On Call,* your first books of poems, to the latest ones, *Body Bee Calling from the 21st Century* and *Time's Now.* The first referred to very specific circumstances dealing with the lives of Puerto Ricans in New York. The latter ones are more universal in scope. The last one also includes the experience of South and Central Americans in their own countries.

MA: What happened was that first I grounded myself in the Lower East Side. The *persona* that speaks in *Mongo Affair* is a Nuyorican that is not yet free to understand the political and emotional relationship between a place—which is the tar and concrete jungle of Manhattan—and the cosmos, which is where that tiny little speck of tar and concrete-covered land is in relation to, first, the state, then the nation and the hemisphere, and then the globe. But by the time I hit *Body Bee Calling from the 21st Century*, I create a *persona* that has lifted himself out of locality and has made a trip into the future from where he looks back.

In *Mongo Affair* I was acquiring a consciousness of the universe because as a person and as a poet I found myself in the electronic center of the world. But I had not realized that. I was still seeing the broken glass in the street; I was still immersed in the politics of the sixties and seventies. I was involved with the issues of civil rights, of political rights. I was immersed in a sociological context.

But if by *Body Bee Calling from the 21st Century* I'm in the future looking back, by the time I hit *Time's Now* I'm looking at the whole world. I go from *Daily Dealings in South, Central and North America* (the first part) to *Conversations with Silence* (the third part), going through *Newspapers* (the second part). This time, however, the daily dealings are not just dealings with my own identity but with a larger self which is trying to deal with what it means to be alive or in a relationship. I want to dwell on the war of love. Every one of the titles of those poems signals the condition of which I am speaking.

That book's impulse is to go from the personal to the essence of what it is to be as an *I* and as a *You*: "the sweet and turbulent tenderness of loving" as I say in *Right to the Grain.* I get to a point where I have to identify myself.

CDH: The second part of that book, *Newspapers (radio and television),* is very different.

MA: There I get into the reality that is around us and I analyze it, from El Salvador and Nicaragua to Argentina (through Jacobo Timmerman and the Falklands' War) and to Israel. This summer, I went to El Salvador after several years, and I found that two of my poems had been written on the walls of the city. I was surprised and moved.

The Nuyorican mentality has acquired a consciousness of the misery that has been digested and compacted by commercial news. Nuyorican consciousness has become universalized.

CDH: Has it also become religious? The last part, *Conversations with Silence,* seems to be very spiritual.

MA: When I finished the section about the newspapers, I found myself facing the reality that my personal mentality had risen to a level where I needed to speak directly to the Creator. I talk to the Holy Spirit in those poems. The word becomes a chemical element: it changes me or it does not change me. I also converse with Jesus. I explore, grammatically, the relation between the *I am* and the *You are* in the poem *Conversation number two with Jesus.*

CDH: There is a mystical tone in these poems.

MA: This book has been translated into Japanese and has been read by Buddhist monks. They have said that it shows how the human mind goes into transparent space. These are monks who have not gone out of the convent for sixty-five years. An 89-year-old monk wrote to me and said the experience of my being goes up to a point where the flame is not seen and it turns into transparent space.

CDH: Were you ever in contact with Oriental spirituality?

MA: I was at the Naropa Institute, a Buddhist institute. Since I am a friend of Allen Ginsberg, he introduced me to the monks and the great teachers there. I talked a great deal with one of the Masters who was descended directly from Buddha.

These monks find that when I want to talk with God I go into the grammar of language, I don't use metaphors. For me God is not the same as for Saint Theresa or Saint John of the Cross. For them He was a tongue of fire that licked their personal souls and enveloped them in fire, providing a moment that is both sensual and sexual. For me it is the entrance into transparent space, but into warmth, not into empty space.

CDH: Well then, Nuyorican poetry has attained mystical heights. From the streets of the Lower East Side to the heavenly realm. In this poetry you do not mix the two languages. It is much simpler in style than that of your first books.

MA: I wrote the same book in two languages without translating. I didn't set out to write that book in either Spanish or English. It's not bilingual in the sense of mixing the languages. They are completely separate.

The book was also designed to be read in a little over twenty-nine minutes.

CDH: The change was already noticeable in *Body Bee Calling.*

MA: I referred in that book, published in 1982, to things that are happening today: organ transplants, alien tissue in our bodies, and so on. We the Nuyoricans are in a position to be at the cutting edge of science, at the cutting edge of grafting an arm, of transplanting a heart, of artificial blood. We will see it, and the speaker in this book is projecting himself into the future, when a person will be able to reach 150 years of age but he can be three-quarters replaced parts.

CDH: Did any North American help you when you were starting out as a performance poet?

MA: In 1972 Joseph Papp gave me a space at 4 Astor Place. In 1969 or 1970 he was interested in our development as playwrights, but the poetic impulse manifested itself first. It was through him that we had the opportunity to go into theaters, to use the Delacorte Theater for poetic recitals on Monday nights when there were no shows. That man had a very sharp eye and saw the possibilities of our movement.

CDH: It was a pioneer movement for Puerto Ricans in New York.

MA: There had always been poetry recitals, but it was more a refined thing. This is a dramatic type of poetry. The Chicano theater and the Nuyorican theater have some points in common. The Chicanos and the Nuyoricans have a much closer bond than the one that exists between the Puerto Rican from the island and the Puerto Rican from New York. We used to go to Arizona, to New Mexico, to Texas way before we were invited to come to the island.

CDH: Did you establish ties to North American poets?

MA: I have a strong relation to North American poets. Allen Ginsberg, William Burroughs, they all discovered the Nuyorican Poets Café when it really got going and they were aware of our activities, and it was clear to them that what we were doing was very much in the tradition of bringing poetry into its popular mode and returning it to the people. Poetry has always been an art of heightened communication between people, and I don't mean between readers of poetry but between people. They were instrumental in making us feel that we were doing what we were supposed to be doing. But they were not in any way our inspiration. Ginsberg is a Jew, Robert Creely is an Anglo, Burroughs is an Anglo. They are all aware of our work, and Nuyorican Poetry means something to them.

If you went into a mainstream literary poets' meeting and you said Nuyorican Poetry, they would recognize it as Puerto Rican poetry. That has to do with the fact that we write in English, and that has to do with the fact that we are accessible culturally to them.

CDH: So you are much closer to the mainstream poets in New York than to the Puerto Rican ones from the island?

MA: Undoubtedly, yes.

CDH: Have your relations to Puerto Rican poets from the island improved over time?

MA: The electronic frontier has reduced space so much that there are no distances. If I can be in Chicago, in Los Angeles, and in Tokyo simultaneously in a Friday night poetry slam broadcast from the Nuyorican Poets Café and in all those places they can hear what happens in the Café, well then, the distance between New York and Puerto Rico will definitely be much smaller also.

The island's experience will continue to grow when our experience is added to it. If those on the island want to add up what we do in New York and to say that because we are Puerto Ricans that also belongs to them, well then let them do it, but only if they are going to grow because of it.

The Nuyorican Poets Café is a central place not only to New York but also to the island because the island Puerto Ricans should recognize that we in New York are not enemies but that we are, because of the nature of the era, at the electronic frontier, and that our mentality is developing at a speed that is awesome. We are accelerated because of our placement in the hemisphere, because we are not in the Caribbean but we are Caribbean-rooted, we are North American and therefore not in any way having to deal with the polemic of *Am I a Puerto Rican or not?* But the real deal is that I am a North American, but also a Caribbean man by birth, and in mentality I carry the emotion of an island people into the cutting edge of the electronic frontier, of the scientific frontier in the North. And we cannot go back into concerns with an idealized Taíno Puerto Rico. It's irrelevant. It's not to the point.

CDH: In your introduction to the anthology *Aloud: Voices from the Nuyorican Poets Café,* you wrote that the slam could be called "Prime Time Interactive Literature." Could that be also applied to the relation that may be established between the Puerto Ricans in New York and those on the island?

MA: What's interesting is that you can be with me today, with the woman who raised me while living in my mother's home[6] and you see how rooted I am in Puerto Rico and how ironic it would be that the Puerto Rican *intelligentsia* from the island not be open to that reality, open to what I do. I am open to what they do because I am constantly aware of what's happening on the island. During the time of the plebiscite,[7] I couldn't go anywhere without hearing about Puerto Rico. PUERTO RICO was looming as this important reality in New York. And there was a plebiscite taken in Manhattan, in the five boroughs, because there was a question about the Puerto Rican here not wanting us to involve ourselves in their world, in their business. They wanted us to have nothing to do with this island. or maybe they thought that our politics would upset Puerto Rico's precarious balance. Maybe they thought Puerto Ricans in New York were more radical, less central in their politics.

CDH: Was it so?

MA: As the thing turned out, the plebiscite, the way we did it up North, voted in favor of the status quo. But anyway, it seems to me peculiar this attitude that we should not participate because we do not live on the island. It seems to me peculiar because this island is not a sovereign nation. It is an island that has to import 99.9 percent of all its food. If it was an independent island in agricultural or industrial terms, maybe we could all agree to talk about the matter. But that is not the case.

CDH: Is this situation painful for some New York Puerto Ricans who are rejected in both places?

MA: I meant it when I said the New York Puerto Rican has evolved mentally to see himself as a man that belongs to many worlds and that I am really 400 years old. I was not born in 1941 out of the clear blue. There was something that preceded me that had all the complexities of a leprous grandmother, a suicide, birth cousins marrying, all of that, all that is humanity. All the people had been around here, on this island for hundreds of years. They didn't come here yesterday, two generations, ago, four generations ago. They came here twenty generations ago. See? We were based in the center of the island, in Juncos. What was this black woman, Julia, doing in Juncos where there are not so many blacks because they colonized the coasts?

It was probably a case of women picked up by men of the center of the island, and when they had children they were kept apart from the familial heart because they were racially a throwback. I do see myself as old in spirit and old in culture connections. I wasn't born yesterday, I was not born fifty-three years ago. There are all those people involved in my world.

I am aware of that continuity of history, and without it I would be very confused about myself. When you think about the Afro-American reality, the Afro-Americans were raped completely of their dialect, of complete cultural identity altogether. But the Caribbean black held on to a lot more, and therefore we can today bring *santería* to the North. These are Caribbean-based religions. The monster from the North didn't have the power to squelch it. So when a Polish man in his seventies speaking heavily accented English says to a young boy of 12, "Go back to where you came from," that young boy does not understand, but as a man that young boy comes to understand that going back to where I came from was going back to another part of America, not to somewhere other than America but to another part of America. That old man's problem was thinking that America was the North. He had a problem, "go back to where you came from." Here were white trash from Europe telling a black Puerto Rican to go back to where he came from, and he had been in the Caribbean for 400 years.

And these white trash had been leaving Europe for the New World seeking ways of survival. The white man in America has been here only several hundred years. We have been here a long, long time. The average white American can, however, egotistically command you to leave his country and go back to where you came from. And you are an American.

Once you understand these things you no longer have to be so violently disturbed. So when the Puerto Rican *intelligentsia* wants to bicker with me and raise issues about whether or not I'm a Puerto Rican writer, that's bullshit in comparison to what you really deal with in the North of the Americas and with white people. And anyway, the person usually raising that issue here is a white Puerto Rican intellectual. Just one more white person trying to introduce dissension into your world.

Photograph of Sandra María Esteves, *El Nuevo Día* newspaper.

3

SANDRA MARÍA ESTEVES

Sandra María Esteves's hands seem to take on a life of their own as she recites her poetry. As much as her chant-like intonation, they speak of rituals, of feelings; they tell ancient stories. To hear and see her is, therefore, an experience in total communication. In her poetry she has condensed the trajectory of a people displaced and seeking meaning in memory, new fusions, and a universal understanding amid the small circumstances of daily life. Silent and strong, she herself resembles the Earth-Mother who sometimes appears—directly or indirectly—in her image-laden poems that are rich in myth, rhythm, and feelings.

Born in the South Bronx in 1948 of a Puerto Rican father and a Dominican mother, Sandra María Esteves first wanted to become a graphic artist. She studied for some time at Pratt Institute in Brooklyn. She has published three volumes of poetry, *Yerba Buena*, which she also illustrated (Greenfield Center, N.Y: Greenfield Review Press, 1981); *Tropical Rains: A Bilingual Downpour* (New York: African Caribbean Poetry Theater, 1984), and *Bluestown Mockingbird Mambo Houston* (Houston: Arte Público Press, 1990).

Her poems have also appeared in many anthologies and literary journals, such as *Nuyorican Poetry: An Anthology of Puerto Rican Words and Feelings,* edited by Miguel Algarín and Miguel Piñero (New York: William Morrow 1975), *Herejes y mitificadores: muestra de poesía puertorriqueña en los Estados Unidos,* edited by Efraín Barradas and Rafael Rodríguez (San Juan: Huracán, 1980); *Puerto Rican Writers at Home in the US*, edited by Faythe Turner (Seattle: Open Hand Publishing Co., 1991); *Papiros de Babel,* edited by Pedro López Adorno (San Juan: University of Puerto Rico Press, 1991); *In Other Words: Literature by Latinas of the United States*, edited by Roberta Fernández (Houston: Arte Público Press, 1994); *Aloud: Voices from the Nuyorican Poets Café*, edited by Miguel Algarín and Bob Holman (New York: Henry Holt, 1994); *Currents from the Dancing River. Contemporary Latino Fiction, Nonfiction and Poetry*, edited by Ray González (New York: Harcourt Brace and Co., 1994), and *Boricuas: Influential Puerto Rican Writers*, edited by Roberto Santiago (New York: Ballantine Books, 1995).

Esteves has received numerous awards and fellowships and has read her poetry in New York and on the campuses of many U.S. universities and colleges as well as at poets' festivals. From 1983 to 1988 she was executive artistic director of the African Caribbean Poetry Theater, a company that staged plays, poetry performances, and other literary events.

"SOMETHING WOKE UP INSIDE OF ME; THE DOOR CAME OPEN AND OUT OF THE DOOR CAME POETRY"

CDH: Where were you born and where did you spend your childhood?

SME: I was born in the Bronx in 1948. My father was Puerto Rican; my mother is Dominican and they met in New York. My parents were never married. My mother was too dark, and my father's family didn't accept her, especially my father's mother.

I was brought up in the South Bronx, but when I was 5 years old, I was sent to a Catholic boarding school in the Lower East Side because my mother was a single parent and she was extremely protective. She didn't like what she saw in the public schools. One time my cousin came home without her panties on. So she decided it would be best to put me in the boarding school. It was a nuns' school. I lived there from Sunday night to Friday afternoon, and then I would go home on the weekends. It was like living a double life because the school was like a military school except that it was religious. We went to church often, at least three times a day and sometimes more. There was Mass and different celebrations. Lent was a serious ritual: we made the Stations of the Cross every day.

CDH: Do you feel that experience has had an impact on the person you are?

SME: It had a lot to do with it. Before I went to the school I only spoke Spanish. When I started going to the school, I was not allowed to speak Spanish. I was forced to speak English. By the time I reached the third grade I knew the languages, I knew what words were what, but I didn't know which language they belonged to. There was a confusion as to what was English and what was Spanish, so I would sit for hours repeating the words to myself, trying to savor and taste the words and to figure out if they were English words or Spanish words. It was clear to me that Spanish was very sweet and English was different, so I would savor them over and over and try to decide that way. It was such a traumatic thing to go through that by the time I was 7 years old I knew I wanted to be a visual artist because I didn't have to talk; I could just draw. So I didn't talk. Basically, my vocabulary was "yes," "no" and "I don't know." Up until I was 13 I didn't talk much. I read a lot, I read furiously. I read all the comic books that were available over and over again, and I drew and drew constantly.

There was also a nun in the first and second grades: she used to draw these elaborate chalk drawings on the blackboard, a special blackboard. I learned a lot from watching her draw; that was an education. I was the best artist in the class. I was good in academics, but I wasn't interested. I even got writing awards in school, but they didn't mean anything to me. I wanted to be an artist.

CDH: So in a way you lived a double life, with the nuns and at home.

SME: I also had a triple life. During the summers I lived with my godmother, who was a maid for some rich white Wall Street financiers. I would go stay with her at their estate in Connecticut. I had my own room, it was the only time I had my own room. I used to go walk barefoot through the farm and see the animals and the flowers, and I would become a nature child.

I think that that was also important because it was very different from the city, the South Bronx, and from the school.

When I was starting out I didn't question, I just accepted everything. When you're a child you don't understand, you don't intellectualize. Life was what it was; I was in boarding school, I didn't want to be there; I wanted to be home with Mami and my family.

CDH: Did you relate to other ethnic minorities at this time?

SME: Even at the boarding school, there was a mixture of Irish, Italians, and a lot of Latinos and blacks. There was a lot of everything except Asians. There were no Asians then.

CDH: What books did you read?

SME: I read the usual children's literature—*Rebecca of Sunnybrook Farm, Huckleberry Finn, Little Women,* all those classics. I didn't read any Puerto Rican books or anything like that. In fact, I didn't know anything about Puerto Rico other than that I was Puerto Rican. I didn't know what that meant.

CDH: But you define yourself as Puerto Rican and not as Dominican.

SME: I grew up with my father's family around me. Even though my mother was born in Santo Domingo, she left there when she was 4 years old because her mother died and her father, who was an engineer, relocated to St. Thomas. My mother lived there for ten years, but in her family they spoke Spanish. When she was 15, she went to the United States to study and decided she was staying. My mother is the only one of her family who is in the United States that I know of. A short time ago I met my aunt, my mother's sister, whom I did not know. So I didn't know that family, I was not aware of them. My mother never really took the time to teach me the history of all of that. Because my mother was busy being an American, becoming an American, she wanted me to be American and thought I didn't need to know anything about my roots, my history, or my past.

Also my *tía*,[1] from my father's side, lived on the first floor of our building. Before I went to the boarding school, while my mother worked I stayed with my tía and she was a homebody. I used to help her cook *empanadas* and *alcapurrias* and *pasteles*.[2] Because of her I identified myself a lot with Puerto Ricans. Her name is Julia. I have a poem, *A Julia y a mi*,[3] and it does not refer only to the poet Julia de Burgos.

My father also lived some four blocks away from where I lived, with his mother, my grandmother, and I used to visit them regularly.

CDH: When did you first come to Puerto Rico? Did you feel you were "coming back" to something that was yours even though you had never been here?

SME: I knew that Puerto Rico was the land of my family. When I was 17, I decided that I had had enough of New York, and I made my mother pay for the *pasaje*[4] to come here. I had a tía with a house in the Condado sector of the city, by the beach; another tía had a boarding house. I came with the intention of staying. I decided it just like that. My cousins would come every summer, and they stayed and I felt I wanted to come but we never had the money.

CDH: When was this?

SME: This was around 1964, 1965.

CDH: What were your feelings once you got here?

SME: Well, I was expecting to find something . . . *algo bien campo*.[5] And I was surprised to find how much it reminded me of Queens. I was surprised to see the life here, how it was. There were highways, there was McDonald's. In fact, I remember that I went to the store because I wanted to buy some *criollo*[6] food. What I found in the store was Campbell's soup with Spanish labels.

I came to San Juan because my tía was over here, my *prima*[7] was in Guaynabo and my other cousin was in Bayamón, so I would rotate between their houses. I went looking for a job. I started going to the hotels. They wouldn't hire me because I couldn't read and write in both languages. I could read and write in English, but my Spanish wasn't so good and I really had a hard time speaking it. I had to think a lot before saying each word in Spanish.

But the thing was that besides the fact that I couldn't get a job, they also called me *gringa*.[8] I was surprised; I was hurt. In New York I was Puerto Rican, and that was something shameful. When I came here, the first thing

I realized was that everybody was Puerto Rican and it was OK. It was actually nice, and there was respect and people treated each other courteously. There was no shame in being Puerto Rican, but in New York you were relegated to certain communities, to certain jobs, and even in our education they tried to push us in certain directions. And here they called me *gringa*.

CDH: So you were a *gringa* here and a Puerto Rican over there?

SME: It was like being rejected in both places. I would say to people: *Yo no soy gringa.*9 I would try to defend myself, but then I would have to say it in English, which didn't make sense.

I stayed here for two and a half months. The only job I was offered was with Arthur Murray Dance Studio. They were willing to teach me to be an instructor because I had a sufficient sense of rhythm to be able to learn, but I couldn't take the job. I earned more than twice those wages working as a waitress in New York. And also I had decided to stay with my cousins because my tía was too old fashioned. One day I came in after the sun had gone down, and she chewed me out: *Tu vas a desgraciar el nombre de la familia; no puedes entrar a esta hora, eso es una poca vergüenza. Yo no se cómo son las cosas en Nueva York pero aquí las cosas son diferentes.*10 And I moved out and went to stay with my cousin in Guaynabo. But the last bus to Guaynabo left at 10:00 and the job lasted until midnight so that was that.

CDH: Did you feel pain at the rejection?

SME: It's like being an orphan; like being abandoned. I put that together with being abandoned by my father before birth in the sense that my parents were never married. Then I was sent to boarding school when I was only 5 years old and felt abandoned by my mother. For many years I felt my mother didn't want me. I didn't understand that she had to work. When you are a child, the only thing you understand is that Mami is not around. Then the rejection from my father's family. They had parties and we weren't invited; we were sort of relegated to the back rooms.

CDH: Did you come back often after that first experience?

SME: I didn't come back for twenty-five years. I didn't come back until two and a half years ago when *Papiros de Babel*11 was presented. I always wanted to come back. I had many dreams, for years, of jumping on a plane and coming for the weekend. It was always like coming home even though I was born in the Bronx. But two and a half years ago, when I came to read my poetry, I felt that was the right way for me to come to Puerto Rico. I come now with dignity, and I come knowing who I am and I come to bring the wisdom I have acquired and to fulfill my family's circle.

CDH: How did you develop your strong sense of identity while living in the States?

SME: Well, I was born there; I had no choice in that. But I do feel there was a deliberate conspiracy to keep me ignorant, to keep my history away from me. Because in the school system there were no Puerto Rican Studies. It was as if I had no past. We were kept feeling powerless. What we learned about our own history is that we were slaves, we were savages. It was a very negative viewpoint.

Now, when I was growing up, being a visual artist and being talented and having that talent acknowledged by many, that empowered me. Then as I got older and grew into womanhood, I confronted a world that sees me as just another dark-skinned Latin. So I'm full of myself, and I'm confronting a world that wants to keep me held back and down.

And early on I began to say "Wait a minute, I know who I want to be. Why do they insist that I be this other entity? Why do they want me to be a slave . . . someone *less than* . . . ? Why can't I be equal? At least I can be equal; if not better, I can be equal."

CDH: Do Latina women have a different situation from Latino men?

SME: All young Latina women in the States are seen as sex objects. I didn't want to project that: I didn't want to be considered *sucia*, a slut, maybe because of my upbringing with the nuns. And when I used to walk down the streets and hear all that about '*Ay Mami, ven p'aca*[12] I used to wonder, "Is it the way I look? Am I projecting this?" And I would try to dress properly. I couldn't figure it out. I thought it was me. I took everything very personally. It took me a while. It wasn't until I began understanding the political context of Latinos in the United States that I began to see that it wasn't me at all, that this was a social condition and that all women were basically in the same position, that we are held down and oppressed. In a sense both men and women are victims. Certainly, Puerto Rican men are not held in the same esteem as Anglo men. And that's ridiculous. We each have our own special character. What we don't have are the opportunities to develop ourselves to the degree that we should. We have to fight for those opportunities. When I got to Pratt there were three Latinos, even though there were over two thousand students there.

CDH: When did you first think that you might become a writer?

SME: When I got to Pratt, after the first year of college I experienced an identity crisis which some people say is the typical thing that students go through, especially Latino students. I knew who I was in a personal way but not who I was in a larger way, in a social way.

I was in a serious search for something, I didn't know what. While that was happening, someone had given me a gift of an IBM electric typewriter, the new kind, with the soft-touch controls; it made typing very easy. Also, I went to a community poetry reading at the National Black Theater in Harlem. It was something they had once a year, what they called Community Day and everyone in the place—and there were between thirty and forty people there—everyone got up and read one or two poems that either they had written or someone else had. All except me. I was the only one who didn't. But I was blown away. I never heard poetry that was connected to me so immediately. I went home and wrote my first poems.

The other thing that happened was that I had a Japanese sculpture teacher who one day came into class, and he wrote things all over the place and he woke me up to the realization that words could be a tool for creative visualization. That was important because at that point I started experimenting with combining words with visual images.

CDH: Do you feel that the fact that he was not Anglo had something to do with his making you more aware of who you were?

SME: Well, I did have three Japanese teachers and several Anglo teachers. My Japanese teachers were sensitive to my personal being because of their alien status. In this society I am also an alien, even though I was born and raised here. In that sense, there is an understanding of me as a colonial person, as a child of a colonial society. They affirmed my identity; all three of them. They gave me a different way of looking at the connection between art and our lives. The ones that negated my being and my identity were the Anglos because they had a bias, a European focus. But not all of them.

CDH: So Pratt was important for your development as an artist?

SME: At Pratt my Anglo instructors were very critical. That was their job, they're supposed to break down your work to analyze it. I didn't understand how to handle that criticism. It was devastating to me because up until then I had only received praise for my work, and awards and acknowledgment.

And there were things with which I couldn't agree. I felt, for instance, that I had a wonderful sense of color; it was very Caribbean, very bright. So one day I came in with a painting with that kind of color combination, and the teacher used my painting as an example of what not to do because it wasn't muted, toned down, there were no natural earth colors. That devastated me. I didn't understand that out of criticism you take what's useful and throw away the rest. I didn't understand that. So it totally devastated me, and that was when I began going into the crisis.

CDH: When did you actually begin to write?

SME: I had started writing about 1972. In 1973 I went to an ethnic writers' conference in Wisconsin. I met some wonderful writers, like Ricardo Sánchez, a Chicano; some Asian Americans, including Lawson Inada and Frank Chin and some Native-American writers. It was my first multicultural encounter. One thing I realized—it was an important realization—was that even though we all had different roots, we all shared a common condition. We were all oppressed. We were facing a similar kind of crisis: we were all second-class citizens; we were all disenfranchised people. That's what brought us together.

CDH: So in a way, writing became something like a homeland for you.

SME: The artist began writing as a different way of painting. But what I was writing about—the themes—had to do with a process of self-discovery. And even though you do that with painting, you don't do it the same way because in painting I was just recording things that I saw around me and painting from life. I didn't have to have an identity in order to be able to do that; I just had to have a photographic view of whatever I was looking at. But when I began writing I had to define, to name things. And that's when the process of discovering my Puerto Rican side started happening. And that's where the self-transformation began.

But when I first started writing, I felt my work was primitive; I was intimidated about sharing it. I didn't believe in the validity of what I had to say because I suffered from low self-esteem. The process of affirming myself happened with the writing, and it took years. Writing was an integral part of it. Not only the writing but the reading, the sharing of what I was writing. It initiated a dialogue with others, and that's when the learning began because that's when people shared things with me. That was truly a dialogue that went both ways.

CDH: Was your family happy with your decision to write?

SME: Now they have a different respect for me, even my mother, who never accepted my choice as a writer and as a poet. She wanted me to be an accountant, a mathematician. When I told her I wanted to be an artist, she said, "That's not a career." For many years she felt I threw my life away.

CDH: Where does she live?

SME: She has an apartment in Chelsea; she considers herself a hip New Yorker now. Her name is Maria Christina, and when she came here and became a citizen, she dropped the María and kept the Christina. So now she's Chris. She talks to me in broken English, and I talk to her in broken Spanish and we argue about things. She says to me, "You're not Puerto Rican, you're an American." To her, I was born in the United States, and that makes me an American. My past, my history, my lineage, all that's irrelevant.

CDH: And yet in your poems there is a very strong sense of past, of tradition, of family, of history.

SME: I'll tell you how I got there. When I went through that first year of college, some of those instructors convinced me that I was in the wrong place because of that criticism I told you about. For four years I stopped drawing and painting. I went on a search for myself because then I didn't know who I was. If I'm not an artist, I thought, if I couldn't paint, if that isn't the gift that was given me, what is the gift?

Then I met some other artists from New York, the first Puerto Rican visual artists I had met. It was in Taller Boricua. In particular, Jorge Soto stands out more than the others. There was also Fernando Salicrup and Marco Dimas. But the one who really kind of took me under his wing was Jorge Soto. I believe that they understood what I didn't understand: this deficit, this void, a cultural void. And they began telling me "Sandy do you know this? Do you know that? Do you know what the *bomba* and *plena*[13] are?" I am 25 years old, I didn't know what *bomba* and *plena* were; I didn't know these things were indigenous to Puerto Rico. None of this was given to me. No one took the time to teach me these things. They began feeding me. Then when I started writing I became involved with El Grupo.

CDH: Was that a group from New York?

SME: It had connections to the Puerto Rican Socialist party and to El Grupo Taoné, made up of people like musicians Roy Brown and Andrés Jiménez. These two came to New York, to Rutgers. I had just started writing, I had been writing for maybe six months when I met them in Rutgers; me and Jesús Papoleto Meléndez and Américo Casiano. They invited us to tour with them. They were touring the New York, New Jersey, Connecticut, and Massachusetts areas. So we did that for the next two weeks, When they left, we decided, "Well, let's continue this on our own." The group also included Suni Paz and Bernardo Palombo, who were Argentinean, and José Valdés: they were musicians.

I hooked up with El Grupo, and they began politicizing me. These were all very conscious, political individuals. I was the baby, politically speaking. I began learning, I began to become aware of what it means socially and politically to be Puerto Rican. That was the beginning of *Maria Christina*,[14] the poem. *María Christina* was my first poem in a social context. Before that, everything was very personal: usually about love.

I began learning the names for things I had grown up dancing: *merengue, cha cha*.[15] When I began learning, it was something that empowered me with my past, a beautiful thing.

CDH: The poem which you just mentioned, *My Name Is María Christina*, refers to a very well-defined female Latina identity, but it also seems to be very traditional in outlook.

SME: Well, the Puerto Rican poet Luz María Umpierre wrote a response to María Christina, a poem called *My Name Is Not María Christina* where she says that she is not submissive as Maria Christina seems to be in my poem. I entered into a dialogue with her in a poem in my latest book. The poem's title is *So Your Name Isn't María Christina*, and in it I explain the moment in which that poem was written. It was a time in which I was not sure of my own identity, and I was looking for ways to define it: "She didn't used to know herself," I say there.

CDH: Your poetry seems to have been born of all those contradictions within yourself as an individual and as a Latina in the States. Would you have been a poet if you had not lived in the United States and felt all those contradictions so keenly?

SME: I don't know. I know that something woke up inside of me, and the door came open and out of the door came poetry. I have many different feelings about my poetry. On the one hand, I feel that I'm like a channel, that consciousness passes through me: I give birth.

I'm bombarded by a variety of factors and circumstances, and they focus through me onto the page. When I write about my personal memories, they are memories that are common to many. In that sense the artist and the writer is the advocate of many in the sense that the feelings we have, as personal as they are, are common feelings. And we become voices for those who don't have or can't find their own voice or how to articulate a particular concept or idea. They may feel it, they may sense it, they may intuit it, but they can't articulate it. The thing is we're all in this society where there is a dominant culture and everyone else is not affirmed, so we're all seeking reaffirmation.

CDH: You were one of the first Puerto Rican women to write in English and one of the first women poets. What models did you have for your writing?

SME: I had no Latina models for my poetry. Whatever I knew of poetry or literature when I began writing was based on European models from the canon, the classics. At the point where I began writing, I began meeting other Puerto Rican, Latino and African-American writers. But when I first started, for many years I was the only woman surrounded by a bunch of men, and I think my work is very reflective of their style and their themes. I adopted them somehow in my own way, even though I may have translated them. It took a while before I began discovering my own voice, my own issues, priorities, and needs and whatever form was appropriate to them. It was definitely a woman's thing that I saw as different, and I was searching for how to put that into my poetry, how to express it. I was around these men, I wasn't around women. Where were the women? What can be said about us? There was a need which I could clearly imagine. I was breaking away from that which I was exposed to and coming into my own.

I did have, at a later point, the knowledge of African-American women poets like Nikki Giovanni, Sonia Sánchez, and Thulani Davis and also Ntozaki Shange.

But Latin rhythms were an influence in my work, and women's influences came through the music, the influence of women like La Lupe, like Graciela, Celia Cruz, and others. I see the voice as an instrument. And the word is another vehicle for expressing music. I remember there were times when I actually would try to compose words to simulate a conga. I would listen to Cubans speak, and they seemed to do so with a conga rhythm.

I used to think it would be nice if somebody would write a poem like a mambo, which I did, finally, in *Bluestown Mockingbird Mambo* ["Mambo Love Poem"]. That was part of my searching for the form. I am a great experimenter for forms; it comes from my art training.

CDH: Did you ever think about writing in Spanish?

SME: I have a few things written in Spanish. People have tried to discourage me because my Spanish is more phonetical than correct. It's a New York Spanish. And it's not even a New York Puerto Rican Spanish; it's my own Spanish, possibly my own dialect.

CDH: Do you consciously code-switch between Spanish and English?

SME: I do some of that with key words: it's not with a conscious intention. This is the way that we speak, so I'm reflecting a common usage in most cases. Sometimes I'm just playing with the language. I was criticized for that, like when I wrote *Tabla de Contentos.*[16] I know what *contentos* means, but I wanted to say it like that. It was a Puerto Rican intellectual who criticized me, but the thing is that control and domination are part of the colonial mindset. I experiment in language; I think that language is constantly evolving.

CDH: When you perform and read your poetry and use the two languages, do you think that people who only know one of those languages feel left out?

SME: Sometimes they feel left out, but then they pick up something along the way because we communicate on many levels, not just verbally. It's the words, it's the form, it's the sound. When I recite a poem like *Oyeme que tu espíritu habla*[17] and I sing it, its not just the words I'm saying, but somehow, this takes us back into the past, to our Taíno[18] roots.

CDH: Do you define yourself as a Nuyorican poet, one of the group who used to perform at the Nuyorican Poets Café during the seventies?

SME: I think people define me that way. I was writing poetry before Miguel Algarín coined the word Nuyorican Poetry. In my case, it may be applicable because I was actually born in New York. But it does not include all those Puerto Ricans who write who were born elsewhere: California, Florida, and so on. So what about them? Are they also Nuyoricans? I think all labels are essentially superficial.

CDH: Do you keep in touch with other Puerto Rican writers in the United States?

SME: I try to cultivate my contacts, to maintain a dialogue with other writers. I do readings and I'm constantly meeting new writers. Just recently, I met four other Latina Puertorriqueña poets. For me it was exciting because now there are finally other Puerto Rican women poets who are strong and talented.

CDH: Who sponsors those readings?

SME: I work with a collective of artists/writers called the Bronx Council on the Arts, Writers Corps Project. All of them are community artists and cultural activists. We want to keep art in the community. Everyone wants fame and fortune, but that's not our priority. Our priority is to empower our community.

CDH: Do you have contact with Anglo writers or black writers or writers from other minorities?

SME: We not only nurture our own Latino writers, but we also interact with other cultures; we deliberately bring all the other writers into our group. We also bring in the inexperienced along with those who are experienced, because we have to empower our youth. That's very important as a way of cultivating the whole community. And not only the community but the whole society.

CDH: Do you have any relation at all with Puerto Rican writers from the island?

SME: It's difficult because of the distance. Maybe we will get closer as computer technology becomes more available. Certainly, we have the desire for that kind of connection. Whenever writers come to New York we try to be supportive. There are writers like Clemente Soto Vélez who have lived in New York and have also lived here on the island. Clemente was in many ways my link to here. And there's Pedro López Adorno,[19] he's another link.

CDH: You have also written for the theater. When was that?

SME: I produced and directed a theater company for five years. I attempted to write for the theater, but I came to the realization that a poet is a poet and a playwright is a playwright. I have a healthy respect for the difference. But I had to come through that to realize it.

I was the executive director/producer of the African Caribbean Poetry Theater in New York from 1983 to 1988. We did a lot of productions. We didn't have a space, we worked out of our homes. One of our productions was *A Rose in Spanish Harlem*. It was a song recorded by Ben King. Our resident playwright wrote a play with that title, and we presented it in El Barrio. We also went on tour around the Bronx. I mostly did theater as a labor of love. My husband at the time was an actor and a playwright; we were partners. I was the business one, I ran the company. All of that has impacted my writing as well as my performance of my writing. The company was predominantly Latino and African American, but there were also Anglo Americans and Asian Americans. It was called the African Caribbean Poetry Theater because I felt that name was an affirmation of who we are, and after years of growing up in denial of ourselves and in low self-esteem, we wanted to turn the tide around.

CDH: What are you writing now?

SME: The working title for my next book is *Contrapunto in the Open Field.* It's my fourth book of poems. I keep experimenting with new forms there. I seek expression in many ways. I believe that the poet is absolutely an advocate for the people, whether or not he or she chooses to be. I did not necessarily begin at that point, but I arrived at it. Every time we say something we represent a few thousand people. The poet also becomes a model, want it or not. We become a model for creative thinking, for progressive ideals, for empowerment.

CDH: What do you feel that the United States has given you as a Puerto Rican born and raised there?

SME: The United States has given me political awareness and opportunities to establish a dialogue with other poets and other cultures.

Photograph of Victor Hernández Cruz, *El Nuevo Día* newspaper.

4

VICTOR HERNÁNDEZ CRUZ

His country accent—in Spanish—defines him as a man who comes from the mountainous interior of Puerto Rico. His measured words reveal a profundity of thought, a dedication to study, and an awareness of language that sets him apart. Victor Hernández Cruz has always tried to find the sense and significance behind life experiences and the music behind sounds and language: his work can be thought of as a quest for a rhythm that combines the different beats of two societies, two cultures.

Of all the well-known New York–Puerto Rican poets, he is the only one who has come back to live for good on the island of his birth. He is content to be back in Aguas Buenas, the small mountain town where he was born. He is a far different person than he would have been if he had not left it, however. The thirty-four years spent in the United States have colored his thinking and his poetry. His art deals with differing contexts, with harmonies and dissonances, with incongruities and strident contrasts. Their impact is transmitted in a playful manner that comes across as surrealistic in tone and manner. The syncopated melodies of jazz, the slow cadence of the *bolero*, and the repetitive beats of salsa music all find room in his verses. It's all a question of rhythm, the poet seems to indicate repeatedly.

Victor Hernández Cruz is one of the best-known Puerto Rican poets in the United States. His ear for Latino musicality is also attuned to the simple, direct, rather colloquial style of quintessential American poets like William Carlos Williams, about whose work he wrote in a poem titled "An Essay on William Carlos Williams." (*I love the quality of the spoken thought/ as it happens immediately/ uttered into the air/ Not held inside and rolled/ around for some properly schemed moment . . .*)

Each of his books of poems, beginning with *Snaps*, is a major commitment to the double scope of the poet's vision, a seeking of understanding of what it is to live between cultures, between rhythms, between languages.

Born in 1949 in Aguas Buenas, Victor Hernández Cruz moved New York with his family in 1954. He studied in New York public schools and then enrolled for some courses in Lehman College, taught by María Teresa Babín and Carmen Puigdollers, two Puerto Rican intellectuals. The greater part of his education, however, has been obtained through reading and through writing his poetry.

He has participated in several school programs directed toward Latino children and has taught at San Francisco State University, Lehman College, the University of California at Berkeley, and the University of California at San Diego, teaching courses and workshops on literature. In 1989 he returned to Puerto Rico.

His poetry books are: *Papo Got His Gun* (a chapbook published by Calle Once Publications in New York, 1966); *Snaps* (New York: Random House, 1969); *Mainland* (New York: Random House, 1973); *By Lingual Wholes* (New York: Momo Press, 1982); *Rhythm, Content & Flavor* (an anthology; Houston: Arte Público Press, 1989), and *Red Beans* (Minneapolis: Coffee House Press, 1991). He is now working on a novel titled *Time Zones*.

With Virgil Suárez and Leroy Quintana he co-edited an anthology of Latino writing in the States, *Paper Dance* (New York: Persea Books, 1995).

Hernández Cruz was editor of *Umbra*, a New York Afro-American literary magazine to which several Latinos contributed. He has published articles and poems in *The New York Review of Books, Ramparts, Evergreen Review*, and *Down There*. He also publishes occasionally in *The Village Voice* and was one of twelve poets selected by *Life* magazine at the beginning of the 1980s as representative of North American poetry. He was also one of the eighteen participants selected by Bill Moyers for the eight-part TV series on PBS presented by Channel Thirteen/WNET in New York between June 23 and July 28, 1995, "The Language of Life," featuring the lives and work of contemporary poets. The series was published in both audio cassette and book format (New York: Doubleday, 1995).

His poems can be found in anthologies such as *Puerto Rican Writers at Home in the U.S.A.*, edited by Faythe Turner (Seattle: Open Hand Publishing Co., 1991); *Aloud: Voices from the Nuyorican Poets Café*, edited by Miguel Algarín and Bob Holman (New York: Henry Holt, 1994); *Currents from the Dancing River: Contemporary Latino Fiction, Nonfiction and Poetry*, edited by Ray González (New York: Harcourt Brace, 1994), and *Boricuas: Influential Puerto Rican Writings*, edited by Roberto Santiago (New York: Ballantine Books, 1995).

"GOING FROM AGUAS BUENAS TO NEW YORK WAS LIKE HOPPING ON H. G. WELLS'S TIME MACHINE AND GOING *ZOOM!*"

CDH: You have spent the better part of your life in the States and now you live in Puerto Rico. Most of what you have written is in English. Do you consider yourself an American or a Puerto Rican writer?

VHC: I consider myself an American writer because I write in English and not Spanish. It must sound like a wild contradiction, but my poetry is in English and thus part of the North American literary landscape. I am not saying that I, the person, is a North American. I live in Puerto Rico and lead a total personal and cultural life in Puerto Rican Spanish. I write in Spanish also, so that I am a Latin American writer as well, but I have published a lot more in English. My English poetry in the United States is full of my Puerto Rican psyche and island vistas. Poetry is first of all a sensation that conjures up images before it encounters a linguistic decision; it's a way of being in the world and arranging it, it could be in Chinese or Persian or Guaraní. Once you scribble it into a language you become part of a tradition. So what I am saying is that I wrote English poetry in the United States, and that body of writing I did there can only be North American literature. Joseph Conrad was Polish, but he is considered an English writer. Some of his sentences are weird, oddly put: that criss-crossing of languages adds to the beauty of his prose. Nabokov was Russian, and if you read his prose it feels like he is constantly diving into the dictionary for the most uncommon words, away from everyday usage. Yet his work is brilliant. This is not the case of U.S. Latino writers who grow up using the English as a Spoken Weapon; what we do is screw with the syntax.

Puerto Rico is a Spanish-speaking Caribbean country, and its literature is in the language brought by the Spanish that was transformed here into something that tastes like guava and has the rhythm of African drums. Spanish is a language that accepts words from many quarters and mixes them in: it has accepted words from the Hebrew, from the language of gypsies, from the Arab. It's a language that is the same as one's own body: it is mulatto. Among us are people who look like Arabs; others look like Indians; others are mulattos and Africans. And their words have been planted in this language. I find that very interesting. When I write in Spanish, especially when I write poetry, I feel that the questions coming out from my soul flow more easily. They seem more important, stronger; I express them more forcefully because Spanish is part of my body, of the history of who I am as a person, of the family I come from, and of the small town where I grew up, Aguas Buenas, which is about thirty minutes from San Juan.

CDH: But you still consider yourself an American writer.

VHC: I think I'm the only one of those who have lived over there who says he is American. The thing is I write in English because I know that language better. Now I'm getting to know Spanish a little more; I've been living here [in Puerto Rico] for six years. But I respect the Puerto Rican language very much. I understand that the Puerto Rican spirit has to express itself in that language, in that Spanish that is combined with all that I just talked about.

Of course, what Puerto Ricans write in English in the States has a direct relationship to us and to our island. They are Puerto Rican, but the literature that they write in English has to be part of American Literature, and we have to say so without fear because even there, they have the feeling that they are on the outside, that they don't belong to the mainstream. Every writer wants to be known, wants to get to publish what he writes and communicate, because writing is his life work; he has dedicated himself to it.

This situation is different on the island. A writer who grows up here, who writes in Spanish, doesn't feel that he is left out unless he comes from the boondocks and wants to get to the capital and know the people there. He may feel isolated. But even in that case, after he gets to where he wants to, he does not feel foreign. But the United States is an empire: fifty states, in most of which Puerto Rico could fit in several times. California is like a different civilization; New Mexico is like another country: it has the infrastructure of a Latin American country. U.S. society is complex and big, and each group backs its own culture. Each one fights for its culture to be included at some point of that kaleidoscope that makes up the United States. That's what the word *multicultural* means: one culture here, another one there and another and another. It's different from Caribbean culture. In the Caribbean there are new things that have come out of the combination of different cultures. We can also talk here of multiracial. But when I use that word over there I am referring to a very sensitive matter. Americans accept the word *multicultural*, and they can even give you funding for a program that develops an aspect of that, but they say to you: "Just don't put in your proposals the word 'multiracial' because you're not going to get funded."

CDH: Their bigger problem seems to be this racial conflict.

VHC: They keep the races separate, even though there is now more mixing by marriage. There are places like New Orleans where people are more Caribbean-looking. That's the only area that had a Catholic background, as opposed to the pilgrims up North. These are the Anglo-Saxons, snobbish and proud. The United States has many divisive attitudes that are passed on from generation to generation. It's part of their national character.

CDH: Were you born in Aguas Buenas?

VHC: Yes, I'm from Aguas Buenas, I come from mountain stock, I am the product of intermarriage, the product of popular culture. I don't have one drop of Italian, French, or Dutch blood in me. In that sense I am a pure mixture of those three ingredients that are at the base of our society: those crazy soldiers, those Taínos,[1] those Africans. Aguas Buenas is all like that.

It has lived from tobacco, and it's not far from the coast. My family comes from all those mixes of blood.

CDH: How come they decided to migrate to the United States?

VHC: I really don't know. It wasn't something I myself chose. I was a 5-year-old boy, and I had to go with the adults. We were part of the situation created by the Commonwealth; I am a child of the Commonwealth of Puerto Rico.[2] I think all that came with the industrialization of the island, especially the lack of jobs, pushed my parents to their decision. Of course, my father was a soldier, and in small towns a soldier was someone who has money, who can get married and have a family and get ahead.

CDH: When was your father a soldier?

VHC: My father was a soldier in World War II. It was important because we had some savings and could get out of the town, and he could get married to my mother. As I said, it was a tobacco town and everybody worked rolling tobacco. My mother and grandmother worked at that. They rolled tobacco near the plaza, where the Banco Popular stands today. Maybe my mother was rolling tobacco there, and two or three houses down, there was a small Edgardo Rodríguez Juliá[3] playing, as a child, in his big house. He comes from my town and was raised on a house in Muñoz Rivera Street. I was born on Muñoz Rivera Street, but in a different situation; it was the section they call El Guanábano. I come from a barrio that has the name of a Taíno fruit: El Guanábano.[4]

CDH: Maybe that's why you mention so many fruits in your poetry. In one poem you say that, during hurricanes, the worst danger comes from mangoes flying and from the possibility of getting killed by a bunch of bananas falling down on you.

VHC: A shower of mangoes upon your head, yes. Too much sweet pulp can kill you.

CDH: Was your family looking for the American Dream when they left for the States?

VHC: I don't think so, because my family never really became part of American society. My mother, who lives here now, came back. She doesn't speak English. She can say two or three words, because she worked over there in a factory, but not much more. My father also worked over there. They did not really want to become something else; they didn't want to change their ways or their language. They never changed their way of cooking. As children, we used to eat rice and beans and stewed codfish and all those things when it was snowing outside and the temperature was below zero and there we were, inside, eating all those things you eat in Puerto Rico.

CDH: In what part of New York were you brought up?

VHC: In the lower part of Manhattan, the Lower East Side. It's like another Barrio. It's called *Loisaida* by the Puerto Ricans.

CDH: I was told the name was given to it by Bimbo Rivas, the street poet.

VHC: Bimbo Rivas, it's possible. Loaisaida was different from the Barrio or Spanish Harlem because it was more open, it was downtown, near the Village, near the West Side. There were cafés and jazz joints and many other things, and I think even the libraries were better. Many students lived there, many artists who were unconventional. I knew all those people when I was 13 and 14 and I used to borrow their books, I started to educate myself that way.

CDH: Was that how you became interested in writing?

VHC: I started writing when I was more or less 14. It's something that goes beyond the person because language is very old and one is very young. Language was there before we were born, and it stays there after we die. And the only thing one can do is apprehend the language, feel it inside of us. I used to read a lot, I became very interested in books. I was fascinated by fantasy and wanted to write something that would come out the same as what I was reading. I began to take notes in a little notebook, I tried to write prose. Also, I had an uncle who was a poet, who recited *décimas*,[5] and we always used to recite the poem *The Bohemian's Toast*[6] the last day of the year. I tried to write poetry in the style of those Puerto Ricans who recited at parties and activities, only mine was in English. It was very difficult.

CDH: Was there any other person who had a direct influence on your desire to write?

VHC: Well, like all mountain people, in my family everybody sang a lot. My grandfather was famous in Aguas Buenas for his singing. They called him Julio, the Bohemian. He was a tobacco worker; all the men who worked in tobacco sang while working. They continued with that tradition in New York.

That's one side of the story, the one that has to do with the popular aspects of my poetry. The other one deals with my interest in language; that comes from books. I feel my poetry wants to strike a balance between what is popular and what is learned. It is a combination of which I also think in terms of the opposition between country and city, the rural milieu and the urban milieu. That tension extends into language.

CDH: You always maintained a Puerto Rican identity, with specific references to Puerto Rico in your literature. I have perceived that in writers from the island who have lived in the States there is a strong desire to keep on thinking of themselves as Puerto Ricans, in spite of the fact that they may even ignore the reality of Puerto Rico today, because the island has changed a great deal.

VHC: The thing is that they all have a sense of nostalgia, because they take with them the Puerto Rico of their childhood, the Puerto Rico of the stories that their family tells them. But that Puerto Rico changed. The same happened to those who went to Hawaii.[7] I was in Hawaii once, and it was the most curious thing. I saw all these men, they were old men, and they dressed with *guayaberas*[8] and they looked like *jíbaros*, Puerto Rican country types. When I approached them, I realized they were speaking in English. They didn't talk one word of Spanish, but their character, their personalities, their appearance were like those of typical Puerto Ricans. When they sang, however, they sang in perfect Spanish. They sang *aguinaldos.*[9]

CDH: But the writer—the Puerto Rican writer—who lives in the States has the advantage of having access to many different cultural modalities. As island people, our literary tradition—even though, as you say in a poem, it comes from many traditions—has limitations, we are isolated. Do you think that being in contact with so many diverse, stimulating, and different cultural elements has an influence on writing?

VHC: Definitely yes. When I was young I used to go to museums all the time. I grew up seeing Picasso, especially *Guernica.* I used to look at that picture all the time, the same as Van Gogh, Velázquez, all those pictures that were in the Met's permanent collection and in the Museum of Modern Art. Other things I heard on the radio. I learned to like jazz from an early age because I was raised in a part of the city where there were a lot of Puerto Ricans and African Americans. There were relations among us, and I learned to like Afro-American music. I knew the music of Duke Ellington, Jack Coltrane, and other people like that when I was 14. I don't think I would have had those experiences in Puerto Rico, especially if we had stayed in Aguas Buenas.

CDH: Maybe not, because even San Juan wasn't as exposed then to that cultural diversity.

VHC: That is always interesting, but I also want to expand my understanding of Caribbean culture. It is one of the most universal cultures of the planet because even at its poorest and more country-like, it is a very rich culture.

CDH: Did the difference you felt as a Puerto Rican in the United States give you topics for your writing?

VHC: We felt the differences because there was a lot of racism then, and our teachers used to insult us for speaking Spanish among ourselves. It was forbidden. That was the language that we used at home, but they kept ordering us *Speak English, speak English!* And then there was television, which was all in English. There was a lot of pressure in that sense in New

York. One always felt different. We ate different food from what we saw on television, we were different in the way we dressed, in everything.

CDH: And does your writing come—in any measure—from a desire to document or validate that difference?

VHC: That will come later, because to write is to write and to write is to think clearly and live calmly. One has to have a certain peace and quiet to sit down and write. Later, one finds a particular way. Some writers like a psychological atmosphere; others are more centered on sexual matters, and they write erotic literature. Others are taken up with politics, like Juan Antonio Corretjer,[10] and others are immersed in the urban situation. One finds a way, a niche, and it comes after you are writing for some time. What I always want to do is fill in that space that I lost because of the migration. That's why I always wrote with images taken from Puerto Rican realities. I wrote about our fruits even though I was in a totally different place: papayas and pineapples in the snow, things that were always out of context. That happens a lot in my poetry and also that situation of coming from a small town where there were not even paved roads when I left. They were paving them when we left for the States. When I was small, I grew up with chickens and goats around me. I used to see the tobacco workers in their Panama hats, their white linen suits and all. There was a time when tobacco was selling well, and they earned more than teachers because the industry was flourishing. To see all this and then go to New York, which is one of the biggest and more advanced commercial urban centers of the world was like going from one era to another. It was like taking H. G. Wells's time machine and going *zoom*! My poetry is about that; I am still recuperating from something from which you can never recuperate.

CDH: So your move to the United States was a voyage in time as much—or more so—than a trip through space? That must have happened to many who migrated like you and who were from small towns or the country.

VHC: It had to be that way. The migrants were country folk because agriculture was the sector most affected when the industries and tourism started coming in. And our coffee, which was one of the best and was sold very widely, and our tobacco, which was also a strong product, and sugar cane, which gave all the world sugar for rum and for cakes, all those areas became depressed in economic terms. That's why the *campesinos*[11] left.

CDH: Those papayas and pineapples in the snow of which you write about give your poetry a Surrealist air. That is intriguing because you may not have that intention. Puerto Rican readers may take those situations as real, but other readers may find those images surreal.

VHC: I lived in the West Coast of the United States for more than twenty years. I went to Berkeley, California, in 1968 to work with a school program called *Other Ways*. The purpose was to bring art to public schools. They organized poetry workshops. I was totally worn out, asphyxiated, in New York so I went to the West Coast. But I used to go back to New York a lot. On one occasion, I came to Puerto Rico. It was in 1971. It was the first time I had come back since I left at 5. It was the greatest shock of my life. I stayed for six months.

CDH: What happened?

VHC: I came without knowing anybody. My family was here, but I didn't want to see my family. I was young at that time, and the last person I wanted to see was my father, who was here. I stayed at a friend's house and later at a guest house on Ponce de León Avenue. I remember that I took my key and went out, and I met the singer, Pepe Sánchez, who had been in New York. He took me to San Juan and to different places. I was curious about everything, I spoke with everybody. Eventually, I went up to Aguas Buenas, and I stayed with an uncle who also worked in the tobacco industry. I didn't go through what many New York Puerto Ricans go through. I think one has to come prepared for some moments of rejection. You have to understand them and place them in context and go on if you want to establish yourself here. I returned six years ago to my town, where I have family. Since then I live there. I didn't settle down in San Juan, I didn't try to become part of a circle of writers and intellectuals and those people. I'm from the popular people of Aguas Buenas, and I went back to that.

CDH: But do you have contacts with the literary world here?

VHC: I have slowly established them. I have a book of poems in Spanish, *Mesa blanca*. It migrated from an English version. The Spanish is not a translation, it is a rendition. The spirit of the poem recurs in the other language. Sometimes the poem isn't even like the original, but I know it has a relation. Sometimes it is only the center of the poem or its root that is alike. It is totally different to write in Spanish; the psychology is different. In Spanish I feel a totally different orientation.

Mesa blanca is about the popular Spiritualist tradition in Puerto Rico and the Caribbean. I know it first hand through my family. I am fascinated by that situation of being possessed by a spirit or by an entity. To me it's the same as being possessed by language. I am fascinated by the thought that conscience does not have a particular seat, a place from which voice comes forth. There is the possibility that perspective does not come from a brain and two eyes but from a golden ring or from a gold tooth. Conscience can come from out of the body, it can be disembodied. All that is in *Mesa blanca*.

CDH: Is it the first long poem you write in Spanish?

VHC: Yes, I have always written things in Spanish, but I never published them. This would be my first poetry book in Spanish. I also have an interview in Spanish in *Boletín García Lorca*, a review published in Madrid.

CDH: García Lorca seems to be a presence in your poetry. There is a playful, graceful air reminiscent of him, a touch of childish glee that underscores the seriousness of the themes and also contrasts with them.

VHC: When I read the poetry of William Carlos Williams and when I read *Poet in New York* by García Lorca, my poetic voice began to be more immediate. I decided that I was here [in New York] and that I wanted to use language that way and not try to keep on writing *décimas* in English because they were not turning out well. I accepted myself as a citizen of that city, as a person who loved its streets. I learned to walk on New York streets reading *Poet in New York*. That's when I brought my language back to reality. It was a big influence, very important for me. García Lorca's relationship with music was also important, especially his relation to flamenco. I am interested in poets who have a relationship with music. T.S. Eliot had it with classical music. I identify myself with Latin jazz.

That's the best of North American music, jazz, I am fascinated by its fragmentary improvisations. I hear a lot of jazz, and it gives me an idea of how to direct my poetic lines, where to stop, how to breathe within the context of the writing. It's like the way you play the saxophone. And the way the city moved was also important for me. *Snaps* attempts to catch that speed in its images; it's like, literally, snapping your fingers rhythmically. I felt the movement of the train, the movement of the city, how the city came unto you. It is a way to feel velocity. That also happens in *Poet in New York*, despite the fact that García Lorca was a poet from Granada, Spain.

CDH: I remember a very interesting phrase you wrote about how the Latinos of the United States would, maybe, never melt into that traditional melting pot into which all immigrants have disappeared.

VHC: I think it's because of the proximity to Latin America and the fact that we are a very strong culture.

CDH: But the Italians and Germans and all the others also had a strong culture.

VHC: We are nearer to our roots, and we can resupply constantly. One goes to certain parts of Los Angeles, and it seems like the Mexicans are just arriving, with their big hats and their vibrant colors. But the Mexicans were there before the Anglo-Saxons. The same thing happens in New York, especially with the Dominicans. The Puerto Ricans are now learning more English, but then the Dominicans and the Ecuadorians come, and they bring another dose of Spanish and the Puerto Ricans and the others who have been there for a long time make new contact with those energies, they renew their contacts with their roots. We are always a new group, and it will stay that way because of the proximity with Latin America.

And in relation to Chicanos or Mexican Americans: they were already there for many generations. We came as immigrants, but the Chicanos were in their country. We migrated with our Caribbean culture, our language, our music, and all these tempos and psychological states have entered the world of our literature. The Puerto Rican spirit is present in another language and is becoming an important branch on the tree of North American literature.

Photograph of Tato Laviera taken by Miguel Trelles.

5

TATO LAVIERA

Tato Laviera seems to bring the gregarious, carefree spirit of Santurce wherever he goes. Ebullient, assertive, talkative, he is never at a loss for words—or for rhythm. The transitions from prose to poetry, from English to Spanish, from factual conversation to an inspired recitation are made in an instant. His body can sway and dance—even when seated—to the marked beat of his verbal emphases. A New York locale—a deli, a coffee shop, or a restaurant—takes on the informal, festive air of a Puerto Rican "cafetín" when talking with him.

He laughs with the endearing brashness of the savvy kid who has grown up in the informality and bustle of a Caribbean city. His poetry has acquired the sensibility, however, of the man who, having entered into a different reality, has had to suffer from unexpected prejudice and discrimination. Wiser, but not necessarily sadder, Tato Laviera has fought back with the most enduring weapon of all. His poetry is a documentation of injustices, of painful dualities, of uncertainties; it is also testimony of the strength of the Puerto Ricans in New York who have defended their distinctness. He himself is certainly not less Puerto Rican by being such a sharp-as-steel citizen of New York.

Born in 1951 in the middle of Santurce, the section of San Juan that was just then growing into big cityhood, he accompanied his mother to New York in 1960, settling in the Lower East Side. He studied in Catholic schools and after graduating from high school attended Cornell University and Brooklyn College for a short while. He soon went to work, however, as director of the "University of the Streets," an educational alternative established in the Lower East Side that offered classes to adults at community centers and helped them get into college. He later also taught basic writing skills at Rutgers University's Livingston College from 1970 to 1973 and entered the Puerto Rican Studies Department from 1979 to 1981. During much of that time he also directed the Association of Community Service.

He has published four books of poetry, all with Arte Público Press in Houston: *La Carreta Made a U-Turn* (1979; it is now in its seventh edition); *Enclave* (1981); *AmeRícan*; and *Mainstream Ethics* (1989).

Several of Laviera's plays have been presented in New York: *Piñones* (1979); *La Chefa* (1981); *Here We Come* (1983); *Becoming García* (1984); *AmeRícan* (1986); and *The Base of Soul in Heaven's Cafe*, (1989). He also has written two other plays, *Lady Elizabeth* (1993) and *Can Pickers*, (1995).

Laviera's poetry has appeared in anthologies such as *Herejes y mitificadores: Muestra de poesía puertorriqueña en los Estados Unidos*, edited by Efraín Barradas and Rafael Rodríguez (San Juan: Huracán, 1980); *Papiros de Babel: Antología de la poesía puertorriqueña en los Estados Unidos*, edited by Pedro López Adorno (San Juan: University of Puerto Rico Press, 1991), and *Aloud: Voices from the Nuyorican Poets Café*, edited by Miguel Algarín and Bob Holman (New York: Holt, 1994).

"I'M A NUYORICAN, A PUERTO RICAN, A BORICUA: I'M A PUERTO RICAN OF MULTIDIMENSIONAL DEFINITIONS"

CDH: Were you born in Puerto Rico or in New York?

TL: In Santurce, Puerto Rico. I'm a true Cangrejero.[1] I was born in 1951, the midst of the boot and the strap[2] during the springtime of the Commonwealth. Culturally, it was the Ismael Rivera and Cortijo era.[3]

My house was in the heart of Santurce, at Bella Vista Street, number 329. Father Junquera, from Sacred Heart parish, baptized me. My mother was very religious. I had to go to Mass at 6:00 A.M. every Sunday. I served as an altar boy.

My father, Pablo Laviera, was a contractor. He helped build the first Tartak furniture store near Stop 24. He also worked out on the island. In Cayey, he worked on the first public housing constructed in that town. This was 1954. Later, he also helped in the construction of University Gardens urbanization. I remember I used to write up his payroll when I was 4 years old.

My sister is Ruth Sánchez. She's considered a great beautician. She does Celia Cruz's[4] hair. She is a true matriarch, the strength of the family. She's like a tree in the center of my family, and I am the strongest branch.

CDH: Did you attend school in Santurce?

TL: I went to Jesusa's little school, near my home, when I was 2. Then I went to Escuela Bacener; to Escuela Padre Berrios; and then to San Juan Bosco School in Cantera.[5]

When I was young, I always won prizes for good behavior, for religion class, and for interest in my studies. But then afterwards I became corrupted. At San Juan Bosco there were attendance cards, and I was put in charge of them. But the students who didn't come to school bribed me. They gave me fruit, gum, bananas, whatever.

CDH: When did your family come to the United States and why?

TL: We came on July 2, 1960, when I was 9 years old. My mother told me, when I was still Jesús Laviera Sánchez, *Negrito, vamos para el aeropuerto*6 because my sister was nine months pregnant. She was the girlfriend of the leader of a very important gang, *Las Calaveras,*7 from Castro Viñas Street. So my mother left without telling my father. My niece was born 27 days afterward.

I didn't know I was coming. When I came here, I didn't know what New York was.

The Lavieras never migrated. Only two women came because of different reasons.

My father's side of the family had come from rich blacks who migrated to Puerto Rico from Maracaibo, Venezuela. They settled in Canóvanas,8 which they preferred to Loíza because there were too many poor blacks in Loíza.

CDH: Did you have any early influences that may have inclined you to be a writer, a poet?

TL: In Puerto Rico I wanted to be an altar boy; I also represented the island on a soccer team that went to the Dominican Republic. When I was 6, I studied under Juan Boria.9 He was asked by the Salesian Fathers, who ran the San Juan Bosco School, to give a Saturday workshop for the students. He recited *Canción festiva para ser llorada,* Luis Palés Matos's10 greatest poem.

I think that was very important for me. Years later I wrote a poem, *Don Luis Pales Matos.* It's in my book titled *Enclave.* It is all in "black" language. It took me two years to write it. I wanted it to be the finest black poem in the history of Puerto Rico. Juan Boria read it for my personal pleasure on a beautiful night in Lincoln Center.

I also remember that my uncle, Felipe del Valle, took me to meet Luis Palés Matos who used to go to *tertulias*11 in 1958 at a club in Stop 17. I was afraid because my uncle told me that Palés Matos was a seven-foot black giant, taller than the giant of Carolina and with a huge *bemba.*12 But he was a gentle man who hailed from Guayama, a town in the south of the island.

CDH: So your own experiences were a starting point for your poetry?

TL: I only have eight autobiographical poems; I don't like to talk about myself.

I have two in my book *AmeRícan*. One is titled *Negrito* and reflects my experience when I came to New York in a Trans Caribbean flight with a plane that had six motors. The first thing I heard from my aunt when I came into this country was *no te juntes con los prietos, negrito*.[13] She used to live in a mixed neighborhood in the Lower East Side. She didn't want conflict. Up until then I thought the United States was all white because of the snow.

The other poem was about something that happened to me as a child. My father was a Nationalist[14] and hid arms in coffins and buried them. When I was 4, I found one of the coffins while playing in the yard. I wrote it down twenty years later in the poem *Boyhood*.

CDH: You do a lot of code-switching[15] in your poetry; sometimes you have whole stanzas in one language or the other. How do you make a decision in regard to language?

TL: Sometimes I write in English and sometimes in Spanish. It depends. You have to select language according to theme. I am cataloged as a Nuyorican writer because of the school of writing I belong to. I write in two languages, and so I have the possibility of writing in either one. I can control both and mix them. All the possibilities of blending two languages are at the disposition of our bilingualism. I have to make a decision according to the colloquiality of the moment.

CDH: But you feel identified with the Nuyorican poets—Algarín, Pietri, Sandra María Esteves—who are older than you?

TL: Bilingually, we are able to have universal friendships. We're all old friends. Algarin's poetry is muscular vision; Pietri's is a linguistic celebration; Sandra María Esteves's is spiritual essence. And one of our great teachers was a "declamador"[16] whose name was Jorge Brandon.[17] He was a great historical figure. He's the tie that binds us to Puerto Rico.

I love the name of Nuyorican because of two things. It's a style of writing. I always say that I'm Nuyorican, even though I was born in Puerto Rico, because of my style of writing. Many island writers gave definitions during the fifties, but the one that stuck, that spelling, is due to Algarín and Piñero. And it's not only a style but a school of writing too.

CDH: You have proposed a new term, *AmeRícan*.

TL: We have two and a half million Puerto Ricans born here. I had to find a new word: Rican. There is a difference because not everybody is from New York. When I began to talk in schools and colleges and people started to ask, I titled one of my books *AmeRícan*: "I-am-a-Rican." American. But our literary language is still bound up with Nuyorican writing, even though we are AmeRícan.

We are all caught up in the dichotomy of the Popular Party[18] and the *jíbaro* who wants to be everything. It's the experience of the Commonwealth. We are a state, we are free, we are associated. There are many Puerto

Ricans being born in Philadelphia, in Cleveland, in Hawaii, all over. In Hawaii, 1 percent of the population is Puerto Rican. They talk in Hawaiian, neither in English nor Spanish, and call themselves "Pokoliko."

CDH: Do you have any trouble with people understanding your poetry written in both languages?

TL: You know, people in Europe see us in a thoroughly different manner than the way some Puerto Ricans and American marginalists see us. They consider that the English language spoken in America has different dialects. In Spanish we have created many new words indigenous to blacks. We have added our own dialects. Besides, twenty-one countries speak Spanish in the Americas. Why should I have to limit myself to English only when Spanish is the dominant hemispheric language?

Bilingualism is not only between English and Spanish; it's a universal situation. It may refer to urban English in Spanish form. It's not the Spanish from the Antilles; it's a Spanish with an English tonality, with an English spirituality, it's a Spanish urbanized. A lot of young writers are into it because they have to deal with a school situation, but they want to deal with a home situation and a community situation. It's an accent in English, it's an accent in Spanish, it is Spanish with an English accent and with urban black tonalities.

CDH: What are your relations with black poetry and writing?

TL: Fifty percent of my poetry, of my recitals, are for the black constituency of the United States for three reasons: they are very interested in my sense of Caribbean blackness, and of urban blackness, and they are interested in the rhythmic quality of my poetry. Whether or not you like it, if you're a Caribbean writer, in the United States you don't write in white verse, you write in black verse. You write with the attitudes of blacks which are very important to the Puerto Rican community.

CDH: So in a way you have established a cultural cross-breeding (*mestizaje*) with the black community here.

TL: Absolutely. I define it in my poems *Salsa in Bethesda Fountain* and *Tito Madera Smith*.

CDH: In the poem *para ti, mundo bravo*, from *La Carreta Made a U-Turn,* you present yourself as a historian who documents events. Is that the purpose of your poetry, to document Puerto Rican reality in the United States?

TL: Always. My first book was that one, *La Carreta Made a U-Turn,* but I started out to write theater. I have written eight plays and knew René Marqués[19] during my childhood. That book is patterned after his play *La Carreta*.[20] It is like the fourth act of his play; I begin with a section, *Metropolis Dreams*, in the place where he left his characters. Then I go to the streets and then to the slums. He started out in the mountains, went to

San Juan and then to the Metropolis. My route is the opposite. And then afterward I make a historical decision to the effect that Doña Gabriela did not go back. The Doña Gabrielas of Puerto Rico stayed here, and they established themselves in all American towns. Even though *U-Turn* means they stayed in the United States, the book had to finish in Spanish. So forty-two of my poems are exclusively in Spanish, even though they have English titles. I'm a Nuyorican, a Puerto Rican, a Boricua: all that. I'm a Puerto Rican of multidimensional definitions. I have five hats, all Puerto Rican: the Latino hat, the urban hat, the black hat, the boricua hat, and the hemispheric hat.

CDH: Is there a connection between your affirmation as a poet and the dislocation you suffered as a Puerto Rican transplanted to New York?

TL: To be Nuyorican is also a return. This is not our problem exclusively. It's a universal problem. The Dominicans have it; the Latin Americans have it; the Africans who go to France and England have it. They have to adapt. The Nuyorican is a displacement. It has to do with people from native countries having to come to mother countries and adapt to them. So the Nuyorican is not a phenomenon of the Puerto Ricans in New York and the Puerto Ricans on the island. It's a worldwide phenomenon.

CDH: We are the ones with the longest colonial history.

TL: But at the same time we are not going to become a state. We won in that. We're against that dream: we rejected them. People ask: "Why don't Puerto Ricans want to be a part of the United States?" To me, that's very important. We had the opportunity since 1917 to go that way. To denounce it is the ultimate state of independence of our people. I call it the ultimate state of *pava*[21] because even though we remain in limbo, we are not a state.

CDH: In a poem titled *angelito's eulogy in anger* from *La Carreta Made a U-Turn*, you seem to express an anger at parents who brought their children from Puerto Rico to the States.

TL: The anger is not only directed at parents. *Angelito* is a bilingual poem. Its structure is determined by the use of English on the left column and of Spanish on the right column. I wrote it in front of my cousin's coffin. I had a conflict, because the poem came out in Spanish and English at the same time. I wanted to talk to the parents but also to the community, to America. It was a challenge. The anger came because I couldn't say everything in Spanish or everything in English. I recited it aloud that night. I didn't want anybody to go without understanding. I didn't want people to say, "It's nice, but I didn't understand it in the other language." So I made a decision that the moment was a bilingual moment. Neither Spanish nor English was sufficient for the opportunity. And as a colloquial poet, neither Spanish nor English was sufficient for the situation in which I found myself.

CDH: Do you perceive any prejudice against you as a Nuyorican when you go back to Puerto Rico?

TL: I have no problem. Everybody receives me well. I introduced Juan Boria to New York audiences. I wrote about him, that's why I have no problems in Puerto Rico; I'm very connected. However, I once wrote a poem titled *Nuyorican* that expresses the feelings of many Puerto Ricans who return and feel rejected. It is very hard, after they have suffered for being Puerto Rican. That's what I say in that poem, but every verse ends with the question *¿sabes? (you know?)* that softens the accusation.

CDH: Do you think you would have been a writer if you hadn't come to the States?

TL: If I wouldn't have come to the States, I would have been the governor of Puerto Rico. There's no doubt in my mind about that.

When I first came to this country and went to school, my teacher was a nun who had left the order but was still teaching there. When I was in fifth grade, I told her my name was Jesús Laviera Sánchez. And she said I couldn't be Jesús because I was black and I didn't know any English. From then on, they omitted my name, Jesús. I immediately became Abraham. So in May of 1960 I was Jesús Laviera Sánchez, and in September, three months afterward, when I started classes here, I was Abraham Laviera. That affected me a lot. That's when I decided to be a writer, to go back to my name. When I became a writer, I said "I don't want to be either Jesús or Abraham"; I used my nickname, Tato, the name my brother Pablo gave me. That's what made me a writer, that moment when they took away my name, Jesús. As a Nuyorican, Puerto Rican, Boricua poet, I needed to write the greatest English poem as a challenge. So I did it: the poem that defines me is *Jesús Papote*. It is totally in English, and it marks my conquering of the verbiage of the English dictionary. That was my purification. I feel, as a poet, that I should have no prejudices about poetry in general. I am totally open to poetry in all the world. I don't have one definitive definition of what it's all about.

CDH: Do you have any relation to writers who live in Puerto Rico?

TL: In terms of Puerto Rico, I personally think that the linguistics that have come out of there marks one of the more authentic integrations of language in Latin American Spanish. The vocabulary of the Puerto Rican repertoire in the last twenty-five years has achieved an incredible amount of openness in identifying the indigenous, the black, and the Spanish groups of languages. It has been respectful of Latin American literature, respectful of the Puerto Rican Diaspora, of the Puerto Rican identity and very open to English suggestiveness and brilliance. Puerto Rican writing has included jazz, has included black American literature. They have developed a patois, integrated linguistics. I do have problems with some thinkers and monolinguals who are opposed to the linguistic vernacular of our people: the ones who have problems with the way we talk. Those who study only in books because they don't have time to talk to anybody. They spend all their time analyzing and categorizing language and not practicing it. They are boring extremists; perfumed educators, consumers of classical seventeenth-century Spanish, racist monolinguists, stuck-up Spanish-only speakers, nihilist philosophers, and misguided revolutionaries.

I especially admire the women writers in Puerto Rico. Ana Lydia Vega[22] is a great synthesizer of language. She's a national treasure. She's the ultimate *sancocho*.[23] She should be on the pedestal of the Ateneo Puertorriqueño and of the Institute of Puerto Rican Culture (ICPR); she should be in La Fortaleza selling Puerto Rican literature to the world.

CDH: You have had considerable success with your books.

TL: The first book published by Arte Público was *La Carreta Made a U-Turn*. It's now in its seventh edition and has sold more than 60,000 copies.

CDH: Have you published your plays?

TL: No; I've written eight. They advised me not to publish until there are "second showings." Some of them are: *Piñones*, a musical with ten songs about Roberto Clemente's accident in Piñones; *La chefa, Base of soul, In Heaven's Cafe, Becoming García,* and *American.*

CDH: How would you define yourself as a poet and as a Puerto Rican?

TL: The poem *Doña Cisa y su anafre* defines me as a Puerto Rican. That poem and that experience was my transition from *jíbaro* to New York. It's about an old woman who is making codfish fritters for a street festival and keeps on even though it is already night and everyone has gone away because nobody has told her to stop. It is there I express the combination between the *jíbaro,* the language, and New York. That is the total coloring, the rainbow of my identity. When I realized that, everything came together and I went on from there.

6

NICHOLASA MOHR

Nicholasa Mohr has proclaimed, over and over again—in her writings, in her words—her great love for New York, the city in which she was born and raised. She is a "Latino" New Yorker whose great warmth and openness, whose wide, welcoming smile embody the best of Puerto Rican social culture in that city.

Born in Spanish Harlem of Puerto Rican parents, she was raised in the Bronx and attended New York City public schools. She became interested in art at a very young age and studied at the Arts Student League, at the Brooklyn Museum of Art School, and also attended the Pratt Center for Contemporary Printmaking. She married Irwin Mohr, a child psychologist, and had two children.

After working as a painter and as an art teacher in New York and New Jersey, Mohr became interested in writing. Her first book, *Nilda* (New York: Harper and Row, 1973), a *bildungsroman* about a young Puerto Rican girl growing up in New York during World War II, was a resounding success. It was selected as Best Book of the Year by the *School Library Journal* and Outstanding Book of the Year by *The New York Times*.

Her other books are: *El Bronx Remembered,* a collection of short stories (it was a finalist for the National Book Award and was published in 1975 by Harper and Row); *In Nueva York,* another collection of stories (New York: Dial Press, 1977); *Felita,* a novel (New York: Dial Press, 1979); *Rituals of Survival. A Woman's Portfolio,* a collection of stories (New York: Arte Público Press, 1985); *Going Home,* a novel (New York: Dial Press, 1986); *All for the Better: A Story of El Barrio,* a biography of Evelyn López Antonetty (New York: Steck-Vaughn Co., 1995); *In My Own Words: Growing Up Inside the Sanctuary of My Imagination,* a memoir of her early years (New York: Simon and Schuster, 1994); *The Magic Shell,* a short novel (New York: Scholastic, 1995), and two illustrated books for children, *The Song of El Coquí,* in collaboration with Puerto Rican graphic artist

Photograph of Nicholasa Mohr supplied by the writer.

Antonio Martorell and *Old Letivia and the Mountain of Sorrows* (New York: Viking, 1995 and 1996, respectively).

Nicholasa Mohr was awarded an honorary doctorate of letters by the State University of New York at Albany. She has been visiting professor at Queens College and has been writer in residence at several universities and institutions, including the Smithsonian Institution and the American University in London.

She has appeared in anthologies such as *Puerto Rican Writers at Home in the U.S.*, edited by Faythe Turner (Seattle: Open Hand Publishing Co., 1991); *Short Fiction by Hispanic Writers of the United States*, edited by Nicolás Kanellos (Houston: Arte Público Press, 1993); *Barrios and Borderlands. Cultures of Latinos and Latinas in the United States*, edited by Denis Lynn Daly Heyck (New York: Routledge, 1994); *Currents from the Dancing River: Contemporary Latino Fiction, Nonfiction and Poetry*, edited by Ray González (New York: Harcourt Brace, 1994); *In Other Words: Literature by Latinas of the United States*, edited by Roberta Fernández (Houston: Arte Público Press, 1994); and *Boricuas: Influential Puerto Rican Writings*, edited by Roberto Santiago (New York: Ballantine Books, 1995).

"MY HEART IS IN NUEVA YORK, WHERE I WAS BORN"

CDH: You were born and raised in New York; how do you relate to Puerto Rico?

NM: I was born in Spanish Harlem and raised in the Bronx. My mother was from Puerto Rico. She was a *ponceña*,[1] Nicolasa Rivera.

Once I attended a conference in New York City with writers from all over the world. They spoke about sounds, foods, smells, all the nostalgia of their home countries. I remember having a sense of envy because I had not experienced the island first hand. I had no childhood relationship with my roots.

Having said that, I must also admit that I'm very grateful to have been born in New York. I don't know how well I would have fared in Puerto Rico as the youngest female in a poor family. Besides, being a woman, I had a lot more choices because I was born in the States. Women's rights are stronger and more equitable in the United States.

I consider New York my home. I love being in the island, of course, and I get great nourishment from its beauty, culture, food, and good friends. But my heart is in Nueva York, where I was born. When one is born into a city with such an immense diversity, one can take advantage of that richness.

CDH: What was it like, to grow up in the Bronx?

NM: I wrote about it in *El Bronx Remembered*. The South Bronx after World War II had many migrants coming in from Puerto Rico. I had never seen so many Puerto Ricans in my life. I was surprised at their loud speech, their unabashed ways, their colorful clothing, and was quite taken with them. I was the offspring of a previous wave of migrants. My mother came at the height of the Depression and settled in New York. The Puerto Rican community was rather small then. It was mixed with other ethnic groups. There were Jews, Greeks, Italians, Irish. There were also black Americans and some other Latinos, like Cubans, Dominicans, and Chileans. The Jewish community was quite prevalent when I was growing up. Some of my teachers and the librarians at my school were Jewish.

And then, almost like a tidal wave, the Puerto Ricans arrived. It was amazing to see it.

CDH: What language did you speak at home?

NM: At home Spanish was spoken, but my six older brothers spoke English. By the time I went to school, I was bilingual.

CDH: Were both your parents Puerto Rican?

NM: My mother's husband was from Spain. My biological father was Puerto Rican.

CDH: Was your mother looking for the American Dream when she came to the States?

NM: She was desperate. She was really looking for work and a way to make a living. She had four little children and had left a miserable husband who was abusive. She had a sister in the States, and so she came to live with her. My mother was very young, about 23.

CDH: How did you learn about Puerto Rico as a child?

NM: What I realize now, in hindsight, is that I lived in the Barrio, in an area where there were so many Puerto Ricans that the culture was always intrinsically there. I was never deprived of my Puerto Rican culture. Within the dominant culture, my own culture was quite strong. I remember when I was a printmaker, many years later, and I was working alongside other artists at Pratt. We started telling Christmas stories. My story about Christmas was about a sow that was roasted, Puerto Rican style, and some *pasteles*[2] and *arroz con gandules.*[3] People began to ask me, "What country do you come from?" "The Barrios of New York City!", I answered.

When I go to Puerto Rico or to the Dominican Republic, the music and also the food there remind me of my childhood. Puerto Rican and Caribbean culture has always been part of my life. As the years pass, you come to have many different realizations. I remember how very moving and beautiful the songs were during my childhood Christmases. I sat listening, imagining, believing every word. It was my earliest exposure to oral literature; poems and stories told with intrigue and mystery. This cultural experience taught me to appreciate the beauty and power of language. It was in great part responsible for my love of books and my love of storytelling.

CDH: Did your mother ever talk about going back to Puerto Rico?

NM: She would have loved to return, especially after being widowed. She considered returning to Puerto Rico. However, she also knew that living in New York gave her opportunities she would not have on the island. Her only skill was sewing. She did not have a formal education. In New York City she could find work. In addition, Puerto Rico is basically a patriarchal culture, and she didn't want to be defined by male dominance. She acknowledged the prejudice that she had felt in New York City; she also longed for the beauty of her island and for her language and her people. Like all Puerto Ricans, she dreamed of retiring on her own plot of land in her beloved island.

CDH: When did you first go to Puerto Rico?

NM: I went as a teenager in the late fifties. It was a surprise because people in New York had talked about a Puerto Rico that existed in their childhood and that didn't exist in reality any more. I did like the countryside and the beauty of the island. I didn't go again for a number of years, and then I returned as a professional writer.

I tackle that reality, how the children of Puerto Ricans who go back to the island are surprised when they find that what their parents talked about is a myth, that it no longer exists. In *Going Home*, my children's novel, a little girl goes back and she's perceived as a stranger, an outsider, a Nuyorican and a *gringa*.[4] She's floating in a sea of ambiguity in terms of status in relationship to where she belongs. There are no answers, just questions that arise.

CDH: Did you feel in any way rejected?

NM: Not the first time because I was quite young. They made fun of my Spanish, but that wasn't anything serious, it was all benign. However, after I started writing, I had a difficult time in Puerto Rico. Many intellectuals on the island could not accept who I was and what I was doing. I soon decided that they were not going to affect my relationship with the land of my ancestors, that this island was as much mine as theirs. The best thing I could do was not subject myself to inane criticism. But I've gone back over the years: in 1987 for the presentation of my book *Rituals of Survival* and in 1989 I was a keynote speaker for a big conference sponsored by the Hispanic Association of Media Arts and Sciences. Island Puerto Ricans often postulated that I was not an authentic island Puerto Rican, but I've never pretended to write as an island Puerto Rican.

CDH: But you feel Puerto Rican. Is there a conflict in that?

NM: When I'm in Puerto Rico, I feel I am an American, particularly a New Yorker, of Puerto Rican parents. I love the island but it's not my place of birth. When I'm in New York I feel my Puerto Rican roots but I'm not an island person. There's no conflict. I was brought up as a Puerto Rican; I didn't invent it, it's my culture. There have been Puerto Ricans in the States since last century. Puerto Rican identity in the States is almost a century old. It's not circumscribed by the island. That's the magic of New York. People come from all over. I feel a citizen of the world. I'm not really a Nationalist. I'm very fortunate; I can embrace any culture in the world and feel quite at home. That's a joy for me. New York gave me a sense of belonging that is not constricted by nationalism.

The island of Puerto Rico is a small but complicated place. It's the only place in the world, I think, where you have a Latin American culture and you're an American citizen. I wrote a paper published by the University of Oklahoma's Department of Psychology about Puerto Ricans being like adopted citizens. I describe myself as an adopted citizen, much like a child who has been adopted by a family. He or she doesn't look like that family and longs to know who his or her parents really are. I was taught in the schools that Americans adopted Puerto Rico, it is not a real country. So, am I supposed to be forever grateful because someone adopted us and took us in? The Spaniards first, and then the United States? How does a child, then, form an identity? I was very fortunate that I could work this conflict out through my art work, initially, and later through my writing. I have enough variety and excitement within my own culture; there's plenty of information and material to write forever and ever. My work is very specific. It comes from personal experience, and yet, coming from that specificity, I can approach anybody in the world and feel I can communicate.

CDH: Do you think that eventually Puerto Ricans will become assimilated into U.S. society?

NM: Well, the Irish were assimilated but not the blacks because of race. With us it's different; we have different colors, but we are all Hispanics. An Argentinean and a Dominican are both Hispanics: The Argentinean is white and the Dominican is brown. Now there are people of color and Hispanics everywhere. We are called Latinos today because it responds more to an acknowledgment of color. They define Latinos as neither black nor white. I define myself as a woman of color.

CDH: Did you read a lot as a child?

NM: I had no TV at home. When I was very small, I began to draw. Soon after, I began to draw words and one of my brothers taught me how to read and write. I was thrilled to get my mother's approval. That was the beginning of my career as a writer. I was also thrilled when I took out my first book from the library. It was Carlo Collodi's *Pinocchio*. I took it out many times and also Grimm's Fairy Tales. I am always glad to express gratitude to the library. I spent my youth there, reading Nancy Drew mysteries, Jack London novels, and the works of Fenimore Cooper.

But I never read about myself or about black people. Eventually, at 14, I discovered Howard Fast[5] and that was quite wonderful. If I had not been a writer I might have been a librarian.

CDH: When did you decide to become a writer?

NM: I never thought I would be a writer, I was not interested in writing. I went to Mexico after high school to study art. When I returned, I got a scholarship for the Brooklyn Art School. After I had become established as a printmaker, I was exhibiting at a gallery when an art agent contacted me. Through the art agent, one of my collectors, who was in publishing and noticed I had words in my art work, asked me "Why not become a writer?" After much cajoling, I wrote fifty pages of vignettes. The collector read them and said I should write something more exciting, about prostitutes, gang wars, and the seedier side of life. But I declined and told them that I led a very dull life, I was only a boring mother and wife. I took back my stories. Some time later I was asked to design a book jacket for Harper and Row. I took the opportunity and asked them to read my work. As a favor, an editor agreed to read the fifty pages. Three weeks after I had given her the fifty pages I got a contract in the mail. That was how *Nilda* was born.

CDH: Is *Nilda* an autobiographical novel?

NM: It has some autobiographical material in it, but it is not an autobiography. It was an instant success: a book for the child and young adult markets. Books like *Felita* and *Going Home* also do well in terms of sales. The language is disarmingly simple, but the context is quite complex.

Nilda launched my career. I was thrilled. The book is never out of print. All my books are about New York and they are based on my experiences, but they also document the experiences of the Puerto Rican community.

CDH: There is a definite presence of different kinds of religious experience in *Nilda*.

NM: *Nilda* takes place during a time when the hierarchy of the Catholic Church was run by the Irish in New York City. Even the Italians had a secondary role, and certainly the Puerto Ricans had a minuscule one. That was also when the Mass was in Latin. There are many kinds of Catholics in the world, and I have found that the way Caribbean Catholics practice their Catholicism is not at odds with practices such as Spiritualism.[6] They practice both in a parallel fashion. The Pentecostals, on the other hand, went dancing, had food, wild confessionals; they spoke in tongues and were lots of fun from the perspective of a child. And then the Spiritualist sessions are given from the point of view of a child who is a dreamer and whose father is a communist, so she's caught up between these two worlds.

CDH: In one of your essays you said your writing was like that of an investigative reporter, that you want to document Puerto Rican experience in the United States.

NM: Yes, because it's my reality, with all its marvelous textures and changes and joys and heartaches. It is all part of being who I am.

CDH: Is it more difficult to write for children and for young people than to write for adults?

NM: I find that whether I write for a child or an adult, I give it as much thought. It's a question of getting locked into a mode. It's just like when I was a painter or a printmaker. I created prints, oils, and watercolors. It's just as difficult to do any of them.

When I write for children, I really write for everybody; anybody can read those stories. Of course, for children, you have to be sure the language is simple: they're not going to be interested in long-winded philosophical monologues. They're interested in immediacy. But within that immediacy, when you make sure you are connecting and communicating, you make it interesting enough so that adults like it too. It must be compelling.

CDH: And the same as your books are not limited to children and young people, they seem to have a widespread appeal that is not limited to the Latino community.

NM: My books have sold in the hundreds of thousands, and many fan letters are not only from Latino children. Those are the last, economically speaking, to be able to acquire them. The books are apparently assigned in schools. And some, like *Felita*, with a fairly simple syntax but an intense plot and interesting characters (they are thrown out of the neighborhood, they come back, there's a fire, etc.), are used extensively for the teaching of English as a second language. Many adults love that book and *Going Home* too, because it deals with perplexing problems they can identify with. Adults can read them and feel they are not just reading about someone getting the wrong lunch box.

CDH: What was it like to work in *Song of the Coquí*, your recent children's book, with Puerto Rican artist Antonio Martorell?

NM: I learned a lot working with Toño Martorell. We decided the high points of the stories, and then we sort of fitted it together. We did the drawings together in the *coquí*[7] book. I sat down at the computer and worked out a lot of the syntax. He was at the helm with the art work and I was at the helm with the writing. We both feel that one couldn't have done it without the other.

However, in my most recent children's book, published both in English and in Spanish, *Old Letivia and the Mountain of Sorrows (La vieja Letivia y el monte de pesares)*, art and writing are totally separate. Rudy Gutiérrez, who illustrated *The Magic Shell*,[8] is also the illustrator for it. I wanted a Puerto Rican who had positive feelings for the island and loved it like I do.

When I wrote this particular story ten years ago, I was staying in Toño Martorell's house in Cubuy, in El Yunque.[9] I was supposed to be writing something else, but I was so taken by the magic of El Yunque that I decided to put everything aside and go with my feelings. The story simply materialized.

CDH: Can you make a living as a writer?

NM: Indeed, I earn a fair living as a writer.

CDH: Did you establish contact with other Puerto Rican writers in New York when you started out on your writing career?

NM: There were some Puerto Rican writers when I started but most were poets: Sandra María Esteves, Miguel Algarín, Pedro Pietri, Tato Laviera, and so on. Ed Rivera was one of the few novelists.

CDH: I notice you do not use code-switching[10] a lot.

NM: I use it sparingly because I feel that the reader might not be getting the point. I am concerned for my readers, so I manage to make my intent clear. With poets it's different. They can read their work aloud and have close contact with their public. When I do use words in Spanish, I follow them up with English in a way that is clear.

CDH: What is your relation with writers from Puerto Rico?

NM: I never strongly identified with Puerto Rican writers from Puerto Rico. My writing comes from a different sensibility. However, we do share ethnicity. What some of them write about doesn't necessarily hold that much interest for me. It's also a question of social class. There is a certain classism in all of this. We are different because we write in another language. We are not living in a void. Some of their writing, as I said in my essay *Puerto Rican Writers in the United States, Puerto Rican Writers in Puerto Rico: A Separation Beyond Language*,[11] is very baroque. I find that hard to relate to. I might have more in common with people writing in places like Prague or Ecuador. I have, however, read and liked very much Julia de Burgos and José Luis González and Magali García Ramis. But things are changing now. Now we have some Puerto Rican writers writing in English, like Rosario Ferré. That seems to indicate change.

CDH: Are there points of contact between the Puerto Rican experience and writing in the States and the African-American experience and writing?

NM: The black American perspective is different. They were brought in as slaves. They use the English language. Latinos have another language.

African-American writing goes a long way back. They developed a black aristocracy, a black middle class. There is a huge variety of writers: Alice Walker, Richard Wright, many, many writers. They cover a wide spectrum of topics. We come from a different perspective, especially the New York group, which is mostly working class.

CDH: You have written plays and screenplays; can you tell me about them?

NM: I did a screenplay in collaboration with Ray Blanco who is the director of *The Cutting Edge*. It was based on my story *The Artist (Inez)*. So far it has not been filmed. I also write plays. I had a play produced when I was in England, *I Never Even Seen My Father*, from a story in *In Nueva York*. It was beautifully produced at Richmond College theater. Antonio Martorell did the sets. I've had readings in New York of my other play, called *Zoraida (Aunt Rosana's Rocker)*, based on a story from *Rituals of Survival*.

CDH: When were you in Mexico and for how long?

NM: I studied art there in the late 1950s for two semesters before I started to write. I was in Mexico City, at the Taller de Gráficas. It was an important experience in my life. Back then, people saved their money to go to Europe, which was what I wanted to do, and then I discovered the Mexican muralists in the library and thought that I would rather go there. For the first time in my life, I saw that art could make strong political and social statements. It didn't have to be only poster art or cheap propaganda; it didn't have to be slogans, it could be very deep, it could be adapted to everyday life, to everything you do in your life. I learned a lot. I was very grateful that I spent time there.

CDH: Did that experience modify your art or your life?

NM: It made me more cognizant of being Puerto Rican, because I had never lived in Puerto Rico, nor was I educated in Puerto Rico. So it was my first experience in a Latin country, and my friends asked me to stay and become a Mexican because I was really happy there. I was pleased and even flattered. However, I said, "No, I'm a Puerto Rican from New York, and that's who I am and that's what I want to be."

7

JUDITH ORTIZ COFER

Slight, with large, sad eyes, very white skin and raven-black long hair, Judith Ortiz Cofer looks like one of the *jibaritas* who were seen so frequently some decades back along mountain roads in Puerto Rico's hinterlands. That impression dissolves, however, the minute she speaks in a clear, precise English, "flavored"—as she herself says—with occasional phrases in Spanish to accentuate her meaning and retain the connection with her origins. An articulate speaker and a thoughtful writer, Judith Ortiz Cofer has evidently thought long and hard about the implications of being both Latina and a writer.

Born in Hormigueros, a town in southwest Puerto Rico in 1952, she moved to the States with her family in 1955. Her father, Jesús Ortiz Lugo, was in the Navy and had to be away at sea frequently. With her mother and her younger brother, Judith stayed in Paterson, New Jersey, alternating with periods when she went back with her mother and brother to her grandmother's house in Puerto Rico. Her schooling, however, was mostly in Paterson. In 1968 the family moved to Georgia.

Judith Ortiz Cofer studied in Augusta College and has an M.A. in English from Florida Atlantic University. She did graduate work at Oxford University sponsored by the English-speaking Union of America. She teaches English and Creative Writing at the University of Georgia, is active in the lecture circuit, and continues writing.

Her poems, short stories, and essays have been published since 1977 in magazines like the *New Mexico Humanities Review*, the *Southern Humanities Review, Kenyon Review, Revista Chicano-Riqueña*, and the *Georgia Review.*

She has published four chapbooks: *Latin Women Pray* (1980), *Among the Ancestors* (1981), *The Native Dancer* (1981), and *Peregrina* (1986).

Her books include *Reaching for the Mainland* (poems, Tempe, Ariz.: Bilingual Press, 1987); *Terms of Survival* (poems, Houston: Arte Público Press, 1987); *The*

Photograph of Judith Ortiz Cofer, *El Nuevo Día* newspaper.

Line of the Sun (novel, Athens, Ga.: University of Georgia Press, 1989–nominated for a Pulitzer Prize); *Silent Dancing: A Partial Remembrance of a Puerto Rican Childhood* (essays and poems, Houston: Arte Público Press, 1990); and *The Latin Deli* (prose and poetry, Athens, Ga.: University of Georgia Press, 1993). Her latest book is *An Island like You: Stories of the Barrio* (New York: Orchard Books, 1995). *The Line of the Sun* has been translated into Spanish and published by the University of Puerto Rico Press in San Juan (1996).

Ortiz Cofer's work has appeared in anthologies such as *Puerto Rican Writers at Home in the U.S.A.*, edited by Faythe Turner (Seattle: Open Hand Publishing,, 1991); *Iguana Dreams. New Latino Fiction*, edited by Delia Poey and Virgil Suárez (New York: Harper, 1992); *Short Fiction by Hispanic Writers of the United States*, edited by Nicolás Kanellos (Houston: Arte Público Press, 1993); *In Other Words. Literature by Latinas of the United States*, edited by Roberta Fernández (Houston: Arte Público Press, 1994): *Currents from the Dancing River: Contemporary Latino Fiction, Nonfiction and Poetry*, edited by Ray González (New York: Harcourt Brace, 1994); *Barrios and Borderlands*, edited by Denis Lynn and Daly Heyck (New York: Routlege, 1994), and *Boricuas: Influential Puerto Rican writing*, edited by Roberta Santiago (New York: Ballantine Books, 1995).

"WHERE IS HOME? I WANT TO GO THERE."

CDH: What difference do you perceive, as a Puerto Rican writer who lives in the States and writes in English, with writers in Puerto Rico?

JOC: As a writer, I had to overcome the usual things, plus the fact that nobody thought that Puerto Ricans could elevate themselves beyond a certain point. I guess what was important to me was that when I write something, people see themselves in it. When I read Ana Lydia Vega and Rosario Ferré, I know what they are talking about because I grew up a Puerto Rican woman, except that at some point our roads diverged. They stayed here and I went away.

CDH: That does not seem to be the experience of all Puerto Rican writers living and writing in the States. Some do not recognize themselves in the work of Puerto Rican writers who live on the island.

JOC: Well, there's a problem there, a certain clash. It's not that I recognize myself in the language of Puerto Rican writers: their Spanish goes way beyond mine, which is a familial Spanish. That is not my fault; that is a result of a choice my parents made.

I recognize myself in the cultural aspects that make us different. For example, in that beautiful story called *Milagros, calle Mercurio* (by Carmen Lugo Filippi). I know exactly what she's talking about; I have enough sense about being Puerto Rican to identify with it. So I don't have to have grown up in the island to understand that. I hope that if she reads a story of mine, that she will for a few minutes say *I can project myself into that girl.*

It's not that I have an idealistic view that I think everybody is going to come together like in a peaceable kingdom—the lions and the lambs—but I think that if instead of instinctively saying *I'll never identify with the Puerto Rican writers* we just actually read them, for them to read us, we will find something in common.

CDH: But there's no sense of there being a community of writers, some in the States, some over here, is there? I think there is a pronounced division or at least an ignorance of each other.

JOC: There is some hostility, yes. When I have done readings in Puerto Rico, in the Río Piedras or Mayagüez campus of the university, not one writer has showed up. I was hoping to meet them, especially the women writers. I am a great admirer of their writing. They are intelligent, inventive. I have read their books. I also believe there is some connection. We are all women writers; we are dealing with very similar circumstances. I don't understand this. I don't know whether there are political considerations involved. I do feel some tension, a division. I hope that at some point this is eliminated. We in the States love the island, and I don't understand why there can't be some communication.

CDH: Do Puerto Rican writers in the States react to the negative vision that exists on the island about them?

JOC: There is a stereotype of all of us, of not being able to speak one language or the other and of other quirks of our personality. The thing is that some people over there do that but some people over here do it too.

I don't consider myself a Nuyorican; I didn't grow up in New York. It's not because I reject them but because it's not my tradition. Nevertheless, I have been to conferences where they complain about the arrogant Puerto Rican writers who accuse them of polluting the language and all that. So the fight is from both sides. I don't consider myself on either side. I'm amazed that they don't stop long enough to think how hard it is to be a writer.

CDH: Now that Puerto Ricans are no longer concentrated in places like New York but are all over the country, maybe a different Puerto Rican–American sensibility will emerge.

JOC: I grew up for the first fourteen years of my life in Paterson, New Jersey, and then we moved to Augusta, Georgia, where I lived from the time I was 16 till I went to college. I got married and moved to Florida with my husband, and now we're back in Georgia. I don't have a New York perspective; I know the New York–Puerto Rican writers, I teach the Nuyorican writers. They have provided a perspective. The thing is, however, that the Diaspora continues. It didn't get stuck in New York. There are Puerto Ricans all over the United States. I have found Puerto Ricans in Minnesota, in California, in Washington State, all over. There is a Puerto Rican Studies Association that groups professionals from all over the United States, with thirty-two states represented.

My vision is, therefore, a legitimate one. I didn't stop being Puerto Rican by changing locations. I use my language differently from other Puerto Ricans; my perspective has to be colored by those differences. There are all kinds of Puerto Rican writing. We don't have to consider ourselves Nuyorican in order to write. Puerto Rican writing does not come only out of Spanish Harlem. That is a colorful part of our heritage, but it's not the only part.

CDH: What has been your experience in the South, as a Puerto Rican?

JOC: I live on a farm in Georgia right now. It has been in my husband's family for many years. There are some similarities between this atmosphere and Puerto Rico. When I hear John's grandmother talking about the problems of the farm, I am reminded of my grandmother talking about "el cafetal."[1]

CDH: Have you had any problems with prejudice in the South?

JOC: Racism in the South is open. In the North, I'm treated in a particular way in which all Puerto Ricans are treated. Down here I'm more of an oddity, a curiosity. It's not a generalized prejudice. They ask me where I'm from and when I tell them, the reactions vary. I've learned the culture; I can deal with the culture.

CDH: So there are not many Latinos there?

JOC: Oh yes! In Atlanta there are over 100,000 Latinos. They even have a Spanish yellow pages for the phone book. There is much interest in Latino literature, even outside of Atlanta. I was recently invited to do a reading in a little town next to our farm. There are no Latinos there, but they want to learn more about that literature.

CDH: When did you decide to be a writer?

JOC: I started writing when I was already an adult. I had a child, I had finished graduate school and was teaching. I kept looking for what was missing in my life and discovered it was writing. It was a question of finding the time and the place to do it.

CDH: Do you feel you have been influenced by a specific literary tradition in terms of genre, language, and outlook?

JOC: What I realize now influenced me most were the strong storytelling narratives like the fairy tales and folk tales of different countries, and then also hearing my grandmother tell her *cuentos*.[2] I was fascinated by the power of the *cuento* to influence people and to move them and keep their attention, so in most of my stories there is a storyteller, and I use a frame story, like a grandmother telling a story or a woman telling a story.

Later, because I did not have any Latino models—being in the South, I was distant from Latino communities—all I knew was that I needed to read.

There are lots of women writers in the South, like Flannery O'Connor and Eudora Welty, who wrap you up in a story. They come from a tradition of storytellers which is amazingly similar to the Puerto Rican *cuento*. *"Te voy a echar un cuento,"* eso era lo que Mamá decía.[3]

CDH: The tradition of oral transmission is common among minorities, especially among immigrants.

JOC: Of course. When you read Flannery O'Connor, you almost hear her. It wasn't until I was an adult that I discovered Latino writers who do the same thing, but by that time I had been influenced by the storytellers of the South and by my grandmother. In my book, *Silent Dancing,* I go back and forth between Puerto Rico and the United States. Many of the pieces of the book are a combination of memory and imagination.

Immigrants transfer culture by oral transmission. When they came to the United States from Germany or whatever, the only way they had of letting their children know what was important in their culture was to tell stories.

CDH: Oral transmission is also something closely associated with women.

JOC: I think that with women it is solidarity. In *Silent Dancing* I use the way that my grandmother and my aunts talked about personal things when the boys were out playing baseball or something. They would begin to tell a story, and everybody would just laugh and my cousins and I looked at each other dumbfounded. Later I realized they were sharing their pain, sharing their problems and teaching us that there are ways to deal with life that women have, and so it is a way of not only passing the culture but of empowering each other.

When my mother moved to the United States, she took that with her. She would get together with the women in her building and they would do the same thing, except that then it became nostalgic: *cuando estaba en casa hacíamos esto y lo otro.*[4] They passed on not only culture but yearning. I grew up with my mother yearning for *la casa, la mamá, la isla.*[5] It's a part of the immigrant experience, this constant feeling of homesickness that you have; it's something that never quite goes away. That's why my work probably has an element of *Where is home? I want to go there.*

CDH: So Puerto Rico for you is bound up with memory and yearning.

JOC: Yes, and also with the knowledge that I can never come back to *la casa, la mamá y la isla* of my mother's *cuentos*. That doesn't exist anymore.

CDH: Is that the origin of your writing?

JOC: What I'm doing is examining the past and seeing what I can gather to explain where I came from. It's not a nostalgic journey; it's more of an exploration. For me writing is self-discovery.

The origin of my imaginative life was in Mama's *casa* [house]. That's where I learned about the power that women have; it wasn't from taking courses in the university. Another source of power is the language. Because I did not have access to the Spanish language, it appears in my work as a sort of energizing force. *Terms of Survival* is a book in which the titles are in Spanish and the poems are in English. It's like a dictionary. When I hear somebody say "la muerte,"[6] it rings bells in my head in a way that hearing somebody say "death" doesn't, because when I would hear my mother say something like *la muerte llegó a esta casa*,[7] it was a dramatic statement. The same as when they talked about "la maldad" or "el mal"[8] or something like that. Since I didn't grow up using Spanish all the time, Spanish is magical to me.

CDH: Because you only heard it in one context.

JOC: Yes, that's right, so Spanish connects me immediately to memory. People ask me, "Why do you use Spanish words?," and I answer, "Well, they're my magical formula for getting back in touch with my culture."

CDH: Would that be a kind of code-switching?

JOC: Not exactly, no. Code-switching is like what the Nuyoricans do when they mix Spanish and English. What I do is to use Spanish to flavor my language, but I don't switch. The context of the sentence identifies and defines the words, so my language is different from that; it's not code-switching. It is using Spanish as a formula to remind people that what they're reading or hearing comes from the minds and the thoughts of Spanish-speaking people. I want my readers to remember that.

CDH: It's a way of emphasizing the value of words.

JOC: Yes, when you hear a word three times in your life, it's not the same as if you hear it every day. So when my mother said something like "el olvido"[9]—I heard her say something one time about a child who had forgotten his mother, and she said, "el olvido"—that just gave me goose bumps because what she was saying was that he had fallen into this "el olvido" like into a pit or something. For someone who hears that all the time, it doesn't have the same power as for someone like me. Words are my medium.

CDH: So maybe to have two languages at your disposal can turn out to be especially enriching for a writer?

JOC: Definitely. It was hard being a bilingual child, but it opened my mind to two different realities, because I understood my mother's world and the world outside too.

CDH: Yet with Puerto Rican writers it is considered the other way around, both in relation to those who live in the States and those who live on the island. The ambivalence between the two languages is generally considered impoverishing.

JOC: For me it has not been impoverishing at all. You have to eventually choose, because I could not know both languages at the same level, living in one place most of my adult life, so I had to choose English as my literary language because I had more words in English. It's like I had more currency. If I had had more currency to spend in Spanish, I would have written in Spanish. But the longer I stayed away from Spanish, the fewer words I had, so I no longer can make metaphors in Spanish. I can make metaphors forever in English when I'm writing a poem. I don't have intimacy with Spanish anymore. I tell people: "My English is not a political choice, it's a choice of expediency."

CDH: You write poetry and you write prose, and in many books you combine poetry *and* prose. In *Silent Dancing* and in *The Latin Deli* you transmit one experience in both ways. Why is that?

JOC: They are different ways of seeing. Poetry allows you to delve into the depths of language. Prose is looser. Poetry is a probe to plumb the depths of language, to explore the hidden meaning of words.

Poetry is to me the first discipline. It empowers me. In a sense one is like a microscope, and the other like a telescope.

CDH: Do you think of your writing in terms of validating an experience?

JOC: Oh no, not validating. I'm not a politician or a philosopher or a historian; I'm a compulsive storyteller. I can't help myself: I make stories, I write stories, I tell stories. What I'm trying to do is something defined by Robert Frost: when he said "a poem is a momentary stay against confusion." When you write a poem you have a moment in which all confusion ceases and you understand one thing perfectly. I like that idea. When I write a story, I write it to try to see what I understand about a situation and what I don't understand. If it is successful, there's a momentary stay against confusion, at least for me. And if it is that for the reader, too, then we have art. If not, then I have it and it's a diary entry or something. I see art as a bridging, an understanding. I don't see it as speechmaking. I'm a very political person, but my politics are in the stories and the poems.

CDH: You mean your writing has a political result, but it is indirect.

JOC: Yes, we lead political lives. Every choice we make is a political choice, but we don't go around saying "I do this because I'm *estadista* or *nacionalista*."[10] I'm doing this because I'm human and I need it. So my characters make political choices that have to do with keeping their dignity and surviving.

CDH: And if you give an understanding of the Puerto Rican situation, that's political also.

JOC: Right, but that was my situation, so I'm not writing about things just because I'm interested in the political situation, but because it was what I witnessed, what I imagined. And it's not just autobiographical: I put myself in the place of the people. Knowing the people that I knew when I was growing up, I think this is the way they would have behaved. If I have a character modeled after my mother, I know how she feels about the Church, about children, about being *puertorriqueña*, so I use that. It's something that all authors do.

CDH: So in a roundabout way you *are* validating the dignity of Puerto Ricans in the United States.

JOC: Yes, in a roundabout way. I don't sit down in the mornings to write and say *I am validating the experience of Puerto Ricans,* because that would make me arrogant, like a politician. Nobody can give dignity to other people. What I can do is record in my stories what I feel are the true characteristics of the people around me, and if I put them in that context, it is the reader who tells me if I'm validating that experience or not. That's what I hope to hear.

I want to give a vision that is not a stereotypical vision of gangs and fallen women, and so on. That certainly exists but there are also decent men and women, and I've lived with them. We were aware of crime in the streets when we grew up, but my parents knocked themselves out trying to protect us from that. And they succeeded at the expense of their own lives, because my father didn't go to college, but he was determined that we go.

CDH: In a way it must have been a heroic enterprise.

JOC: Yes, but in a way that is not acknowledged. In our world heroics are in the movies, it is people with guns. It doesn't have to do with the fact that my father was one of the most intelligent people I knew and he would have made a fantastic college professor, but he didn't go to college. He had to spend his life alone in the Navy, missing us, getting sadder and sadder each year because he could not afford to have the life I have now. He gave up his future for us and that's tragic.

CDH: Yet that is the way immigrants get ahead in a new country.

JOC: Yes, and my daughter's life is already a hundred percent easier than my life, as mine has been a hundred percent easier than my father's and my mother's.

Some people make it out of the barrio,[11] some people stay in the barrio, but the barrio doesn't have to destroy you. My characters have an inner life; they think, they love, they suffer. I want my readers, no matter from where they are, to relate to them.

CDH: Around the time *The Line of the Sun* was published, Christina García published *Dreaming in Cuban* and Julia Alvarez published *How the García Girls Lost Their Accents*. Those were, in a way, three *bildungsroman* coming from women whose roots are in the Spanish Caribbean.

JOC: Well, we're about the same age. It's a new generation of college-educated women who feel secure enough to write books.

CDH: Was it easy to get published?

JOC: I had a hard time publishing my book. The novel was rejected by every major publisher . They thought there was no public for my work. Now my work is in anthologies and is being used in classrooms all over the country.

I had no reason to keep on writing during the first ten years I was writing as far as publication goes.

CDH: Do you think the same thing would have happened if you had not been a Latina?

JOC: I think that if I had been a mainstream writer with a little bit of talent and a lot of perseverance, they wouldn't have been able to say: "This is a beautifully written book but we don't have a public for it, not if the characters would have been North American." I don't want to be unfair to anybody, but publishers thought that people were not interested in the minds and the hearts of Latinos. It took a book like *The Mambo Kings* to show there was an interest.

CDH: Would you like to enter the literary mainstream?

JOC: I don't like to think of things that way. The mainstream is like the river. Some currents go faster than others. My work right now is exotic; people are reading it because it is new and interesting and gives a glimpse of something they never saw before the inside of, but I feel that in another ten years they will be reading my work in recognition. They will be saying "Yes, I knew people like this."

CDH: Do you relate to non-Puerto Rican Latino writers in the United States?

JOC: Something that makes me different from other Latino immigrants is the fact that I can go home. That affects your imagination and your perception of yourself in the world. You think, "Well, I am an American citizen, why am I being treated as an immigrant?" That has affected all of us.

CDH: How about other immigrants?

JOC: America is a land of immigrants, but they all act surprised about a new group. The Italians were rejected by the Irish, the Irish were rejected by the Germans, and so on. They think that there are Americans who are identifiable and the only identifiable Americans that I know are the Indians, the Native Americans, and they were treated as second rate.

CDH: What do you think about the future of the Puerto Ricans in the United States?

JOC: I hesitate to make predictions based on demographics and politics. I don't live where those demographics are available to me. I just came, however, from a conference in Boston where there were 200 Puerto Rican academics, from the United States and Puerto Rico. They are making lives for themselves in the United States, highly complex and intellectual lives, producing Puerto Rican criticism, philosophy, art, literature, and I think that there is a society that is no longer the working class but the daughters and sons of the working class that can now go to college. So when people talk now about the Puerto Rican community in the United States, they can't mean just the factory workers; they have to mean the executives, the historians, the academics, and all that. That has to have a voice. What I see is that more middle-class, college-educated people will make their visions available, so it won't always be Oscar Lewis's *La vida*,[12] the culture of poverty.

Of course, there will always be a Bronx, but even there I just went to a play based on *Silent Dancing*, called *La marcha nupcial*[13], presented by a Puerto Rican group, Pregones. They did it in Spanish and English. It was a beautiful play for which they had composed music. So in any case, it is no longer working-class people accepting their lives; it's people striving to have an art and a culture.

CDH: All this may be the first step to assimilation.

JOC: But it's not an assimilation that rejects the Puerto Rican roots because El Museo del Barrio, for example, has cultural artifacts. El Teatro Pregones puts on plays in Spanish and English. This is pluralism; it is taking the best of both cultures and making a third culture. This is not the future, it is the present, the only thing is that it is not universally acknowledged. It isn't utopia. There are still drugs, and crimes, and welfare and all of that, but there is this thing that exists now that didn't exist before: a call to a voice. They want art, they want poetry, they want people to know that they are thinking people, not just reactive people. I'm seeing that right now, and it did not exist when I was a child.

CDH: What do you think the relationship of that third culture should be to the "two" Puerto Ricos?

JOC: Well, I come here and I renew myself. I hear the intonations of Spanish, I understand my family's worries in the context of modern life, so I think it can be an exchange that is not seen as two separate worlds. I think we're now at the stage where we can have a dialogue instead of rejecting each other.

CDH: Is Puerto Rico in your past or in your present?

JOC: Puerto Rico is always in my present. How can I stop being a *puertorriqueña*?

Photograph of Pedro Pietri, *El Nuevo Día* newspaper.

8

PEDRO PIETRI

Even before he opens his mouth, Pedro Pietri makes a statement. Dressed all in black, with a beard, long—somewhat unkempt—hair, and a beret perched on his head, he has the incongruous appearance of a harmless terrorist. He also parodies the mien of an eccentric clergyman. This *persona* is ratified by the big white letters on his ubiquitous briefcase that read: "Sumo Pontífice de la Iglesia de la Madre de los Tomates" (High Priest of the Church of the Mother of the Tomatoes). The other side of the briefcase reads: "Rent-a-Coffin."

A walking, living metaphor, Pedro Pietri's incongruity with his surroundings is an extension of his own poetry: ironic, full of puns and word plays that can only be understood in the context of two languages, two cultures juxtaposed yet in full opposition to each other. When he does speak, he has the deadpan delivery of a stand-up comedian and the solemn intonation of a preacher. To hear him is to go from one riotously funny—and outrageous—remark to the next. Nothing is left standing after his challenges to conventional—and unconventional—wisdom. All this is punctuated, for emphasis, by occasional loud guffaws that suddenly light up his face.

If one pays close attention to what Pedro Pietri is saying, however, there is a deep internal logic even in his most seemingly absurd pronunciations, particularly if we take into account his perspective, which encompasses the contrasts lived and felt by the waves of poor Puerto Rican immigrants to the United States who arrived in unprecedented numbers after World War II and kept on coming.

Pietri is probably the most widely known Puerto Rican poet in the United States. Born in 1943 in Ponce, Puerto Rico's second city, he arrived with his family in New York before he was 5 years old. One of the founders of the Nuyorican Poetry movement, he is also a playwright and a born performer who has recited his poetry in many forums, academic or otherwise.

His published poetry can be read in *Puerto Rican Obituary* (New York: Monthly Review Press, 1973 and a bilingual edition by the Institute of Puerto Rican Culture in 1977) and *Traffic Violations* (Maplewood, N.J.: Waterfront Press, 1983). He has a narrative, *Lost in the Museum of Natural History* (San Juan: Ediciones Huracán, 1981) and some of his plays have been published: *The Masses Are Asses* (Maplewood, N.J.: Waterfront Press, 1984) and *Illusions of a Revolving Door* (San Juan: University of Puerto Rico Press, 1992), a collection of seven plays.

Pietri is the author of twenty-three plays, most of which have been presented in public readings in New York City and San Juan. Among them, *The Livingroom* was presented in New York by José Ferrer in 1975; *The Masses Are Asses* was presented by the Puerto Rican Traveling Theater in 1983; and *Mondo Mambo/ A Mambo Rap Sodi* was presented within the framework of Joseph Papp's Festival Latino in New York in 1990. *The Masses Are Asses* has been translated into Spanish by Alfredo Matilla Rivas as *Las Masas son crasas*. It will be published in San Juan in 1997 by the Institute of Puerto Rican Culture.

Pietri's work has appeared in anthologies such as *Nuyorican Poetry: An Anthology of Puerto Rican Words and Feelings,* edited by Miguel Algarín and Miguel Piñero (New York: William Morrow 1975); *Herejes y mitificadores: Muestra de poesía puertorriqueña en los Estados Unidos,* edited by Efraín Barradas and Rafael Rodríguez (San Juan: Huracán, 1980); *Puerto Rican Writers at Home in the U.S.A.,* edited by Faythe Turner (Seattle: Open Hand Publishing Co., 1991); *Papiros de Babel,* edited by Pedro López Adorno (San Juan: University of Puerto Rico Press, 1991); *Aloud: Voices from the Nuyorican Poets Café,* edited by Miguel Algarín and Bob Holman (New York: Henry Holt, 1994); *Currents from the Dancing River: Contemporary Latino Fiction, Nonfiction and Poetry,* edited by Ray González (New York: Harcourt Brace, 1994) and *Boricuas: Influential Puerto Rican Writings,* edited by Roberto Santiago (New York: Ballantine Books, 1995).

"WE WERE ALL OPERATION BOOTSTRAP CASUALTIES"

CDH: Where were you born? How was your early life?

PP: I was born in Ponce, Puerto Rico, in 1943, and I think we migrated in 1947. We came and we lived in Spanish Harlem. Nobody there was from Spain, but they called it Spanish Harlem. We were all Operation Bootstrap casualties.

In 1948 my grandfather was disillusioned with this question of the American Dream stuff. He was totally depressed; he had sold all his land, he had no friends, and he couldn't speak the language. He committed suicide. At first we kept it a secret.

In 1949, on New Year's Eve, my father—because he was unfamiliar with the weather and that whole thing—he put on a *guayabera*[1] and a straw hat and went out in the coldest winter there was in New York City. Double pneumonia ended *his* career as a human being. Every week after that there was a different funeral because people were dying left and right, so I figured I might as well be always dressed in black so that I won't be caught unprepared, you know.

It was my mother who mostly raised us up. There were three widows who mainly raised us up: my mother, my grandmother, and my aunt. (Her husband died of cerebral hemorrhage before they were six months married.) These three women were role models for widows: they never remarried. They did a magnificent job with us four boys and one girl. My grandmother is Tata, the one whom I talk about in my poems. She never spoke a word of English: she was a brilliant, brilliant, brilliant woman; she lived to be 90 years old. She was very introverted, like me, but she had a lot of information; she used to turn the radio on to the Greek station.

We were raised in the Methodist faith. A lot of my poems, a lot of my performance deals with the way the minister used to deliver the sermons. They said it good, but what they were saying was no good because most of the time they were just paraphrasing the Bible, mainly the Old Testament.

CDH: Was the congregation mostly Puerto Rican?

PP: They were Puerto Ricans, all colors of Puerto Ricans; we even had a few albinos in the choir. It was a Puerto Rican rainbow congregation, so I was raised up with no prejudice whatsoever.

CDH: When did you first encounter prejudice?

PP: It was not in the schools, because there everyone was from Harlem. I encountered it for the first time in Louisiana. I went to a bar wearing a uniform, and they said we can't serve you here. And here I was going to Vietnam in a few weeks. I got pissed off, but my mother's influence was still pretty strong. So that was why I went into the military, because being her son I didn't want to break her heart.

CDH: Were there other minorities where you lived?

PP: We were raised up with the Irish in Spanish Harlem, with Jewish people; we were raised with Italians. We all got along with each other, but years later they moved to the suburbs and we were left in the housing projects because they tore down the buildings and relocated everybody.

CDH: How was your experience in school as a Puerto Rican recently arrived in New York?

PP: Well, there was this English teacher, she was really an idiot. She was a special education case. And she always used to tell us, "If you speak Spanish, we'll send you back to Puerto Rico." That was a mistake, because I should have spoken Spanish to get a free trip back. They told us, "Don't speak Spanish," but they never really made us articulate in the English language. We were not educated in those schools; we came out semiliterate. Sometimes totally illiterate.

CDH: If school was not stimulating for your creativity at an early age, what was?

PP: At home, we were a very music-oriented family. Songs were important to us, the songs of Daniel Santos; romantic songs. I used to sing a lot, my father used to sing a lot before he died.

Also, I started out from the 1950s right? There was that rock and roll phenomenon with Frankie Lymon and The Teenagers. These are my contemporaries. Frankie Lymon became a sensation overnight. He had this legendary song, *Why Do Fools Fall in Love?* which he wrote, so you know, we all aspired to be famous rock and roll singers because we were too small to be basketball players and too distracted to be baseball players, so rock and roll was going to be our salvation. I wrote some rock and roll songs which I'm glad that they were misplaced because they were horrendous. We were trying to follow in the footsteps of all these famous rock and roll singers who became very famous but made no money. When I became old enough to go on the unemployment line, I would see people from that scene, writers, musicians, and I would go, "Wow, you people are famous! What are you doing here at the unemployment office?" This is just to give you an idea of how they were exploited. In those days we were very naive and innocent, and racism was terrible. I mean, nothing has really changed, but it was worse then. And just to have a hit record and just to be heard on the radio—that was a big deal and you traveled all over the country, but the producers were real bad to you. It was just recently that the two remaining Teenagers finally got what they're due. They gave them about $3 million apiece, something like thirty years later. And Diana Ross made a fortune out of that song. But I was spared that; I never had a hit record.

It was from rock and roll that some of my first influences actually came. I started writing about that.

CDH: How far did you get in school?

PP: I graduated from high school with a general diploma. I thought I was going to become a general in the United States Army, but I ended up as a private. I was in Vietnam also; got killed there but refused to die. That's why I'm here.

Education was important for us who were raised in housing projects; it was important for my mother that we graduate from school and not end up in the factories. We ended up in the factories anyway, in the garment district. But at least I had a diploma.

After graduating from high school with that general diploma, I failed the post office exam thirty-one times. That was a record. I failed all sorts of civil service exams. I took all sorts of jobs: I worked in the garment district, I worked in a pool hall, I worked in a car wash (that was one of the most memorable jobs I had because at lunch time I had a sandwich in one hand and I would be wiping the car with the other hand, and I thought, "Man, that's great. This is ecstasy."

I went through all those jobs, and I ended up working at the Columbia University library, getting the books for the students. It was there that I was enlightened, and I started reading all these books and I found out that blacks wrote, that Spanish wrote. I read books by Langston Hughes and García Lorca, all these people. I read Spanish authors in English because I couldn't read Spanish, and then later I read them in Spanish. But that came years later. So I met all these writers and then I met some in person, people like Baraka. I started writing poems in my head and I memorized them. I had a fertile memory. I could recite these long-distance poems.

I started reading books on vocabulary: all these words I was never taught! I read everything I got my hands on: I read Faulkner, I read *The Wasteland*, I read everybody, everyone . . . *The Love Song of J. Alfred Prufrock.* To me that was music and then I met Roger Paris, an astrologer. Him and me read the Holy Kabbala once together. This guy's a genius; he's still a good friend of mine. He's an astrologer and he writes realistic fantasies. He introduced me to W. B. Yeats. We used to go to his house and read all the time. He's read a lot of Yeats; he's a real nonconformist.

CDH: Tell me about your experiences in Vietnam.

PP: I was a foot soldier in the 196th Light Infantry Brigade during the Tet Offensive and had an M-16 and grenades all over. I had been rejected in 1963 for having a low IQ: I was classified 1–y, which meant I was unable to be adapted to military discipline, but when the escalation of the Vietnam War came, they sent the freaks to the front and that's why they lost that war. I remember my platoon: they sent us to the front, to the infantry. They gave us two months of basic training, and two months of advanced infantry training and we'd go out and fight these people who were born warriors, who had defeated the Chinese, the Japanese, the French, so what were we supposed to do? Do what's never been done? And they were experimenting with us, we were exposed to Agent Orange. The odds were against us.

I survived, but I don't know how; it was very traumatic. It was in Vietnam where I met people like these two Puerto Ricans who had been drafted from Puerto Rico. We were about to go, and they said, "Listen, we're not going because this is not our war. We're not going." This guy's name was Angel Luna. He finally went and he got killed the first month there. I wrote a poem for him in *Puerto Rican Obituary*. I didn't find out he had been killed until

I got back because we were separated. It blew my mind that he got killed. Even now, my head is racing when I think about it.

So it was in Vietnam that my political education flourished. We would burn flags there, and we would ask ourselves, "What the hell are we doing here? This is really crazy." There were a lot of Puerto Ricans in Vietnam, a lot of minorities. We were the grunts; they sacrificed us, and then the cadets would come later on to take credit for whatever was done.

Then for thirteen years after I got back I denied that I had been there because I was too freaked out at first. I was stunned; I was shell-shocked, and for years and years it seemed I would do everything wrong. But then I wrote *Puerto Rican Obituary* and that changed my whole life. I dedicated it to my mother; she slapped me across the face. She was very religious.

I have a manuscript about the war that's not published; it's called *Missing Out of Action*. It's about someone who came back from Vietnam and went totally crazy.

CDH: So Vietnam was important for your development as a writer?

PP: Vietnam was a learning experience; it was an education. I started reading Ho Chi Minh's poetry. It was when I felt that finally I was no longer a casualty of Operation Bootstrap. It was when I started writing poetry.

CDH: You said a while ago that you started composing poetry before, when you were working at Columbia, but that you kept it in your head and memorized it. Did you think at that time that you would write it down and publish it?

PP: No, because I belonged to the oral tradition. I would read my poetry at weddings, funerals, baptisms.

CDH: What precedent did you have for that?

PP: What happened was we were too poor to afford a TV, so we all stayed around the radio and heard radio dramas and the imagination developed. We didn't have the visual thing in front of us. They had those *radio-novelas*,[2] and we just sat around and it was amazing the way they spoke on these radios, the material they used. Comedy was like going to save my life. They were in Spanish: *El tremendo hotel*, with Diplo;[3] this was my education. That's were the humor came from. And that's how the oral tradition came to me, so it was important to make people laugh because there were so many tragedies, so many funerals, so that's why I say that humor saved my life.

CDH: I've heard that the oral tradition in Nuyorican poetry also had to do with a poet named Jorge Brandon. Who was he?

PP: He still is.[4] He's the most oral poet that I've met. I met him when I was 17 and was working in Klein's Department Store. I was a store clerk for a dollar an hour, $40 a week. After taxes they were $35; after $20 I gave my mother, they were $15; after coffee I had . . . TEN BUCKS! This was around 1960. After three years they paid me $1.25. So during my lunch break I'd go to Union Square Park, and during that time the radicals, the anarchists would congregate there and Jorge Brandon would be giving his speech. He had a shopping cart, he had a sign, he would be there with his rhetorical stuff, and then in the middle of his delivery, he would just go into the unknown. It was something totally outrageous. It was poetry. I said, "Wow!" I was really fascinated by him. I was also dealing with poetry, but I was very introverted; I was in the closet and he was out there. He's the only person that I would admit to have been my mentor. Twenty years later he became the father of the Nuyorican Poetry movement. He's still alive; he's 90 years old. He lives in New York; he's a street person.

CDH: I thought *you* were one of the founding fathers of the Nuyorican Poetry movement.

PP: No, no, it was Jorge Brandon, Jorge Brandon. He's the one who influenced me as a performer. At that time he was just a street person. He has this memory, and the way he delivers his poems and the way he reads them; his presence is poetry. He used to carry a shopping bag, and then I thought of carrying a shopping bag. He was fearless when he gave his performances. He's now living with his sister; he's 90 years old and has a full head of hair. He's a character. He reminds me of Joe Goon. You ever heard of Joe Goon? Professor Seagull? He was a good friend of e.e. cummings and he was that type of poet who would just talk his poems. So Jorge Brandon was my main influence, and he's the father, the grandfather, the great-grandfather of the Nuyorican Poets. He's the one who influenced Bimbo Rivas, but Bimbo can't answer because he died about a year ago. Bimbo Rivas is another oral poet, a great guy, man, a great guy. When he died I really missed him because he was a great friend and he had this delivery and he took care of Jorge. Jorge had broken his leg and for about two years had to be taken care of. Tato Laviera also took care of Jorge Brandon. His poetry was transcribed in *Aloud: Voices from the Nuyorican Poets Café*.[5] It's the first time he has been in print.

CDH: How were your beginnings as a performance poet?

PP: At first I would perform at parties, weddings, at dances. From 1960 to 1966 I did a lot of odd jobs; I was the minimum wage kid. I'd go look for a job and stay out for lunch.

The first job was in a jewelry store . . . the boss's wife and me . . . forget it. I quit that job in a week. So then I would recite on the streets. I had this collection can in front of me that said, "Help me, I can see," and I would collect money that way. Then I got a job in a supply room, and I would recite there and became a small-time celebrity among the workers. That's how I started.

During that time I would go to Greenwich Village and I wanted to be a beatnik, but I didn't succeed because my beard wouldn't grow long enough. I was influenced by the Beat Generation or rather one of the influences I had, aside from *el trío Los Panchos* and the *décimas*[6] was the Beat Generation. I'm a personal friend of Allen Ginsberg. We were in Nicaragua together, with a lot of crazy poets. I love this line by Ginsberg that says *I saw the best minds of my generation destroyed by madness*. I said "Wow! He's a great poet." He's also a great guy. He wrote in an interview that I was his favorite Nuyorican poet.

So I would quit the jobs and do a lot of traveling. I went to California once, and when I came back my mother said, "How was California?" I said "It was great." And she said, "Well, you know, some investigator came about an accident that you witnessed at the Bowery three days ago." So you see my mind would go to California, but my body went to the Bowery.

Another big influence on me was Dr. Willy Pietri, my brother. He wasn't a real doctor, but we called him that because he was a free-lance gynecologist. He was the real poet in the family except that he just spoke it and he spent a lot of time in mental institutions. We all loved him because he had this split personality; he was a genius, he would get a job and get to the top and then screw it all up. I have a few thousand of his poems I'm trying to publish. He was a big influence with his type of humor. And sometimes he would dress like me. I would be too freaked out to go somewhere because paranoia was introduced into my life in the seventies. So he impersonated me. He looked like me physically, maybe he was a little lighter. He would dress in black and put this hat on, and he'd go there and forget it. . . . He would say later, "Hey, that was a good reading you gave last night."

CDH: Did your mother like your being a poet?

PP: No, she said, "you're crazy." My aunt would say, "Get a job." Even my uncle, my hero Juan Pietri, who was a Nationalist, a friend of Albizu Campos (he spent time in La Princesa[7] for the Nationalist uprising) would say, "Come on, poets are faggots." I would say, "This is one poet who isn't."

My mother was a Republican. Talk about schizophrenia. . . . When the FBI came around, she would hide my uncle's typewriter in the closet, hide him under the bed. But she was a Republican, for statehood. I went into the military because of her influence. She died in 1971. I'm an official orphan.

CDH: Did the fact that you were Puerto Rican in the United States have to do with your becoming a poet?

PP: No, because the music was always there, the irony was always there. I saw things differently. Had I been Irish I still would have been a poet; had I been any other race I still would have been a poet. That happens before you're born. Before *Puerto Rican Obituary* I had written a lot of poems, but

Obituary had the ones they focused on, that they identified me with. But before, I had poems about the supernatural, evidence of the unseen, they were already there.

CDH: Is your poetry a documentation, a validation of your experience?

PP: In *Puerto Rican Obituary*, in *Traffic Violations* I got into the mescaline, the acid. . . . Whatever I experience, I document. Everything can be traced to some experience that I survived.

CDH: What are your feelings toward Puerto Rico?

PP: I want to move there. I really like it there. I want to live in both places.

CDH: When did you first come back after migrating?

PP: Something like twenty-five years later, in 1969. I was there for a weekend. The culture shock was very big. I had been so inhibited and fearful of the Spanish language, and then I could feel the animosity, people feeling that you're not really Puerto Rican. I had no reception there whatsoever. I went back home in a week.

Then I came back again years later for a weekend, and then after my mother died I went to Ponce to meet my aunt. She was an *espiritista*[8] and I wanted to find out about that world because I had lost faith in everything else. So I came to Ponce in 1971, and that was when I met Alfredo Matilla, Ivan Silén, and all those people and they made me feel good about myself. And they were Puerto Ricans who held no animosity, who didn't say, "Well, you're not Puerto Rican if you don't write in Spanish" because that's bullshit. The thing is we're not from Spain so we don't have to write in Spanish. It was through Alfredo Matilla that I lost my fear of communicating in the language that my mother taught me. Alfredo Matilla, Iván Silén, and Che Meléndez,[9] they said, "Hey, speak whatever language you want to speak, the thing is to communicate." So I lost my fear of Spanish.

CDH: Where do you feel more accepted as a writer?

PP: In the United States people accepted my writing more. *Puerto Rican Obituary* became a big deal. I've been all over Europe. It's been translated to thirteen different languages. I just got back from Milan not too long ago because it was translated into Italian. So the *Obituary* became something that the people who didn't want to accept me as a Puerto Rican, they had to because of the publicity it got. Now I'm well known in Puerto Rico.

I tell those diehards who don't like for Puerto Ricans to write in English: *Mira, si no hablo bien el español, es porque no nací en España; si no hablo bien el inglés es porque no soy hijo de puta.*[10]

Spanglish is what we use. We mix both languages, and that's not the sign of an inferior mind but a sign of an advanced mind. Being chauvinist about a language, that's not very intelligent.

CDH: What happens when you recite poetry in *Spanglish* before a monolingual audience?

PP: They have to wait until I recite in a language they understand. But the thing is my poetry is not just with words. I have established a communication through body language. I carry props all the time; it is visual poetry that I walk around with. It is a performance.

CDH: Do you feel more poet or playwright?

PP: I'm a poet who writes plays through the eye of the poet and the ear of the poet. A lot of people who read the play just say this isn't theater. But Ferrer directed *The Livingroom* and *Lewlulu*. Raúl Juliá did the first stage reading of *The Masses Are Asses* in 1983. I knew him quite well, it blew my mind when he disappeared because we were good friends. I met him when he was in *Two Gentlemen of Verona*. Joseph Papp was also a good friend of mine.

CDH: When did you get started in the theater?

PP: In 1971, after the Young Lords[11] disbanded and the Black Panthers were on the wane, that's when I got into theater. Because all those political organizations—the Black Panthers, the Young Lords, the Movimiento pro Independencia[12]—wanted to control your mind, control your thoughts, I said, "The hell with all of you!" And it was people in the theater that got back my trust in human nature. I started writing. My first play was *Illusions of a Revolving Door*. I started working with people again, and I started feeling good about myself over again.

I'm working on a musical now with Paul Simon. It's about the youngest inmate on Death Row in 1959. He was a Puerto Rican, called "the umbrella man." He killed these kids, they were gang fighters of the fifties; he killed two Polish kids and he was sentenced to death, and then, when his sentence was commuted to life in jail, he became a poet. Simon is doing the music; I'm doing the book.

CDH: *Illusions of a Revolving Door* is a strong satire of religion. What is your position on religion?

PP: It's organized religion I'm against. I don't believe in the New Testament or the Old Testament. I mean, how many times can you read one book? Read other books also. I am against the religion that was shoved down my throat, but I'm very religious, extremely religious.

CDH: What is the Church of the Mother of the Tomatoes, of which you are the head, according to the portfolio you carry around?

PP: *La Iglesia de la Madre de los Tomates* is a nonprofit, profit-making organization. It's something that happened fifteen years ago. I found a crushed piece of paper under my desk. It said: "Do this." That's when I started with the Church of the Mother of the Tomatoes. I've been dressing in black for thirteen years. I haven't taken off my hat in thirteen years except when I take a shower. I'm very religious.

CDH: Could you speak a little more about that religiosity?

PP: I'm not a Christian. I'm undefinable. But there's a spirituality. I think there's more of *espiritismo* than of anything else, you understand? That's what saved my life when I was going crazy. I didn't trust anybody. My mother had just died, so I went to Ponce and Cangrejos, where people can actually communicate with the dead. My mother was raised up with this religion, but she protected us from it: voodoo, black magic, the African religions. . . . Like I went to Santiago de Cuba with Che Meléndez and there was this high priest who made me a member of his religion; it was really great. It's a religion of the earth, although there are also supernatural issues. I like to hold candles, I like the incense, the dances, the people going through possession. That has always been in me. Christianity just interfered with that.

When my brother had his breakdown, we went to this psychiatrist, that psychiatrist. . . . When nothing worked my mother went to my uncle, a high priest, to ask if they could practice a *despojo*[13] on him. His name was Juan Oppenheimer, he died recently in Ponce. We wouldn't stay with him because we thought he was weird. He didn't read or write, but what an intelligent person he was! He brought me back to my roots and to some of his religious beliefs, you understand? Because when science fails, magic comes to the fore. So after my mother died, I went to him. He was a big influence on me after 1971.

CDH: Can you tell me about the beginnings of the Nuyorican Poets Café?

PP: Around 1975 Miguel Piñero had written the play *Short Eyes*. We all used to go to Miguel Algarín's house, all these poets would congregate there: Jesús Papoleto Meléndez, Lucky Cienfuegos, Bimbo Rivas, Shorty Bonbon, my brother, Dr. Willy. We used to stay in his living room and recite poetry. We felt really good about it because at that time we didn't have a space, we didn't have an audience, we were all we had. It was exciting in the beginning; we were young, struggling artists. It was like magic; everything was so important.

So then his living room got a little too small, and that's when he opened up the first Café at 6th Street. Miguel being who he is and with all these other people—Ginsberg being one of our main supporters; others like William Burroughs and Bob Dylan made an appearance there—the place became very popular. And we finally had an audience, we finally had this recognition. Then we moved to 3rd Street, but it was great because you had people who were poets all the time; you had older people who were poets, and Jorge Brandon was our leader there. The first Nuyorican anthology for me was the real deal because it was us. Now we got a little out of hand. I was supposed to be the co-editor of this anthology (*Aloud*), but this guy Bob Holman, he had the money, the influence, whatever, and I was phased out.

But Miguel said, "When we do another anthology, I want you to be co-editor of it." I don't hold it against him because you do what you have to do, but I was supposed to be co-editor. I was phased out of this one, which pisses me off because Miguel Piñero was the co-author of the first anthology, and even if he wanted to include Bob, I could have still been part of this anthology. This guy Bob, he's a show-off. He's the master of ceremonies at the slam and to me the slam,[14] is also a disgrace. You know, you get up and read and then you're judged on a scale of 1 to 10, come on. . . . That's how Bob got his claim to fame, and he's all over the country. He never got along with me because I don't slam.

Some of the people in the anthology did a twenty-six-city tour and he didn't include me because I can't be manipulated by him. And I'm one of the founders of this Nuyorican Poetry movement. Another one was Jesús Papoleto Meléndez. He's the one who got Sandy out of the closet. I told Bob Holman to get Papoleto to publish in the anthology, but he was left out. Bob said, "We'll include him in the next one." You know, ten years from now. The thing is that Papoleto was living in Tijuana, but people like Jimmy Santiago Baca are in the anthology, so he did go out of his way to include some people.

And Papoleto was one of the founders of the Nuyorican Poets Café; it was him and Tato Laviera who had the first anthology and gave it to Miguel Algarín, and Miguel swished it around. Tato Laviera's *La Carreta Made a U-Turn* was going to be the first anthology of Nuyorican poetry.

CDH: Was Nuyorican poetry the first definitely Puerto Rican literary movement in New York?

PP: Yes, it was the first. Now it's a business, before it was a real movement. A lot of the people from the old school don't go to the Nuyorican Poets Café anymore. They feel uncomfortable there because it's been yuppified. But that's where we started, that's where we got the publicity. Joseph Papp was one of our main supporters, and Papp was a big thing, you know? Now I don't really want to be into that. Now we're looking for our own space, a place where we can again come together and read our own poetry. Right now there isn't that space, but we're working on it. This is something that belongs to us, we'll share it, but there are limits. Bob stated in *The New York Times*, "Anybody can be a Nuyorican." That's bullshit.

9

LOUIS REYES RIVERA

He walked into the trendy lobby of one of New York's most sophisticated hotels, a man seemingly from another time and another place. Small in stature, with a long, sparse beard, flowing, colorful robes, and a curiously shaped cane (a gnarled sapling used as a walking stick), he looked like a Chinese sage or a Shaman.

Nothing about him, neither his aspect nor his somewhat incongruous New York accent, signaled his Puerto Rican roots. When he began to speak, however, the extent of his interest in Puerto Rican—and Caribbean—history and sociology identified him as deeply committed to the study of his culture of origin and its convergence with black culture in America. Here was, truly, a learned, thoughtful man.

Louis Reyes Rivera was born in 1945 and raised in the Marcy Projects, an African-American community in Brooklyn. He went to local schools and read copiously, educating himself in the process. He graduated from City College in 1974 after majoring in Sociology and English. He has worked as counselor, college professor, and lecturer, and has read his poetry widely.

His decision to become a poet has led not only to his publishing three books of poetry, *Who Pays the Cost* (1977), *This One for You* (1983), and *Scattered Scripture* (1996), but also to his founding a small publishing house called Shamal Books in which he has edited his own and other poets' work. Shamal's editions include simple, pamphlet-like books, that are functional in their purpose and inexpensive.

Rivera has edited several anthologies, among them *Poets in Motion* (New York: Shamal, 1976), *Love, a Collection of Young Songs* (New York: Bronx Museum, 1977), *Womanrise*, an anthology of six women poets (New York: Shamal, 1978), and *Portraits of the Puerto Rican Experience* (Bronx, N.Y.: Institute of Puerto Rican Urban Studies, 1984).

Photograph of Louis Reyes Rivera taken by Miguel Trelles.

His work has been included in several anthologies, among them *Herejes y mitificadores*, edited by Efraín Barradas and Rafael Rodríguez (San Juan: Ediciones Huracán, 1980); *Papiros de Babel*, edited by Pedro López Adorno (San Juan: University of Puerto Rico Press, 1991), and *Aloud: Voices from the Nuyorican Poets Café*, edited by Miguel Algarín and Bob Holman (New York: Henry Holt, 1994).

Rivera has translated Clemente Soto Vélez's *Caballo de palo* ("The Broomstick Stallion") and the collected poems of Guatemalan Otto René Castillo under the title of *Por el bien de todos* ("For the good of all"), both still unpublished.

"IN THIS COUNTRY, YOU'RE A PUERTO RICAN, PERIOD. OVER THERE, YOU AREN'T PUERTO RICAN ENOUGH."

CDH: Mr. Reyes, where were you born?

LRR: First of all, let me tell you that my first name is Louis Reyes. It's my last name that is Rivera. My grandfather was born on January 6, so he was named Reyes Rivera Vega and he named his oldest son Luis and his oldest son named *his* oldest son Luis Reyes, but it came out Louis Reyes in the birth certificate. My last name is Rivera Pardo.

I was born in New York. My mother was born here in 1927. Her mother comes from Ponce. She left in 1924 to come to the States because she had gotten an illness from cutting sugar cane, from breathing it in. The best way to handle that was to get out of Puerto Rico.

CDH: She was a woman cane-cutter?

LRR: This was prior to the 1920s. And then, of course, she had a child before she had a husband, so she had to get out for other reasons too.

CDH: So your family didn't come with the Great Migration of the forties.

LRR: You'd be surprised to know how many Puerto Ricans don't belong to that migration. Puerto Ricans in New York are traceable to the time of the American Revolution and even before, given that Puerto Rico was New England's single largest customer for smuggling operations which were intended to avoid paying British taxes. Under the Spaniards, Puerto Rico acted as a conduit for the slave trade in North America, a trade that also included sugar cane and molasses. So when you look at that, then obviously there were merchants here, which is the beginning of every form of migration anywhere. There were merchants involved from both ports of entry. So throughout New England and the Mid-Atlantic States you have a scattering of Puerto Ricans coming from Puerto Rico to do business. You have Puerto Rican sailors staying here, you have Puerto Rican slaves being sold. . . . So at the very least, Puerto Ricans have been in the New York vicinity since the 1750s, 1760s.

Further proof of the longevity factor of the Puerto Rican community here is that when Betances and Belvis first go into exile, they come to New York. And there is a thriving Cuban, Puerto Rican, Dominican community that is willing to receive them and assist them in organizing what became known as *El Grito de Lares* and *El Grito de Yara*,[1] which were conjointly organized. So in order for you to have a community willing to support you and that community is in exile, then, obviously, that exiled community has been in existence for a much longer time than most folks tend to think.

When you consider that following the Ten Years' War[2] there is a buildup of the Cuban Revolutionary party that manifested itself in 1891 but that had been in organization since the early 1880s, you see that through the life of José Martí and Eugenio María de Hostos[3] the organizational efforts were made from New York.

CDH: So New York has always been a crucial place for the Antilles?

LRR: That goes all the way back to the 1860s as a formal organizational attempt. People usually tend to miss that because they don't read a cross-section of books. You see, one of the problems with people from the Caribbean, generally, is that because we are dominated by four competing cultures—the Netherlands, the French, the Spanish, the English—we absorb the provincialisms and arguments from those people. Consequently, when you have a Spanish-Caribbean historian, his tendency is to focus on the Spanish Caribbean. And even, in a more provincial level, the Puerto Ricans concentrate on Puerto Rico, the Cubans on Cuba. So you have to be willing to research across cultures and inter-islands. You have to be more regional than provincial. If most people are not that broad-minded, the information that they get and the perspective that they develop is short.

CDH: Arthur Schomburg, the Puerto Rican black scholar who came to the United States at the end of the last century, was part of that Puerto Rican–Cuban connection that flourished in the States.

LRR: He came here in 1891, with letters of introduction to a fellow named Flor Baerga.[4] He immediately joined the Borinquen Club, which was part of Martí's form of organization. He was educated by tobacco workers—the cigar rollers—and they in turn were the underbelly that financed the Cuban Revolution of 1895. But they also were the ones who principally attempted to finance and execute the Ten Years' War, the Grito de Lares, the Little War.[5]

As early as 1850 and as late as 1950, Puerto Rican, Cuban, and Dominican cigar-makers would use popular poets and orators to read to them. From my standpoint, that's poetry all the time. What they were looking for was the ability to make those sounds alive while workers worked. Schomburg lived near a tobacco factory. He grew up listening to all of that. But he had limited formal education. The basis for his intellectual curiosity was nurtured by the readings in cigar factories. African Americans here had a problem with Schomburg because of his lack of formal education. He defended himself by saying that he had attended the University of St. Thomas but that his records had been destroyed in a fire. It was a way of gaining acceptance here.[6]

CDH: There is a Schomburg Center in New York that is dedicated to black scholarship, right?

LRR: Yes, it's at 135 Street and Malcolm X Boulevard AKA Lenox Avenue. The architectural style selected for it is not exactly inviting. For my money, it is a little too secretive and bourgeois to be of any real service to the community. But once you get past that door, there's a load of information in there.

CDH: I discovered Arturo Schomburg[7] very recently; a tremendous discovery. Is he well known here?

LRR: He's highly respected here, particularly among African Americans. Some Puerto Ricans will point to him with a little pride, but most are rather ignorant of the connection and of the identification.

CDH: Because of the name, which seems to be foreign?

LRR: Partly, but also because of the provincialism. You know, Pedreira,[8] I think, did us a lot of harm. Because of his *Insularismo* notion, while it was geared against Anglo-Saxon absorption, it also was a little on the racist side vis-à-vis that we should be discarding that which is lethargic in us, which translates to we should discard our indigenous cultural identification. And of course that also means, definitely, our African connection. And so in the process of becoming Hispanophile, as a way of combating the Anglo absorption, he helps create another problem. And since he becomes the leading authority and his book is required reading, then you're permeating people's perspectives with distortions and self-defense both at the same time. This has had its consequences, here as well as on the island.

Even here we still suffer from phrases like "dañando y mejorando la raza."[9] So that's not exactly coded language, it's very clear.

CDH: You spoke about your mother's family, but when did your father come to the States?

LRR: In the mid-thirties. He was the oldest son of twelve children. They were farmers from Yauco. And as you should know, the Depression forced a lot of Puerto Ricans to be recruited by U.S. corporations and U.S. governmental programs. So he joined the Civilian Conservation Corps (CCC) under FDR, and that was his way of earning some money to send home. He worked as well in the Merchant Marine, and eventually, when World War II breaks out, he was inducted into the Army. While he was in the Army, he dated my mother's sister and started writing to her. My mother's sister was really not interested in answering his letters, so she asked her sister to answer the letters for her. My mother started writing to this strange person, and they developed an interesting kind of relationship by mail. They fell in love when they finally did meet during one of his breaks from military duty. It happened that my mother's aunt was also a very close friend of my father's oldest sister, who was already here since the early thirties. That was how my aunt and my father met initially. My grandmother on my father's side comes from Río Piedras. My grandfather, on my mother's side, comes from Fajardo. So I come from all four corners of the island. And yet I was born and raised in Brooklyn, which is an interesting contradiction.

CDH: Were your parents pursuing the so-called American Dream?

LRR: No, my grandmother on my mother's side, as I said, was getting out of a difficult situation, and my father was trying to carry out his responsibilities to the family back home during the Depression. The only thing they were interested in was making it the best way they knew how in terms of feeding their families. They were not necessarily ambitious people in the sense of entrepreneurship or petty bourgeois thinking; they were simple people. I'm not sure if the term peasant is correct. I'm not sure if the word *jíbaro*[10] is the best to describe them. But certainly "campesino"[11] adds a little local flavor to their perspective. "Jíbaro" in the sense of roots, yes, but "campesino" in the sense of outlook. They were from the land. My aunt, the oldest sister, was the only one of the girls who survived (there were six boys and six girls, but five of the girls died before they were 5 years old), so there's only one aunt on my father's side. She used to tell me about how she would have to walk 6 kilometers every day to get to school in Yauco. They lived in a barrio.[12]

CDH: Was your community in Brooklyn entirely Puerto Rican, or was it a mixed community?

LRR: That sort of depends on your geography. The area that I lived in was the exact borderland between Williamsburg and Bedford-Stuyvesant, so it was a meeting ground for the leftovers. I'm talking about 1945 through 1954. To the west of us were the last remnants of an Italian community; to the south of us was the fullness of Bedford-Stuyvesant, which is African American; and to the north and east of us was the fullness of the Latinos, mostly Puerto Ricans, in Williamsburg, and the Orthodox Jews. So I was exposed to all of that. I lived in a housing project that had been built specifically to make room for returning veterans. So initially that housing project—in which we lived with 17,000 other families—was mixed. But the whites eventually moved out; there was a small contingent of Puerto Ricans and a large contingent of African Americans. And so being in that project, mostly around African Americans, my social life was African American, outside of my family. My family life was strictly Puerto Rican and bilingual. In the house, Spanish was spoken, and as the older people got hipper to English, we mixed the languages. This, by the way, is the first stage of Spanglish.

CDH: Did you feel a difference in respect to African Americans?

LRR: Not at all. I did a reading once, a few years back, in 1988 or 1989, when López Adorno[13] invited me to his classroom with José Angel Figueroa[14] and we did a dual thing because Pedro wanted his class to see the range of Puerto Rican poetry in the United States. Figueroa is much more the Spanglish poet with a heavier Puerto Rican emphasis, and I'm much more the Brooklyn Afro–Puerto Rican. So it happens that after the session, the entire class was walking through the corridors and a young lady comes up beside me and says, "It must have really been difficult to be caught up between the two worlds: African American and Puerto Rican." And I answered: "Why do you say that?" A problem that I had is that I have never been able to distinguish exactly what the difference is. We came to use the language as difference, but language is not a difference because all five languages that are spoken in this hemisphere were imposed on all of us. So we cannot really use Spanish as a defense because it is not genuinely our language. Whatever language we may have spoken originally has been lost to us as a direct result of the imposition. And English is an Anglo-Saxon imposition on everybody here. What we are talking about here is the Anglo-American arrogance, not the cultural necessity of any given people, much less the political and social necessities of those people.

I explained to her that there are almost as many light-skinned African Americans as there are dark-skinned African Americans. There are as many white-minded African Americans as there are white-minded Puerto Ricans. And there's as much African American and Amerindian in the Puerto Rican as there is throughout Afro-America. You see it among the Brazilians, you see it among the Central Americans, and certainly you see it in the United States in various degrees. So I could never really understand what the difference is. And she smiled at me because it had been troubling her, the notion of "what side am I on."

CDH: It is slowly becoming understood that in Puerto Rico we all belong both to a white tradition and to a black tradition.

LRR: There was a case in Louisiana about twelve years ago where this woman was suing the state so that she could have her birth certificate changed to read "white." She had married three times and all to white men; from all intents and purposes she was—she looked like—a white. Well, the state brought in all of her relatives to testify that she was black. And according to law, in Louisiana, if you are one thirty-second part black—that's one out of thirty-two grandparents—then you are black. What happens is her attorneys proved that any white person in the United States who has been here more than a hundred years has one-twentieth part black in them. But she lost the case.

What we're really doing is reacting—as opposed to responding to—a sickness of perspective that is 500 years old. Proof of that is seen in Columbus's letter in regard to how easily the Indians could be made into slaves. He imposed a quota on every Indian of Hispaniola; they were required to produce a cow's bell full of gold every three or four months, or they would lose their hands. At that same time, there were coming into the Spanish colonies people of African descent—Muslims, Jews, and others—among them, many who came as slaves or servants in the second voyage. When they ran away, they were called *cimarrones,* the same term used for wild beasts. After 1497 there was a sprinkling of people brought in directly from Africa. Later on, by the way, blacks and mulattos could buy their "white papers," which officially made them "white." So you see, those two manifestations: Columbus looking at the Indians not as converts but as slaves and the government allowing people to "buy" their racial status, we absorb all that.

As an ideological illness, racism is barely 200 years old. It's only since the cotton gin that there's a concerted effort among the intellectuals to "white-out" black history and to push the notion of inferiority on the basis of what they call race but I would call ethnic grouping. And only since 1795 does it become an ideological type of tool. You can find books from that period that have no problem with—even up to 1903—making reference to the "black" ancient Egyptians. It's only in the twentieth century that you see an argument on whether or not the ancient Egyptians were black or whether or not Mexico was visited by Africans. The argument is mostly a twentieth-century argument as a result of that disease and some form of response to it.

CDH: So you were always sure that there was no difference.

LRR: I've always wanted to search for understanding what I was and what it meant, and while I couldn't understand the differences people put on me, there are several moments in my life when the contradiction was confronted or confronted me. The most compelling can be summed up in two stories: I was 8 years old and my family had broken up—my mother and father—and my father did not like the idea of another man raising his children—you know this is quite Puerto Rican—so my mother could leave, but she couldn't take the children with her. But he couldn't take care of us because he was working at night and we were day people. So he sent us to Yauco[15] to live with his mother while he got his act together. So we lived in Yauco at the very top of a hill; it's built in a circle up against the mountain, and you have this slope with streets on its side and roads. Directly across from my grandmother's house was this house where a very, very dark-skinned couple lived. And the youngsters that I was going to school with, the boys, once in a while they would come running through that area, right by my house, and make fun of the black woman when she would step out of her house. That happened twice, and it was something that was very strange to me because of the notion of elder. And like I say, I never understood the difference of coloration, so I never understood why you would want to disrespect this woman, that's a grown woman. The second time that I saw it happen, I was standing on my porch and I asked, "Grandma, why are they doing that to her?" They were running around her—"haciéndole burla"[16]—and she says: "Because there are some people in this world who just don't understand."

So I kept that with me and when I was 11, which was three years later, I'm back in New York and I'm confronted again, but this time more clearly. Back then we didn't use the word "racist," we used the word "prejudice." All around me, even among people in my family, were people who would try to pass for white. And of course I was becoming cognizant of that white omnipresence, of the authorities all over the place. And it was devastating to me, and I was wondering if I was the one who was wrong and all the world was prejudiced. And I looked around me, and I couldn't ask anybody what I needed to ask. But there was one person who I knew would give me an honest answer. And it was one of my maternal grandmother's sons, my uncle. He was about eight years older than me. So I'm 11, he's 19, he's hip and mean and streetwise and of course it was obvious that he was of African descent, so there was no question about that. So I said, "Well, I'll go to Uncle Mario. He'll tell me." They lived up in the Bronx—my mother comes from the Bronx; my father comes from Brooklyn. So I went up to the Bronx and after greeting my grandmother, I immediately went to Mario's room. He was standing in front of a mirror with a brush, brushing his hair, and I said, "Mario." And he says, "Hey man, what's happening?" And I says, "Can I ask you something?" and he says "Sure, go right ahead." And he's brushing his hair, and I said, "Are you prejudiced?" And he stopped. And there was this long silence. And then he say, "Yeah, I'm prejudiced." And he keeps brushing his hair. I says "You are?" And he says, "Yeah. . . . " and he adds, "Against ignorance." And I looked and I thought—I was 11, mind you— prejudiced against ignorance. And I said, "That's it. That's exactly what the problem is. We're looking at ignorance." And I said, "Hey, man, thanks a lot, man." And I didn't stay there but a half hour. I went right back for an hour and a half ride. And from that moment on, to the present, I have kept that beside me, and eventually I remembered my grandmother with what she had said, and that, added on to what he had said, clarified for me why I understood there was no difference.

CDH: I find the prejudice or racism in Puerto Rican society inexplicable.

LRR: Well, it is explicable. It was not as such prior to 1898. There is a difference in what we call racism before and after that date. I agree with Fanon in *Black Skins, White Mask* when he says there is no such thing as being the least racist or the most racist among us. Either you are racist or you're not. However, the Spaniards in Puerto Rico—the Catholic element in the Americas—allowed for things (and you see it in Brazil, another Catholic element at work) where you would absorb the African into the European in such a way where even though there may be a little gossip about it, there's no problem about the black and the white marrying, because the marriage is sacred.

So it is as a result of the inundation of Anglo-Saxon and North American propaganda and "divide and conquer" tactics on a class-caste level that we get this idea that to be human means to be white. The kind of prejudice that Puerto Ricans have suffered or exhibited since 1898 is different. We are infiltrated in terms of our psyche with the modern, white Anglo practice of racism. You know the expression "una abuela en la cocina" (a grandmother in the kitchen). That doesn't come from the Spaniards but from trying to impress the North Americans. The white-looking girl who was going out with a North American man would ask her mother to stay in the kitchen and would play her as a maid. It's a question of your parts of speech. In his autobiography, Malcolm X says that when the Arab describes himself as white it is merely an adjective, but when the North American says he's white, he means he's the boss. This he said after he had been to Mecca and had sat down to eat with whites for the first time. It opened up his eyes.

CDH: So there are nuances in regard to prejudice.

LRR: Bernardo Vega and Jesús Colón[17] were both from the same town, Cayey.[18] One describes himself as white, as an adjective, not as a noun and that's the difference. Here, it becomes a noun. And so you're misplacing your part of speech. And that's what we're really talking about. Now prior to 1898, the Ten Years' War and the Lares revolt were to end slavery and to establish independence from Spain and to establish a republic of the Greater Antilles: all three in the same breath. That was white, black, and mulatto fighting together. The word *Creole,* in fact, was used among the French and the Spaniards to designate those who were not born in either Europe or Africa. It is peculiar to the Americas. What it means to imply is that you're not purely African or purely European because you were born in the Americas. And since the ratio of men to women coming from Europe had a serious imbalance and since men do not go anywhere without their women unless there are women waiting for them, then the assumption was always that if you were Creole, that not only meant that you were born in the Americas but also that you were probably mixed, which means that you're not quite European enough or you're not quite white enough.

And when you check out Spanish and French Caribbean history, then you see the notion of peninsularist versus insularist in terms of the gradations of favor and authority. If you and I were to go to court back then and you were a peninsularist and I was an insularist, the judge would move in your favor automatically; the odds would be against me because you had more rights than I did because you came from France or Spain. We're talking gradations here. Now what we're also talking about is that our perspective is based on the quality of the information we receive. And when the information we receive is distorted, the quality of our perspective is distorted. Many things are not absolute, they're in degrees. That's why, here, you have more of an accent on what we refer to as racism or prejudice on the basis of color. And interestingly enough, of all the "Latino-Americans" living in the United States, Puerto Ricans and Dominicans—second generation—more easily identify with the Afro-United States scene than with the Anglo-United States scene. And that's not only because of the similarity in music but also because of the similarity in spirit and in social conditions. It's not just a cultural thing, it's an ethnic recognition. and it's a social response to similar conditions.

CDH: I find what you're saying especially fascinating in terms of literature because the African tradition, in a sense, has been assimilated into Latin literature—into Puerto Rican literature—without a definite break in terms of rhythms, expressions, even perspectives. But here, African-American literature seems to be isolated; it is defined as something apart from mainstream "white" literature.

LRR: What is genuinely United Statesian, what the United States is known for, culturally speaking, is rooted in the African tradition.

CDH: But it has been kept apart, isolated from the so-called literary mainstream.

LRR: Until they absorb it. Take the case of George Gershwin's music, for example, where did he learn his rhythms? He went uptown and took it back downtown. Similarly, by the way, what is referred to as Nuyorican poetry is as much rooted in African-U.S. urban poetry as it is in an attempt to redefine or reclaim the Puerto Rican culture.

And you know Desi Arnaz, he was a descendant of the *gallegos*[19] of Cuba. When he used to go on in "I Love Lucy" with the conga drum and the African mask and calling out *Babaloo-Aye!*—the name of an African god—what he was doing was (the United States didn't understand it, they were ignorant then) he was accentuating the African component. He was a latecomer to a phenomenon that had been under way: the birth of what we refer to as "salsa." It is the mingling of the bebop era of American Jazz and the Latin music that was filtering into New York.

CDH: It comes from the same roots.

LRR: Machito and Celia Cruz and Graciela and Chano Pozo . . . Basically it was the same, but in the United States the drum was outlawed from the Africans whereas in the Caribbean—Catholic again—the drum was absorbed. It was outlawed here because of the Amerindian. They used the drum. And nobody understood what the drummers were drumming. You would be surprised to know how many Amerindians from the Atlantic seaboard were shipped to the Caribbean to be sold as slaves. It was a way of getting rid of problems and making profit out of it at the same time. So it wasn't just killing them or chasing them off their lands, they were also sold into slavery.

CDH: I think we in the Caribbean can recognize the Harlem Renaissance as something very familiar, even though it's in another language.

LRR: During the same period that the Harlem Renaissance was jumping off, French Négritude[20] was also jumping off. Luis Palés Matos and De Diego Padró with their *diepalismo* in Puerto Rico; Juan Antonio Corretjer with the *criollismo*; Clemente Soto Vélez with his *Atalaya de los Dioses*[21] were all fairly simultaneous. It was a time for rebirth. They were all claiming something at the same time. Slavery ended in the Americas in 1888 when Brazilian slavery came to an end. It was then that the Afro-Brazilians began what we refer to as Négritude. The Afro-Brazilians who were writing poetry praised the natural beauty of being black. There began a growing movement for the previously dispossessed to give voice to their own. It was the rise of an intelligentsia that culminated in 1910.

One of the first signs of literary and political self-esteem for U.S. African Americans goes back to David Walker's 1829 book, *Appeal to the Coloured Citizens of the World,* a call to arms against slavery using religion and history as focal points.

After slavery was abolished, the underclass could assert itself intellectually and culturally. By the 1920s, 1930s, it is a hemispheric phenomenon that reaches into West Africa as well. So the Harlem Renaissance was really a national Negro Renaissance because it wasn't just limited to Harlem. The Négritude movement increases; the *criollistas* and the *atalayistas* take on the nationalist perspective vis-à-vis Albizu Campos. And then there's of course the socialist and the anarchist movements that are also questioning capitalism and challenging it on all fronts: cultural, economic, political, and so on. So I'm saying that there's an easy identification given when you check into your own background and see what was happening at the time.

CDH: Is there a specific connection between African-American and Puerto Rican writing in New York?

LRR: The African-American–Puerto Rican connection in New York City can be seen immediately by Felipe Luciano[22] coming into his own as a poet, as a member of *The Last Poets,* a black group. Similarly, people like Piri Thomas and Nicholasa Mohr studied under John Oliver Killens. It was an intellectual and semipolitical relationship. This was during the fifties and sixties. Piri Thomas worked with the Harlem Writers Guild which Killens headed.

Another point of contact between African Americans and Puerto Ricans was in politics. The Young Lords[23] fashioned themselves after the Black Panthers. It was this connection between Puerto Ricans and African Americans that led to ethnic studies, which began as Black and Puerto Rican Studies in 1969.

CDH: Can you tell me more about John Oliver Killens, who I understand was your father-in-law?

LRR: Killens is probably the most ignored novelist in the United States, but he had a tremendous impact on the last three generations of writers. He was connected to the Socialist movement and was one of the few black writers who didn't write for white audiences but for his own national group. He's not appreciated by whites because they are not included in the "conversation" he establishes with his readers. He's different from, say, James Baldwin, who writes directly to white people and so was accepted by the yardstick of the fifties and sixties.

Killens helped fashion a national literature that's not acceptable to the whites. His book *And Then We Heard the Thunder* was nominated in 1963 for the Pulitzer Prize, but since they didn't want to give it to him, they gave it to no one that year. His best-known book is *Youngblood.*

CDH: There seems to be a close connection between Palés Matos, Emilio Ballagas, Nicolás Guillén[24] and Langston Hughes.[25]

LRR: You know Hughes translated Guillén, his book *Son.* It has the reputation of being one of the best translations from Spanish to English because you got poet to poet. Langston Hughes spent time in Mexico as a young man before he came to New York, so he had a grounding in Spanish and when he went to Spain as a correspondent for an African-American paper during the Civil War, he met Nicolás Guillén and Pablo Neruda and Ernest Hemingway who were also writing for their respective newspapers. The poet-to-poet affinity grew out of that. Hughes and Schomburg made it possible for Guillén to come to the United States after the Spanish Civil War.

Hughes understood things because he had traveled; when you move around and see things, you begin to understand a bit more.

Interestingly enough, in Puerto Rico, you folks down there are not Puerto Ricans. You are from Yauco or Ponce or Mayagüez, and you have attitudes about Cayey or Fajardo. It's when you step out of Puerto Rico that you begin to understand that you are Puerto Rican and that there is a national identity and a national culture that is peculiar to you. Now, interestingly enough, one of the things that I found most intriguing, is that—including Toussaint L'Ouverture, even though he never left Haiti, except when he was taken to France, but he read a lot of books, which is another way to travel—every single person in the Caribbean who has made any real impact on Caribbean history, is a person who left the Caribbean either to be educated elsewhere or because economic or other conditions forced them out, like my father and my grandmother. And so they get to see what the Caribbean is in relation to the rest of the planet. And then those who understand it enough return to the Caribbean, but more resolved. So you have Belvis going to Spain, Betances going to France, and Martí going to Spain and throughout Central America and Hostos moving around like he did, and Marcus Garvey, who developed his perspective in Central America, of all places, and he saw that the African condition was not peculiar to a British condition; it was a worldwide phenomenon. Even Muñoz Marín, as much as I disagree with him, he was educated in New York. Albizu went to Harvard, and Julia de Burgos, whose greatness comes as a result of having been exposed to New York audiences, lived here.

CDH: That's exactly what I want to explore in this book of interviews: what the American experience does to Puerto Ricans who are writers.

LRR: Ancient Athens was not a white city. It was a mixed city, it was the center of the Greek city-states, and consequently what that meant was that everybody, from everywhere connected to the Mediterranean, had its community in Athens. The foreigners outnumbered the Athenians, but they were not permitted to vote because they were foreigners (besides the slaves who could not vote and the women who could not vote). Only Athenian-born citizens had the right to vote. When Rome defeated Carthage, it became, slowly but surely, the center of the Mediterranean world. Everybody had his representative in Rome. Rome was a mixed city. Paul, from the Bible, cannot be put in jail or tried by the local authorities because he was a Roman citizen. He must be taken to Rome to be tried before Caesar himself. He was obviously not an Italian. He's not white because he comes from the Middle East.

What I'm saying is the reason why New York is that type of place is because it is the center of this hemisphere, and you find every community of this hemisphere in New York City because the United States is, especially since 1898, a world power and New York City is the center of that world power, attracting every group from every curve of the globe. Every empire has a center and since the United States is the latest attempt at resurrecting the Roman empire, and New York is the center of that empire, consequently it is going to attract the citizens and denizens of that empire. So you have a Vietnam War and you have a whole lot of Vietnamese in New York as a result, never mind who won or lost. And you have a World War I and World War II, and you're going to have a lot of French and British and Scottish and Russian émigrés in the United States.

CDH: I sometimes think it is like the barbarians entering Rome.

LRR: Exactly. And don't forget that the Chinese Wall was built to keep out the barbarians.

CDH: Nevertheless, isolated peoples have different perspectives; they see greater differences than peoples who have received a great many immigrants.

LRR: One of the most interesting assets of the human being in terms of self is self-preservation, and one of his greatest weaknesses is provincialism: the degree to which he is narrow, the degree to which he is a *Heil Hitler* type. And what we are looking at in relation to the United States has another problem to it. On the one hand, there's a European mentality that is Mediterranean-based, and the interchange in the Mediterranean world allowed for a lot more tolerance. But, on the other hand, what you're looking at here has been Northern European: the Scandinavian Norsemen, the Teutons, and the Celtic English. The Northern Europeans didn't have the prerequisite contacts. They were latecomers to the development of Mediterranean civilization. So, they have their own hang-ups as a result of knowing that in many ways they come more out of barbarism than the rest of us.

Now, of course there's a philosophical problem too, in relation to the African and the Amerindian, who have a greater respect for life, for nature. You see that in their relation to nature (what we mistakenly call "animism"). They respected the land they abused. They always tried to give back as much as they attempted to take, whereas the Northern European has been hardly respectful of life and land.

CDH: When did you begin to write?

LRR: When I was 9, 9 and a half, my cousin—she was three years older than me—had a typewriter and when she introduced me to it and I discovered she could type, I wanted her to type something out for me, so I recited a story I made up on the spot about cowboys. And there was this bank robber, a bad guy, and there was this sheriff dressed in white. But the bad guy, who was dressed in black, escaped and actually killed the sheriff. And it bothered her. She said, "Are you going to let this guy get away in the story? He did the wrong thing." And I said, "I get tired of seeing the bad guys always go to jail."

When I was 15, my best friend betrayed my trust. I didn't want to fight him and I went up to my room, and the anger and disappointment came out in tears. For some reason, I pulled out a sheet of paper and started writing, and afterward I felt good because I had written a poem and I discovered, in writing that poem, that I had a proclivity for writing. And then I decided that, number one, I would be a writer and, number two, that there was a lot about writing that I didn't understand, so there was a lot to learn and, number three, that I would never write anything that would lie to the people. Obviously, at that point I had recognized that there are distortions in books.

And from the time I was 15 till I was 29, I studied every form of writing I could. I studied grammar, content and approach, logic, substance, image development. I read all of the British poets that everyone said that you're supposed to know about, and I found them lacking, including Shelley and Byron. I became more interested in the Irish writers of the turn of the century, with their nationalist fervor. I read Yeats and also Joyce. I read philosophy, and the Transcendentalists impressed me, particularly Walt Whitman, Emerson, and Thoreau. Nineteenth-century women did not impress me whatsoever. I found them a bit too personal, and there was not enough substance. American novelists, except for Steinbeck, I found to be lacking in perspective. I studied journalism; I prepared to be a journalist, actually. Journalism also had its problems because of the control the publisher has over the perspective that you'd like to engender. And so, at 29 it was time to decide. I decided to be a poet. I entered college at 24, so from 15 to 24 it was self-study. I graduated at 29. It was after college that I began to fully understand the range of literature written by people of color. And then I discovered another world that was much to my liking because it was more human. Not humanistic; I shy away from that too. The problem of humanism, as luring as it is, is that it makes man out to be the center of the universe, and that's not true. Man is a manifestation of life like every other manifestation of life. We are all manifestations of the totality of what we refer to as life. In terms of all of us, I have a problem with the way we look at things philosophically and politically, economically, socially, and culturally. I look for a planetary perspective. We are all elements of the planet; we are not universalists but planetarists.

In terms of being Puerto Rican or African American or European American, the fact is that we as Americans, hemispherically speaking, have yet to define ourselves. We have inherited and absorbed the arguments and perspectives of Europeans, Africans and Asians, in that order. But Europe,

Africa, and Asia are three different places that do not necessarily dictate or define the essence of what it means to be American. So what we lack is a genuinely American perspective, which means pain because America, hemispherically, was born out of pain.

We have yet to define the planet, not the world, because the *word* world signifies that it is human-made, while the word *planet* signifies that there's something larger than what humans make. When you speak of the world, you speak of what humans have made; when you speak of the planet, you speak of what humans are born into.

CDH: Do you go back to Puerto Rico often?

LRR: Only when invited, which is not often. Poets don't make any money. A Puerto Rican poet who identifies with the African-American community would be even less invited. So if being a Puerto Rican born in Brooklyn doesn't help much, being a Puerto Rican born in Brooklyn and coming out of an African-American perspective helps even less when there is this refusal to even consider the possibility that stateside Puerto Ricans can write well and contribute to thought. So while one of the reasons is that I can't afford to go as much as I'd like to, the other is more complicated.

But a couple of years ago I went with Tato Laviera, Sandra María Esteves, and Pedro López Adorno. In 1980 I had to go bury my father; that was the only other trip since I was a child.

CDH: Do you feel part of Puerto Rico? Do you feel accepted there when you go?

LRR: My perspective is that when I walk into a situation with which I'm not familiar, I'm not exactly wide-open, I'm cautious. When a hand is extended to me, then I'm much more open. I don't have a problem with identification if you speak honestly and if you'll at least accept the fact that I have opinions and therefore I have a right to express them. If we can engage in really honest play, I have no problem. I'm not worried about that. I'm not intimidated or threatened in any way by it. My problem is that I don't like to impose. And the moment that I see people's defenses go up, I have no problem at all being quiet. I read poetry in Puerto Rico and audiences loved it, but one of the eggheads got funny on me saying, "Well, your poetry is so nineteen-sixties. We've gone beyond that." And the funny thing about it is that I'm trying to explain that poetry has a tradition that is greater than the moment. The poet's responsibility is to write a Scripture. Who else wrote the Scripture? The Popol-Vuh was written by poets, the Egyptian Book of the Dead was written by poets. The Kitabu—the African Pygmy Bible—was written by poets. The Bible was written by poets. It represents a thousand years of Jewish poetry. Even Jesus' sayings are manifestations of the poetic effort.

My grandmother made me read the Bible in Spanish every day before I could go out. From the time I was 7 to the time I was 11, I was not allowed to go out to play unless I read the Bible and explained it to my grandmother. She taught me how to read in Spanish, and I taught her how to speak in English.

CDH: Do you find Puerto Ricans prejudiced against those who migrated and go back?

LRR: It's a question of ignorance. There was no dialogue between mainland and island Puerto Ricans from the 1920s through the 1970s. In 1980 Efraín Barradas and Rafael Rodríguez conspired to put out an anthology, *Herejes y mitificadores*, which was the first full attempt at establishing a literary dialogue between the island and the world. What we have is an insular community that has no intellectual or political connections to Puerto Ricans in the mainland, even though the familial connections are thriving. Still, New York Puerto Ricans are not considered real Puerto Ricans, as witness the problem with having Puerto Ricans from the mainland vote in the 1993 plebiscite.

Puerto Rico fails to see how The Other is seeing it. I agree with anybody who sees the world from the point of view of self, but self is not enough from the point of view of the person. We must also recognize that an Other is also looking at and measuring us.

Now there's another problem here too. If you come from New York, if you come from the streets of New York, it's another culture. And this fast-paced, neck-breaking, peacock-strutting type of New York stuff is something island Puerto Ricans look at and say, "Well, that's a violation of our insularity." So there's a misunderstanding in that too. But in dialogue, you find communality. You can't find a more staunch Puerto Rican than Clemente Soto Vélez no more than you can find a more staunch New York Brooklynite than me. And there's absolutely nothing wrong with understanding notions of common differences. We're different, but we also have a lot in common. The funny thing about it is that in this country, you're Puerto Rican, period. Over there, you aren't Puerto Rican enough.

10

ABRAHAM RODRÍGUEZ, JR.

Abraham Rodríguez, Jr., is an angry young man. When he speaks about his parents' native Puerto Rico, he seethes with rage at what he perceives as its spinelessness. When he talks about the South Bronx, where he was born thirty-four years ago, his voice chokes up with ire and frustration, describing the desolate human panorama of wasted lives. He lashes out at fellow Puerto Rican writers, at "Hispanics" in general, at the system that maintains the violent status quo. He questions everything: politics, history, even himself. He speaks articulately, incessantly, and with passion.

Yet there is more than rage behind Abraham Rodríguez's words. To anybody who talks at length with him, it soon becomes clear that he has given much thought to the complicated processes that drive contemporary society. A great deal of what he is saying ultimately makes sense. What he is denouncing is even now under scrutiny in diverse forums: state control over individuals' lives; institutionalized violence; structural poverty; disguised imperialistic motives; the psychology of dependency.

His writing is impassioned in its relentless portrayal of "little" lives immersed in the huge tragedy of urban chaos, particularly in its South Bronx version. He creates characters that are memorable in their smallness and in their total ignorance of the unleashed societal forces that are ultimately running their lives. Some of his stories—and parts of his novel *Spidertown*—are, strangely enough, touching when they reveal the pitiful efforts of his characters, mostly young people, to copy the external trappings and rituals of "normal" life in a developed, capitalist society.

Rodríguez's stories and his one published novel tell and retell the same tale over and over again, many times from a perspective that focuses on the most exploited among the exploited: the young girls who have a limited recourse to power and who must depend on emotionally unstable, delinquent boy-

Photograph of Abraham Rodríguez, Jr. taken by Miguel Trelles.

friends for recognition, respect, and well-being or the young punks who are used as expendable carriers and messengers for the pushers who are higher up in the drug business hierarchy.

Part of Abraham Rodríguez's success as a writer is his wonderful ear for dialogue, his ability to offer the seemingly imperturbable surfaces of deeply disturbing realities, making these come across through suggestion rather than outright manifestation. The ghetto ambiance which he holds before the reader constantly has new and subtle nuances—including accusatorial undertones—that reflect a mirror-image of established society.

Abraham Rodríguez was born in the South Bronx to Puerto Rican parents in 1961. He studied at neighborhood public schools and dropped out of high school when he was 16. He became a punk rock band leader, playing the guitar and writing the songs for his group. He eventually obtained a high school equivalency diploma and attended City College of New York for four years. During that time he was twice awarded the first prize in the Goodman Fund Short Story Awards.

Rodríguez's first collection of short stories was *The Boy Without a Flag: Tales of the South Bronx* (Minneapolis: Milkweed Editions, 1992). In 1993 Hyperion in New York published his first novel, *Spidertown*, with an 18,000-copy first printing. The movie rights were purchased by Columbia Pictures shortly afterward.

Abraham Rodríguez's stories have appeared in the magazine *Story* and in the anthologies *Best Stories from New Writers* (Cincinatti, Ohio: Writers Digest Books, 1989); *Iguana Dreams*, edited by Virgil Suárez and Delia Poey (New York: Harper, 1992); *Currents from the Dancing River: Contemporary Latino Fiction, Nonfiction and Poetry*, edited by Ray González (New York: Harcourt Brace, 1994); and *Boricuas: Influential Puerto Rican Writings*, edited by Roberto Santiago (New York: Ballantine Books, 1995).

"THE ISLAND IS A MYTH TO ME. IT DOESN'T EXIST FOR ME AT ALL."

CDH: What is your relationship with the older generation of Puerto Rican writers?

AR: I think that for the most part this older generation of Puerto Rican writers didn't do anything for the younger generation coming up, particularly myself.

Take Piri Thomas, for example. I'm very angry at him. The reason is because when I was young, when I was in high school, I told a teacher of mine I wanted to be a writer. I was already writing at the time. I used to put out fanzines, magazine-like publications. I told this old, jaded white teacher that I wanted to be a writer and he laughed. I couldn't figure out why he was laughing, but he was just laughing. I asked him, and he says, "There's no such thing as Puerto Rican writers." Just like that.

Of course, I didn't know about Piri Thomas. I didn't know about any of these people. And Piri had lived blocks from my school in Spanish Harlem, on 116th Street. So I was very angry to learn not only that he came from the area but that he lived in the community. This has to be taken with a grain of salt, of course. Every writer has a life, and I don't know about that whole thing about obligations, but dealing on an emotional level, that's how I felt about him. He never visited my school, Franklin, and I always thought that was a failure on the part of Puerto Rican writers. Later, I met a lot of these older writers and have sat around the table with them, seeing the spite, the anger, and the alibis, the whole thing—"Oh, you don't get published because it's a racist society," and this and that. My feeling is the reason they don't get published is because they're not saying anything interesting. Nothing that they're saying matters, especially to young people growing up now. What they're writing about is forty years old. It's sort of like the Puerto Rican Traveling Theater doing *The Oxcart* by René Marqués.[1] It's an amazing play and I love it, but that was then. It asks the crucial question, "OK, we as a people, where have we arrived? What's going to happen to us?" I think that at this stage we can no longer ask, "What's going to happen to us?" We've already arrived in the situation, we've been here, and we're seeing the fruits of all those political decisions and misdecisions.

They seem to be stuck in another era. The last time I was with those people, we were all sitting at this table, and they were all criticizing Oscar Hijuelos because he had just gotten a Pulitzer. It's just a waste of time. I don't see why writers do that. They should go home and write something. If they didn't sit around at a table drinking, talking about other writers so much, arguing about Faulkner all day, maybe they'd get some work done.

CDH: Do you think that your differences with them may be due to a generational gap?

AR: Oh, yes. The younger generation has to piss on the older generation, and I can't think of a generation that deserves it more. To be honest with you, this motley generation of old Puerto Ricans hasn't done shit for the young people. And it's getting worse. Then they get mad at me because I write a book like this[2] and they say this is negative.

It's more important to show young people that you can piss on the older people and get away with it. That's a good example for them, I think, as opposed to being so formal and nice. You'd think that I'm coming from a different place than these people. And while I respect literature, I don't see any use in stories about the blessed Diaspora forty years ago or of the first time I saw a snowflake. I think we should go beyond that now. We've got young 14-year-old kids blasting each other to hell with automatic weapons, and the island has the same problem. I think these are bigger things, and we've got to find a way. . . . This is not at all about politics. These are the dynamics of writing, but of course politics has to do something to it.

CDH: You said, "We have arrived." Does that imply that these other writers are still preoccupied about the time when they were trying to get somewhere?

AR: They're still trying to come to grips with something that—from their work and from what I've seen—I think has already passed them by. And while I love that ability, some writers have to capture certain moments of our time—that's always important—I really am not surprised that this stuff doesn't sell. This doesn't interest people for the most part, I think. As a young person I was never interested in this kind of book. They had nothing to offer me because I didn't see anything I could really relate to inside of them. In terms of the voice, in terms of the language, in terms of the subject matter, nothing. It's like writing about the island. It's a myth to me. The island is a myth. I like reading about it, but it's a myth. It doesn't exist for me at all.

I don't know any young Puerto Ricans who write. I don't know any young Puerto Ricans who do this stuff. This is old stuff, it's not about anything that's happening. I'm afraid that these older writers lost the ability to create the dynamic to which young people could be encouraged to write, to do anything, to do films, to be actors, to go out and do artistic, creative things. That's not happening.

CDH: After all these things that you've been telling me, do you still identify yourself as a Puerto Rican?

AR: Of course, I am Puerto Rican. I am also American. I'm both. It's really stupid for anybody to say that they're completely Puerto Rican. There isn't a Puerto Rican alive that hasn't been affected by American culture, that hasn't had America inflicted upon him. My big deal was coming to grips with it because I had an identity crisis for long. Coming to grips with it was what *The Boy Without a Flag* was about; it was about coming to accept something. The United States is an integral part of me, just like Puerto Rico is. Puerto Rico was always the smaller part. I kept going back and sort of reclaiming that, reexperiencing it, trying to understand what it is to be Puerto Rican and what it means to be Puerto Rican in these times and what kind of a context can I be Puerto Rican in, in a society like this. That's why I ended up questioning everything, really. A lot of Puerto Ricans don't understand what I say.

I like to recount the story of a friend of mine in Seattle, a Mexican. He gave me a T-shirt that had the Puerto Rican flag on it, he thought that it was a nice thing to do. And I dug it, but after he had left my house, I gave it to my girlfriend and I said "tear it up." And I got the scissors and started cutting it. She said, "Why are you doing this to the shirt?" And I said, "It's because I always thought that the flag was a dishrag, so here's a dishrag, it's for the dishes." And that baffles a lot of Puerto Ricans. Puerto Ricans don't really think about what that flag represents or what it means. It makes me angry, it makes me feel very frustrated. It makes us seem very spineless and superficial. People are very naive, very unaware of their history. And the stupider you are about where you come from, the more likely you are to end up at one end of a gun on a street somewhere selling rocks.

CDH: So in a way you are saying that it's necessary to know about Puerto Rico?

AR: Well, sure. Culturally speaking. It's just like the black people, who have been discovering a sense of themselves. And however militant they might get, it is a positive thing because it makes them stronger and puts them in opposition to a society that oppresses them. I think that Puerto Ricans used to think that way. When I was growing up in the seventies, there was a lot more of an Afro-American kind of experience within the Puerto Rican community: more Afros, more raised fists, Young Lords, all that.

CDH: But not any more?

AR: It's nothing like that now. I don't know of any group out there that's really doing this kind of work on a major scale; maybe on a small scale—never like it was in the seventies. And I think that aggressiveness was always stronger in the Afro-American community than among Puerto Ricans. Puerto Ricans turned to music to express themselves, which was positive. But we don't really have that now, Everybody's busy trying to be Hispanic.

CDH: Being Hispanic is not important for you?

AR: What does the word "Hispanic" mean? It means shit to me. I don't like the word. It means from Spain. I'm not from Spain. We're Taínos, we were natural Taínos; they came over and they screwed us. And so why should I feel like I am from Spain? I learned this from Mexicans when I started going to the Northwest and meeting a lot of Chicanos. I went to Colorado and I couldn't believe it. I thought that in Colorado there were cowboys, white people, but it's Mexicans, man. Mexicans and Chicanos who are strong, politically active. If there is something they don't like, they go out on the streets in front of City Hall. I'm not talking ten people; I'm talking thousands of Chicanos . . . organized, going down there to pro-test . . . what? School lunch, for example. Something happened at school and they're going to protest. This is unheard of in the South Bronx, this is unheard of in the areas out here. Latinos out here have no sense of community, of political awareness. I remember talking to somebody about

Hispanic and how I felt it was another American attempt to categorize people. She said, "We Mexicans don't like the word Hispanic, we refuse to be Hispanic. We don't want to be from Spain because Spain oppressed us, so why should we be from Spain? We're just lower-case Hispanics to the Spanish; they're racist as all hell. So why should I think, *Oh, I'm a bastard son of the Spanish empire?*

CDH: But don't they use the word "Hispanic" here more or less like a catch-all?

AR: It's a category. It's like when I used to apply for jobs, it was always *White, Black, Hispanic, or Other.* . . . Some Hispanics are white, some Hispanics are black, some Hispanics are even Asian. Hispanic is not a race. It's a historically inaccurate terminology used to categorize people. In a society that's supposed to be a tapestry of cultures and peoples, we are the most intent in categorizing and grouping and labeling and separating people. Because really what that does is separate. So, no Hispanic *no me gusta.*[3] And I've had arguments about the word "minorities," too. It's a category-rife society.

We grew up with it. I grew up with that idea that I'm a minority, I'm Hispanic. I threw it off. I don't need somebody else to define me. I don't need somebody else to tell me what I am or what my concerns are, or the concerns of Hispanics. I'm not Hispanic.

When I was growing up in the South Bronx, everybody thought I was a Jew. I used to have these Nazi dreams at night where the Gestapo would come and get me. I dreamed the SS would come. My name is Abraham, I use my hands a lot and have a big nose, so I was supposed to be Jewish.

CDH: As a writer, do you want to express something about the Puerto Ricans from the perspective of a younger generation?

AR: I don't know. These things are all unconscious. I don't have a set program. I write. I don't think about messages or telling people anything. At the same time I'm aware of coming from a different reality. I know what bored me when I was a young kid. And I know what bored me about books. Being a writer, I'm very sensitive to that kind of thing, but in terms of a message, I don't have one general message. I think there is a lot of outrage, a lot of anger, and a lot of pessimism in some of my work. *Spidertown* really isn't pessimistic, it's an angry novel. It's coming from the more angry place.

What do I have to say? I have everything to say about everything. I think a lot of what I do is at odds with the current of a lot of people who are writing about the so-called Latino experience, about the so-called Puerto Rican experience and are still showing this incredible inability to face front and realize that the times have changed. When I was very young, I remember I didn't even know where to go to get books about Latinos; I hadn't read books by Latinos. Then I started ordering books from Arte Público, and I was very disappointed because they all read the same to me. And later, when I almost got a book deal with them, I found out why. They edited my book down to the point where it didn't even seem like my book any more. I was very upset.

CDH: What book was that?

AR: When I was looking to get published, I used to send out my work, and that brief time I spent trying to get published I hit upon Arte Público. I had sent them a short story called *Babies*, and they liked it and told me, "Do you have a collection?" I put together a collection, half city stories, half island stories. I sent them and when they came back, they'd been totally changed. They totally ripped up the language, and I got very angry. The contract had this little thing that said "we edit for felicity." I remember when I first saw that, I said, "Felicity, who's felicity? Who could that be?" I couldn't figure it out. Means that they edit it to make sure that it reads nice.

Well, if we're going to be cultural about this, I don't know a single white company that I've ever signed with or white editor or white anything that's treated my work with less than respect. And here comes a Latino man and he treats my work like crap.

CDH: Then you went on to publish your writing with Anglo companies?

AR: It was a long road from there. I stopped sending things out. They always tell you when you're a writer that you send things out, and they come back and it makes you strong. I don't agree at all; that made me feel bad, it was keeping me from writing. So I stopped sending them out. I eventually got published in one magazine in Chicago that a friend of mine started and which really happened because of my band. He knew me because of my punk band.

CDH: You had a punk band?

AR: *Urgent Fury*, for eight years. We were sort of like a Tri-borough experience. I was from the Bronx and the other two were from Brooklyn. We played for eight years. We put out a record. We played a lot of clubs. We were very big in Chicago, I don't know why. It was in the eighties, 1983 up until 1989. I split it up around 1990.

CDH: So what happened after that story was published in Chicago?

AR: About a year or two passed, and one day I heard from this editor at *Writer's Digest Books* and she was doing a book called *Best Stories from New Writers*. She had seen my story, *Babies,* and she loved it. She wanted it for the anthology. That was my first appearance in print. That led to Lois Rosenthal at *Story* magazine, which had just started again—they resuscitated that short story magazine. It used to be famous; it started off some great American authors like J. D. Salinger and Truman Capote and Gore

Vidal. It is known for not only finding new writers but for helping them get fixed up with agents and helping them get deals. They did it for Flannery O'Connor also. So this Lois Rosenthal called the editor at *Writer's Digest* and says, "Do you know of any new, exciting young writers?" And she said, "Abraham Rodríguez." So then Lois calls me and says, "Do you have stories? We saw *Babies* and we really liked it." I had them all just sitting there. I sent them some stories and they liked them. They bought two of them, and they published *Baby with a Baby*, which later became *Elba*. After I got into *Story* Lois found me an agent, the one I have now. So it sort of came for me because I had stopped looking; that was keeping me from writing.

CDH: This kind of thing could only happen in the States. In Puerto Rico I don't know how many young writers are wasted because there is no real publishing industry.

AR: Well, there seems to be a mutual blockade between what happens in the island and what happens here. When positive things happen up here, nobody hears about it there, and over there the positive things that happen, we don't hear about it here. There's not an inch of communication between the island and here, and the experiences between the two populations are getting differenter and differenter.

CDH: You were born in the South Bronx, right? When was the first time you went over to the island?

AR: I think it was 1968 or 1967. I was about 8 or 9, the first time. I went again when I was 15. But that's about it; those are the only times I've been on the island. The first times I loved it, the last time I hated it. It was all concrete. I was staying in San Juan, I hate San Juan.

CDH: Did you have an idea of what the island would be like from what your parents had told you?

AR: No, I was really young when I went and to me it was paradise; it was green hills and freedom. When I was young here, I couldn't do anything. I was always sick, I had asthma. I couldn't go out. When I went to Puerto Rico, I could do everything. I could stay out, I could run around, I could be bare-footed in the grass. It could rain on me. I never got asthma in Puerto Rico. My feeling was that I couldn't get sick in Puerto Rico. It was just magic or the air; I don't know what it was. But when I went back in 1977, my father was staying in San Juan, a congested city with condominiums, lots of asphalt, lots of cars. And I got sick, I caught the flu, and then I got asthma. I hadn't had asthma in a long time. And suddenly I felt, "Ah, San Juan is just another city, another big, congested city. We should've gone to Fajardo or something."

CDH: Are your parents from Fajardo?

AR: My mother's side of the family. My father is from San Juan.

CDH: Besides your experience, what did you think about Puerto Rico and its problems when you were growing up?

AR: Puerto Rico, for me, was sort of an enchanted place. But I knew too much about politics to be too excited about it. My father always told me about politics. When I was young, I fell in love with war and war movies and comic books and European history. My father was always trying to get me to understand more current history, to him all that was almost Ancient History. To him more important was the history of Puerto Rico and Chile and South America and the CIA and all these things. So he made me very aware of politics, power politics.

I sort of always had a political head. I always felt a sense of shame about the political situation in Puerto Rico because I felt that we did not do what was right. There was no Nationalist kind of feeling. That's why I don't like that flag. You know what mystifies me? Madonna goes to Puerto Rico, and she takes the Puerto Rican flag and she puts it between her legs for a little hanky panky. The situation that Puerto Ricans find themselves in here, in the inner city, or in any inner city in this nation, or even in Puerto Rico, where you got drug traffickers attacking police, is a problem directly imported from the United States, and this is a result of a political decision that was made on the island. It's ironic to me that Puerto Ricans have these amazing problems, and the one thing that makes them get into an uproar is when some white woman takes the Puerto Rican flag and puts it between her legs. Let's face it: Congress has been doing that to the island now for how many years? I remember that movie that came out about the Cerro Maravilla. They made a big deal out of it, and it wasn't even about Cerro Maravilla. It was about the reporters who uncovered the story, and of course they put in an American so as to say it was an American who discovered the story. The movie comes out and they protest it. But why do they protest it? Because it made Puerto Rico look like a Banana Republic. That's why they were angry. But what the fuck is Puerto Rico? Who's dealing with reality here? We have bigger problems to confront than our depiction in a movie or that Madonna plays with the Puerto Rican flag. Those kinds of things upset me because it shows how narrow-minded and ignorant Puerto Ricans are about their own dilemma. That ignorance leads to 12-year-old kids out here carrying Uzzies and killing each other.

CDH: But why does that ignorance in Puerto Rico lead to that situation here?

AR: Because it starts in Puerto Rico. Because the political decisions that have been made by that motley crew, that old generation of idiots, is what led us to this confrontation now with narcotraffic, with the kind of society that you have in Puerto Rico, the polarization that you have in Puerto Rico, and I haven't even been in Puerto Rico and I know some of the problems that are happening over there. Traditional problems of colonialism. There's nothing unique about the kind of problems that are happening in Puerto Rico right now. The only thing unique about it is the Puerto Rican politics of ability to hoodwink itself into believing it still has a special relationship with the United States. The whole machinery on that island is built around the premise of fooling people into believing that. But you know what? That's not my problem. I'm not there. I live here. The bigger problem is here. This is where Puerto Ricans are getting killed, this is where it counts, this is where it hurts the most. Nobody on the island is doing anything about the kids here, and nobody on the island is doing anything about the Puerto Rican generation that's over here, stranded. The political decisions they made on the island exacerbated the great Diaspora that we had here in the fifties that led to the inner-city problem.

If we were going to be cheap labor, well, the labor ran out. What happens next? What's Puerto Rico doing to create an intelligent pool of workers so that we can compete as a nation? We can't compete as a nation, we are not a nation. Look in the almanac for our flag. Where is it? The trusted, beautiful Puerto Rican flag. It's not there. We don't have a flag. You know why? We are not a country. We're a territory. These are little things that don't matter that much, but people have to become conscious of what they are. I can't stand it. "Puerto Rico, my country." No: "Puerto Rico, my territory." Get real. You want a country? Do something about it. The cowardice! In a nutshell that's my attitude. I love Puerto Rico, but it's been marred by the politics of the situation and by the ignorance of a lot of people.

I mean in this country here now, how many Yankees know who Lolita Lebrón[4] is? I dedicate my next book to Lolita Lebrón, one of the characters, who is killed in the first chapter but keeps appearing throughout the book. How many people know about her in the South Bronx? How many young Puerto Ricans know? We have a school called Albizu Campos[5] but how many people know about him? They just know him as the first Puerto Rican to go to Harvard. It has no impact. These people are just forgotten. The Puerto Rican "pueblo,"[6] they're always going to take the easy way out. They've been doing that, and they'll continue to do that. Just the easy, comfortable way out. Like my aunt. My father is a Nationalist, and my aunt is the total opposite, very conservative. Her feeling about it is that it's fine the way it is now, and you don't want more. We don't want anyone to be hurt. The ironic thing is that in this manic need to avoid violence in the name of revolution or political solutions, they now have violence in an untold scale where the young people, instead of dying for their country or dying for ideals, are now dying for little rocks and Mercedes and *lujo* and *prendas*,[7] and all of that.

CDH: I've rarely heard the situation described like this.

AR: I blame the older generation completely; that's why I have a chip on my shoulder the size of Cleveland. Some people say, "Oh, he hates Puerto Ricans." No, I am remorselessly merciless when it comes to myself and what I demand of myself. Therefore, how much more merciless am I going to be with my own culture and my own people? I'm very disappointed. I grew up with *dominicanos* and *cubanos*[8] around me, and I see their different orientations as Latinos. There's this feeling of Puerto Rico being the lapdog of the Caribbean. That upsets me, that we were seen as lapdogs, historically speaking. To a degree it's not true and to a degree it is true, as far as I am concerned. But where do you go with that? OK, if you want to get really systematic about it, the Puerto Rican people were betrayed. OK, now what? That's where real politics comes in. Then my American side comes in and says, "Well, Puerto Rico is obviously important to the United States," and they're going to keep Puerto Rico in the same position it finds itself in now. Just like they're going to keep the South Bronx in the same position it finds itself in. You can't tell me, as a person who lives in the South Bronx, that these problems can't be eradicated. I think there are people who are really benefiting from the situation, and that's why it stays that way. I've seen this, I've seen this in the posses, I've seen it working on the street level. It's not just something that happens; it's a system of control, and the more you're out there, the more you see what's happening, the more you realize that's what it is. It's a system of control and it works perfectly.

CDH: By whom? By society, you mean?

AR: By whom is not even important. It can be a whole class of people, it can be white patriarchy, it can be a little old man. It can be William S. Burroughs. Who knows? Who can really say? The fact is that there is a power in this country that makes these decisions and some people who go against the power get zapped. From top to bottom. Look at what happened to the Kennedys. The Kennedys got zapped for a lot of reasons. Who zapped them? Eisenhower talked about the military-industrial complex. Was it them? I don't know. It's a system that's built a certain way. Look at the story of the FBI and J. Edgar Hoover. A marvelous example of a power-entrenched organization that's supposed to serve the people and becomes entrenched for itself, develops this amazing mystique of having fought underworld crime when in fact the FBI lives side by side with the Mafia which grew in proportion to the FBI. The FBI never touched the Mafia. It's a whole system of interrelations. And we Puerto Ricans are really small in the scheme of this; we are really very, very tiny. The normal American citizen is very tiny: White, black, Latino or other, just the normal American citizen counts very little in this scheme of things.

I'm not talking conspiracy, I am talking real politics. There's a system that's used to keep things under control, and that system works. Notice that at the time of the LA riots, they destroyed their own property. They didn't destroy anybody else's property, they destroyed their own cities. If the day came when young Latinos and black people took their rifles and their guns and went out and got in the car to shoot up other burroughs, then you're talking big trouble. See? It's a system of control. It does sound conspiracy, but I'm not talking conspiracy. It's just a system and it takes different ways to get around it, but the first thing is recognizing it. And these city kids already know about it. Some kids that I know who work in posses and sell drugs on a regular basis deal with the cops on a day-to-day level; they deal with cops almost like supervisors. These are the people we pay to keep our city streets safe. They are, in fact, *working* for posses. Posses pay them to leave them alone. And believe me, look, I understand the cops. If I'm going to work in a combat situation with the kind of pay I'm getting . . . , I mean, the cops are like an occupation army in some areas. Is it any wonder they shoot 14-year-old kids just because they turn around too fast? Those kids are probably outgunning them. Some of these kids have Uzzies. The cops have 9-millimeter guns.

Where are we headed? Obviously, toward some kind of police state. People are walking around saying, "Oh, we don't mind giving up our Fourth Amendment rights." There was a guy on TV yesterday talking about drug testing high school athletes. What's next? How many more violations of people's rights? Computer technology is going to make it impossible very soon for you to buy anything without it going into a computer bank somewhere. We will move to this system inevitably. The Army's already tried it out during the last conflict. It's a system where you don't need cash; you use a card for everything. This card has everything in it; all the information about you. So if you buy something, it's going to go in some big computer bank. If they're looking for you, all they have to do is look you up in the computer. We're getting there; we're there already. And that is control.

CDH: Is this something you would write about?

AR: I should be doing a different kind of book. This is not fantasy science fiction. Twenty years ago, Ray Bradbury would write about this kind of thing. But we're there. What if Hitler had had IBM? If Hitler had had a computer network in Nazi Germany? OK, they used to use index cards and they slaughtered 11 million people. Can you imagine? They would have finished every last Jewish person. They didn't get to them. There were still maybe 6 million Jews left in Europe. They almost wiped them out. Imagine the efficiency they would have had if they had a computer system. And IBM would have sold it to them. So that's what I'm talking about.

CDH: Tell me about your father. You spoke about him before, he seems to be very important in your life. Is he a Nationalist? When did he come to the States?

AR: He was always a Nationalist. He used to write poetry. He was in the Army at the tail end of World War II. He joined the Army in Puerto Rico to get off the island and ended up fighting the Japanese in 1945. He wanted to be a poet or an artist, an actor or something.

CDH: Did he take part in the Nationalist uprising?

AR: No, he didn't take part in it, but I think he felt deeply about it; he felt deeply about Albizu. He always used to tell me about him, about the radiation treatment they gave him. The first book I read about a Puerto Rican was by Federico Ribes Tovar, *Albizu Campos: Puerto Rican Revolutionary*.[9] Before, I read only about Germans; I knew more about Rommel than about any Puerto Rican. I fell in love with Albizu, walking up on stage in 1931 at a meeting and tearing up an American flag. That is just classic. Too bad that the Puerto Ricans did not admire him and did not follow him as they should have. Though he was a fool too. They arrested him in his house. I had an argument once about Albizu because I said he was an idiot and everybody has this very romantic notion about him. I tend to be very realistic; I do admire him, but he was an idiot. Unlike Castro. Castro was more of a smart man. He started a revolt and he went to the mountains and said, "Find me." Albizu was too bourgeois and too trusting; the police arrested him in his house. A lot of the big Nationalist moments overtook him. He was never really in control of what was happening; things happened beyond him. When Lolita Lebrón did her thing, they went to him for comment; he didn't even know about it. This is very sad to me. He ended up getting the blame for a lot of these things. They used it as an excuse to shut down the Nationalists. He was a very intelligent man, but he was no fighter. He trusted too much in the democratic process. You are never going to have a revolution trusting in democracy and the idea that people are going to elect a Nationalist movement when there are so many vested interests in the community that have the money and the capabilities to destroy you; you have to fight them on different terms. It's something really complex; I haven't studied it as much as I would like.

CDH: Was your novel *Spidertown* a success from the beginning?

AR: I just got a lot of attention from the politicians. They wanted to meet me. I got into this fight with a lady from *New York Newsday*. She's Puerto Rican, a reporter. She was very psyched because it had just been discovered that Puerto Ricans and Latinos are 34 percent of the voting population in New York. She's like, "Don't you think this is wonderful?" And I: "This means shit." What do you mean this is going to change? Do you think that the white man will be smart enough or dumb enough to set up a system that can outvote him? You can unseat him by just having a certain percentage of Puerto Ricans? Get real. It's foolishness to believe in the electorate. I've lived in the South Bronx all my life. I've seen Democrats and Republicans go. I've seen liberals become a bad word. Nothing's really changed except the advance of real estate interests. There's been a lot of new housing and stuff going on in the Bronx. It's obvious what's happening. In the Lower East Side they call it gentrification. What does it mean? Why are people so blind? And people in the South Bronx are grateful for this housing. Where are the people going to go who can't afford to buy into a house that costs a hundred thousand dollars?

CDH: You seem to be hurt by all this.

AR: I'm hurt more by the experiences I've witnessed, the lives that I've seen. The reason I write is because of the island. In one way, being a Gemini there's two of you, right? In one way it's like fuck the island, the island never meant anything to me, the island never cared about me or my situation here, I was dumped here, I have to fend for myself, and no one on the island has raised their voice in terms of the problems of the Puerto Ricans here.

CDH: The situation has been ignored even in history books.

AR: I wonder why? Operation Bootstrap! Muñoz Marín,[10] you know. The fucker is on a stamp. I'm not licking that stamp. Crazy. The first governor of Puerto Rico . . . The guy was lucky if he could move the guard outside his office without asking Congress first. There was a congressman in the early thirties that said, "Puerto Ricans are war booty." That's why I have no respect. I'm war booty, what do I care? I don't need to follow laws or regulations. I was won in a war. They had a war, they won me, and they're still trying to figure out what to do with me. It's a bad feeling, just like the feeling of being a minority. I got mad at somebody at a meeting one time because they were talking about minority issues. Why that insistence on classifying me as a minority? In Philadelphia you have small areas where there are Germans and Italians. Would you call Italians a minority? Would you call Germans a minority? Minority is a word you use for certain races; certain people are minorities. Latinos are minorities and black people are minorities. Black people have been here longer than a lot of the white people. So why are they a minority? Because there's less of them? There's less Germans too and you don't call them minorities. It's a certain training that you go through. I remember being a student in Colorado, and when asked if I was a minority I said, "I refuse to be called a minority, there's nothing minor about me." The whole school went "Yeah!" Because they had been dealing with that issue about minorities. It's a conditioning, you grow up with the conditioning.

CDH: Where did you study?

AR: I went to the first bilingual public school in New York, P.S. 25. After that I went to high school in Spanish Harlem, then Franklin High School. It's now a science lab; they turned it into a math lab or some creepy thing like that. But I dropped out of high school.

CDH: You didn't go to college?

AR: Later. After I dropped out I spent four years finding myself, being in bands. And I was going to be a musician, so I dropped out of school. I dropped out for a lot of reasons, and I think in retrospect one of them was that teacher saying what he said because all I really wanted to be was a writer.

CDH: Even then?

AR: Since I was 11, I wanted to write. Writing was it.

CDH: Why?

AR: I just loved it. It was an emotional release.

CDH: Did you like to read?

AR: No, it wasn't about books. It was about writing. My father, it's all his fault really. He used to write poems, these beautiful, long, longing, yearning poems about Puerto Rico: beauty, the loss, not being in Puerto Rico anymore, romantic things. He was into Neruda.[11] My first memory is hearing the typewriter. He used to rent these really big typewriters and type on them, and I remember that *clack, clack, clack*. When I was little, I used to sit on his lap and bang on it. Really, the whole writing thing is about typewriters; it's got nothing to do with literature at all. I love typewriters. I have about fourteen of them, manuals, I only use manuals.

CDH: You seem to have an extensive education. Where did you get that education?

AR: When I went for a job at a jewelry place during the seventies, they made me go through this lie detector test (I don't know if it was because I was Puerto Rican or if it's standard). I started talking with this guy, we started talking about Germany. The guy was in the Ardennes, in the Battle of the Bulge, and I went: "Oh, the Sixth SS Panzer Division . . . " and we started to talk. He was so amazed. "You dropped out of high school? I really feel that you should go back to school." A lot of people were telling me this, which is why I eventually went back. It was mostly for writing. My sister told me, "You should go back to school and see if you can be a writer." The guy was saying, "You're self-taught." He got me the Milkweed book deal and the Hyperion book deal and then the movie deal and all that. I was into books. I liked books. I didn't read fiction. Even though I was writing, that was mostly because of comic books. I love comic books, they're terrific.

Comic books were a big part of my growing up. The book I'm doing now is written like a comic book. Like a graphic novel. I am trying to get Puerto Rican artists to do the illustrations.

CDH: Are you aiming for a wider readership than with *Spidertown?*

AR: I don't know. I've had some bad experiences because being the good boy who came out of the South Bronx, all they wanted to do was exploit the South Bronx to sell books, and I refused to do that. All the major networks wanted me that summer a year ago, a year and a half ago. ABC, NBC, CBS, all these companies were calling up and wanted me, and Hyperion never forgot that I turned them down because I told them there are certain things I don't want to do and the primary thing I don't want to do is to become a pimp for the South Bronx.

But you never really think about those things when you're writing a book. Somebody told me they thought *Spidertown* was a Puerto Rican fairy tale that kids read to see that they can get out. I like that, but I hated the idea that I was being typecast into this role of social uplifter.

I did an interview with *The New York Times*, and they came to my house with a photographer and they said, "Why don't we go and shoot you in a place where some of the action takes place in the novel? Find us Spadgie's." I said it might be dangerous, and they said, "OK, take us to a place that might look like Spadgie's." So I said, "All right, fine." So we went over to the Westchester El, to a little spot under there. And I said, "This is a good place," and guess what, there was a Spadgie's there. We were taking pictures, and this big man comes out and says, "What are you doing here? Why are you taking pictures here? What do you want here? What are you doing in front of here?" I told the guy, "Listen, this is dangerous, let's get out of here, because I live in the community and you're putting me in a bad place." "No, one more picture, one more picture," they said. OK, all right. They took a picture where I look grim. And then what happened was the photographer ended up getting his car crashed. A 4×4, when he was trying to pull out from under the El, comes out of nowhere and smashes into his front side. And I said, "I know what this is." I thought of the headlines, "Young writer killed . . . " They didn't know what was going on. I thought, "You are so stupid and so dense. That's their way of saying *Don't come back here! Go away!* " I know their language and when I got back I was mad. I told the journalist, "If anybody in my family gets hurt because of you, I'm going to teach you a lot about journalistic integrity."

CDH: When you were growing up, Abraham, did you interact with people who were not Puerto Ricans?

AR: When I was young, I didn't have a lot of friends. I was very different from everybody. I had some friends in school, but I was a loner because nobody wanted to be with me. I was very freaky. I was into the Beatles. I was a rock and roll freak. I had long hair. Nowadays, probably because of the advent of MTV, you have young Puerto Ricans that are into metal, they use leather jackets, long hair, the works. When I was growing up, it wasn't like that. You weren't into rock music. Rock music was honky music, it was whitey music, and all the kids I knew were into soul and what later became disco. I was into the Stones, I was into the Who, I was into rock and roll, guitars, so that made me apart from everybody. By the time I got to high school, I was a one-person entity. High school was a bad trip. I dropped out. I got sick of being on my own. I figured if I had to be on my own, I'd rather stay home. I wasn't learning anything there. I dropped out, which really killed my parents. They had visions of me being something useful, you know, like a lawyer or a doctor. And then I was in the rock and roll thing, and my father thought, "I lost him to the world of drugs." Rock and roll meant drugs to my father.

CDH: Do you keep in touch with young Puerto Ricans now that you are a published author?

AR: Over the past two and a half years I visited a lot of schools. I try to make it fun for the kids, I want them to express themselves. Writing is about expressing yourself. The best thing you can do is get kids to express themselves. At first they don't want to talk. They are a very silent generation. You learn to be quiet on the streets, you don't talk too much. They go like: "You talk too much, man, you're like a woman." I do, I talk a lot, I emote. And they're more into the Clint Eastwood thing. Nobody speaks. All these kids, they're scared to speak up. This whole system, the whole educational system, is teaching them to shut up. They treat them like idiots, like they can't talk right; that's why they develop their own language. These are skills to me that teachers don't recognize.

I talk about things they feel about. I start mentioning cops, and the minute that I say cops, the ripple starts. Everybody wants to talk. If I told the kids, "Oh, I sit at the typewriter three hours a day and type," I know the reaction: "You sit at a typewriter? What the fuck is wrong with you?" I know the feeling like I invented it myself. I'm not going to tell the kid what a joy it is to write because the kid already has a problem dealing with why I would waste my time. Except for the money, that they relate to right away. But the idea of writing just for writing as I did all my life with no money. No! Writing is expression; the reason I like it is because I express myself. So if you get the kids to express, they go ape-shit, they go nuts. So I tell them, "You were asking me what it is about writing that I like: writing is expressing myself. Do you like to express yourself? Well that is writing to me." See? You got to show them. You have to show them something that they can relate to.

CDH: Is there a younger generation of Puerto Rican writers in New York, your age or younger?

AR: No. If there were any that were writing that were my age, I would know. I don't know of anybody doing this. There are some young poets. No prose, no fiction writers. I think it's indicative of our community that it is not into the arts, especially in the South Bronx. And I think it's the only thing that could save it, not politics, politics won't do a thing. I think art can go a long way in saving young people. It's just not happening in the inner city.

Photograph of Esmeralda Santiago, *El Nuevo Día* newspaper.

11

ESMERALDA SANTIAGO

Esmeralda Santiago's extraordinarily mobile face, her rapid, sure way of speaking perfect English in modulated tones that can go from oral caricature to deep emotional intensity, and her poise, reveal the training that she received at New York's Performing Arts High School, where she studied to be an actress. That school opened up the path that was to lead her out of Brooklyn—where her mother had settled with eleven children after migrating from Puerto Rico—and into Harvard.

Born in 1948 in Santurce, Puerto Rico, she spent several years of her childhood in a barrio in rural Toa Baja, on the northern coast of Puerto Rico. She also lived for a short time in one of the capital city's poorest slums before her mother decided to take matters in hand and provide a better life for her children, a wish that prompted the move to New York.

When I Was Puerto Rican, Esmeralda Santiago's account of those first years of her life, was first published by Addison-Wesley in 1993 and attained considerable success. It is one of the few memoirs written by a Puerto Rican woman living in the States or on the island. Her first novel is *América's Dream* (New York: HarperCollins, 1996).

Before publishing her first book, Esmeralda Santiago had written screenplays for shorts and documentary films. Together with her husband, Frank Cantor, she owns Cantomedia, a film production company. She has also contributed short pieces to various newspapers and magazines, among them *The New York Times, The Boston Globe, The Christian Science Monitor,* and *Radcliffe Quarterly.*

Esmeralda Santiago graduated from Harvard University in 1976. She has an MFA from Sarah Lawrence College (1992) and an Honorary Doctor of Letters degree from Trinity College, Hartford, Connecticut. She is included in the anthologies *Boricuas: Influential Puerto Rican Writings,* edited by Roberto

Santiago (New York: Ballantine Books, 1995) and *Home: American Writers Remember Rooms of Their Own*, edited by Steve and Sharon Fiffer (New York: Pantheon, 1995).

She currently lives in Westchester County, New York, with her husband and two children.

"MY WRITING IS WOMAN'S WRITING"

CDH: When did you begin to write?

ES: I've always been a writer; my father is a poet, and so words and writing were always an important part of my life and the life of my sisters and brothers. The first publication I ever had, however, was in eighth grade in the school newspaper, and it was five months after I arrived in the United States. It was written in English, and it was about a girl newly arrived in Brooklyn from Puerto Rico who had it all figured out when she left the island. All of a sudden she's in Brooklyn and she's totally confused and she doesn't know what to do with her life, but she decides that maybe she should be a hairdresser.

It took me a long time after that to really be confident enough to write for publication because the more English I learned, the more I realized I didn't know as much as I wanted to know in order to write. And so I got the feeling that I had lost my language, that I had lost Spanish because I wasn't learning it anymore. I was learning English, but, being a perfectionist, I didn't feel that I knew enough to write in it. So the idea of being a writer went into the background.

CDH: You did write screenplays before writing *When I Was Puerto Rican*, didn't you?

ES: Yes, I wrote the screenplays for short films like *Button, Button* and *The Beverly Hills Supper Club Fire*, and I always wrote in my jobs. For a time I was a proposal writer, writing proposals for district attorneys and government agencies. This was after I graduated from college. I had a job writing proposals for Alianza Hispana, a multiservice agency in Boston for *puertorriqueños*. (That was before, now it's for all kinds of Latinos.) From that, I was hired by a district attorney in Massachusetts to write proposals in his office in the area of domestic violence. That's when I started getting an inkling that I probably should write fiction because when I'd go to defend my proposal, people would say: "Your proposals are so readable, you had me crying." That sort of led me to write for a more general audience. I started writing personal essays and opinion pieces for newspapers and magazines. It was through a personal essay that I wrote for the *Radcliffe Quarterly* that an editor discovered me.

CDH: What was the essay about?

ES: The issue was women and work. I knew the editor very well, so she asked me to write about that. The original thought was that I would write about the thirty-two jobs I had had since high school. But when I began to write, what came out was: "When Mami worked, we were happy because we didn't have to be on welfare." So I wrote this essay which was very emotional and hard for me to write because it was the first time that I had written about that experience, about being the oldest of eleven children and my mother really wanting to work desperately. But at the time she was working in New York—she was a garment-worker—the garment industry was moving out of the city. I had this very strong image of Mami all dressed up, and she'd put on her makeup and she did her hair and she had her nice clothes on and she'd go to work and she'd be home two hours later because she'd been laid off. They would never give her notice. That's what happened to people; the owners would move the factories out of New York, and they wouldn't tell you because the workers were not unionized and there was no protection. She would be home when I came back from school, and she would say: "Tomorrow you can't go to school because we have to go to the welfare office and apply for welfare until I find another job." It was very hard for us to go through that; it was a constant up and down. It was that essay an editor at Addison-Wesley saw and asked me to come in and talk to her about my work. It was really her idea about a memoir.

CDH: Your mother comes across as a very strong woman in your memoir.

ES: She was very strong, independent, and stubborn, and she was very proud. If there's a flaw in her character it is this pride that will not give in. Because she was so proud, there was this sense that "yes, we're on welfare," but it was going to be only a temporary situation. We didn't like it; we didn't like taking what she thought was charity.

CDH: Is she still living?

ES: She lives in Florida, and it always strikes me that nobody has ever interviewed her. She's worth interviewing. She's the mother of eleven children; she does not have a formal education (she stopped going to school when she was in sixth grade), but considering the circumstances under which we grew up and the communities in which we grew up, we all turned out all right. All of us have ended up having jobs and families; not one of us landed in jail. I mean, none of those things that people expect from Puerto Ricans in the ghettos of New York City happened to us. That, I think, is a result of her influence.

CDH: So, *When I Was Puerto Rican* started out when the editor called you?

ES: Yes, what the editor recognized when she looked at my work was that I was a writer wanting to burst out of writing these short pieces, wanting to be more expansive. She really did discover me; she had a vision of me as a writer that I didn't have for myself, and she helped me develop it.

CDH: Was the book well received?

ES: Extremely so. Now I can think of myself as a full-time writer. It also gave me the confidence to describe myself as a writer.

CDH: Have you tried to write in Spanish?

ES: The only thing I have written in Spanish is poetry, and if I say so myself, I'm the world's worst poet. The only thing I have written in poetry that I like is a 200-word prose poem for a poetry course at Sarah Lawrence, and it was in English. But even then I kept thinking that I was going to make it into a short story or novel. I don't write short stories: I need the broader canvas. I read big, thick books, and that's what I want to write. I have also translated *América's Dream* into Spanish, like I did with *When I Was Puerto Rican*.

CDH: What do you like to read?

ES: I like to read great literature; I read very few best-sellers or contemporary fiction. In fact, I have spent the last five years reading eighteenth- and nineteenth-century literature: dead white women. I'm not as interested in dead white men.

CDH: Do you read in Spanish?

ES: I read in Spanish whatever I can get because I don't live in the city and so there's only a very small bookstore about thirty minutes from where I live where I'm able to get "los grandes": Manuel Puig, Unamuno, García Márquez, Allende, all these people, but very few Puerto Ricans, very few of the writers who are not best-sellers. I'm a great believer that the classics, even if they're about China, have something to teach you about life. I can read any good writer's work and learn something. I think that's the marvelous thing about great literature, which is something that gets lost in this discussion about the canon. Why are we only reading white men? Now we have the opportunity to read Chinese men, Indian women, Sri Lankan poets . . . it doesn't really matter anymore. We have access to all, and you don't need to be so parochial about it. It's not true that you can only learn from your own culture.

CDH: But do you relate to Spanish-speaking authors?

ES: Very much. What I try to find is women writers. I have read Luisa Valenzuela, Gioconda Belli, Elena Poniatowska, Rosario Ferré, Ana Lydia Vega. I am really interested in women's lives, mostly because I'm a woman. I think my writing is woman's writing. I write for women: I don't care if men read my work; it doesn't matter to me. I'm very deliberate about that. There are times when I'm writing something and I think, "Well, men are not going to like this" and immediately I go, "I don't care." It's women's lives I'm interested in. A man said to me some time ago: "I'm a Puerto Rican man and it's really hard for me to read this book" (*When I Was Puerto Rican*). It was a very interesting comment, and I appreciated it so much because it took a lot of courage to say that. He saw that the book was somehow meant as a comment of how girls and women view Puerto Rican men, which was not necessarily my intention. My intention was to be as truthful as I could, but it was great for me to hear that from him.

CDH: He thought you were holding up a mirror to men and in a way you are.

ES: Yes. It was not my goal to make Puerto Rican men look bad by any means because I don't think my Dad comes off looking bad (although he was a little put out by the book), but I think it is important for men to know how their actions affect women. That's something that men can't get on their own, they have to get it from us. And it's important for women to know how their actions affect their daughters, and so that in itself is something we should be aware of. We are the ones passing on the traditions.

CDH: I think you display a very definite feminine outlook. The details you give regarding the chores of daily life, the relations between mother and children, and those between the couple and with the rest of society, those are all things that would not be noticed or recognized in the same way by a man. Curiously, it gives the book a *costumbrista*[1] projection.

ES: I'm very conscious about looking at the world through a woman's eyes. It's really what my work is about, to see as a woman. A woman notices more details, subconsciously. In novels by men there are not so many details. It's sort of the big picture.

América's Dream is about a maid, and a maid looks at the world in a very different way from an accountant, for example. And even though I hate housework, personally, I liked to write about her doing it. I'm fascinated by someone whose whole life is picking up after other people. That's the kind of detail that a woman appreciates. One of my editors remarked that the main character didn't seem to change very much, but the thing is that I don't think women's lives are that dramatic, and if they are, they sound melodramatic and then you get into the world of *telenovelas*.[2] When many things happen and there are big changes, then it's unbelievable. We see the world in detail, and because of that it has to go a little bit slower instead of taking it all in fast.

CDH: Do you feel an affinity with Puerto Rican writers in New York?

ES: I don't live in New York City. I'm not connected to a community of writers; I'm not even very connected to the general Puerto Rican community there. After a year and a half of being in New York, I went to Performing Arts High School and I became a sort of actress, and after that I lived in midtown because it was close to my work and my school. Then I went to Texas and lived there for a couple of years, and I lived in Syracuse for a couple of years. None of those communities were Puerto Rican communities. I was outside of that experience, and the Puerto Rican community was whatever I brought with me. My Puerto Rican community is my family: my mother and sisters and brothers. But it's not a long network.

Now, after publishing *When I Was Puerto Rican*, I have come into contact with some Puerto Rican writers there: Nicholasa Mohr, for example, with whom I've become friends.

CDH: Have you gotten any feedback from the Puerto Rican community in the States about your book?

ES: I've had the most poignant moments when I have gone to speak at some places. I went to a little town in Tennessee, for example, and a group comes in, about twenty persons. They were all Puerto Rican, and they had come from Nashville, an hour and a half away just to hear me. Another time I was at a Seattle book store and in comes Abraham Rodríguez with a whole bunch of his "home boy" friends. This kind of thing is important for me because I don't live in a Puerto Rican community.

CDH: Do you think you would have been a writer if you had not had the experience of going to live in New York?

ES: I don't know. I might have, because books and words are so important in my family. I would have been the kind of writer my father is; my father is a poet who has not really been published extensively, but he still is a poet and he still writes. I may not have had the confidence to send my stuff out anywhere. But what made me a writer was not necessarily the experience of going to New York but the experience of returning to Puerto Rico.

CDH: How is that?

ES: I left Puerto Rico in 1961 and I came back in 1976, right after I graduated from Harvard. I discovered that Puerto Ricans did not consider me Puerto Rican because I had lived in the United States for so long and I was so Americanized. That experience was devastating for me. I spent four months in Puerto Rico crying. I was trying to understand what I had done wrong; why people who were strangers could pick up on something that had happened to me, but that I didn't know showed. I didn't feel Americanized, I felt very Puerto Rican.

I came, Harvard degree in hand, to stay. My family lived in Bayamón. I tried to find a job, I came with my magna cum laude degree thinking that everybody was going to be so proud of me in Puerto Rico. But the only job I could get was as a typist at $3 an hour. In New York I was at least a bilingual secretary. My boss said to me: "You can have ten Harvard degrees, but you're still a woman in Puerto Rico." And I said: "I'm out of here. This I'm not going to fight." I would have fought everything else, but being seen as a lesser human being because of my gender, I had already fought that.

CDH: Now that you have come back as a successful writer, everybody claims you as a Puerto Rican.

ES: Now it's different. But the thing is that in 1976 I was disappointed because I was very naive. I had been away from Puerto Rico for thirteen years, and when you are away, you always expect home to be the same when you come back. I was disappointed because it was so different, and that disappointment colored everything for me. Home was no longer home; Puerto Rico was so Americanized. That threw everything off for me, especially since Puerto Ricans kept telling me *I* was Americanized. I thought, How can *puertorriqueños* who have never left the island accuse us when they allow the American contamination I was seeing all around? There were McDonald's, Pizza Huts, and so on. I used to think this was not our culture. Big Macs are not our cultural legacy. We in the States at least have an excuse for being Americanized. This ambivalence was part of what drove me away from here. There were so many questions and they couldn't be answered.

That was hard for me to understand: if I'm not Puerto Rican enough and in my eyes Puerto Rico is not Puerto Rican the way it was Puerto Rican before, then what is Puerto Rican and what am I doing here? I couldn't compromise. It was really tough. What I'm talking about is degrees of Puerto Ricanness.

A lot of people have told me they have had that same experience. I always say it's a lot harder to be Puerto Rican in Boston than to be Puerto Rican in Puerto Rico, so the Puerto Ricans who are in the United States maintaining their culture and going out of their way to keep it alive should be celebrated instead of being put down for it. That was my big argument. I tell them: "You take it for granted because here you don't have to work at it, but I have to work at it. I have to drive 25 miles to find yucca." For me being Puerto Rican is a conscious act.

CDH: So that experience was linked with your writing.

ES: That experience really set me to thinking and to writing about it. I would write for myself, in my journals, which were not for publication. But the more I wrote, the more I realized that it had to be public. It was not only my experience but an experience that a lot of immigrants are facing, not just in the United States but in any country that they go to: if you leave your "village," when you come back your village is going to know you left and they are going to challenge you. So as I go around the country talking about this experience, I meet people from all over the world who are relating a very similar one. They left their cultures to go to the States as students or to work and when they go back to their communities, they find out from them that they are now changed. They are asking themselves, "Wait a minute, what did I do? How am I changed?" It's a very superficial change, I think, what people see. I think it's something about the way we behave that's different from the way we behaved before we left. The first to notice are the people who care about us: our families, and then total strangers start picking up on it.

When my family first said to me that I wasn't Puerto Rican anymore, it was devastating. But when I started hearing it from total strangers, that's when it really started to hurt a lot. You have to start thinking about it then and looking at yourself and wondering what it's all about. I discovered that there are degrees of Puerto Ricanness. And that in Puerto Rico the people couldn't tell me what a Puerto Rican was. They could tell me what a Puerto Rican was not, and I was one of those who wasn't. It was a fascinating experience for me: I realized that it's not just here, that somebody from Ghana experiences the same thing. A man from Washington, D.C., stood up sobbing in the middle of a reading, literally sobbing. He was saying: "I read your book, it really touched me. What you're talking about happened to me. I'm a graduate student here; I came to George Washington University for a year to study. After a year I went back to my village in Ghana and was told I was no longer Ghanaian because I was Americanized." So he sat down, and this woman from Guadeloupe stands up and she says: "I came here with my family when I was a teenager. My father was a diplomat in Washington, D.C. I went to school here for three years, and then we went back to Guadeloupe and people began to tell me 'you're no longer Guadeloupan, because you're so Americanized.' " And so people started relating these stories: *mexicanos, costarricenses*, Venezuelans, Vietnamese. . . . And then I realized that this is not just something that happened to me, it's something that's happening.

CDH: I think that given today's mobility, many people are going to be "between cultures" at some point in their lives.

ES: As the world gets smaller, it doesn't matter what culture you come from or what the whole culture is, you are going to take on some of the trappings of the culture where you are and when you go back to your community you're going to look different from those who never left. We're not even aware of it, but the people who pick up on it are the people who know it. This is something that is going to be a big part of our psychology: having to deal with living in two cultures. The ironic thing for me is that in Puerto Rico I was considered American. In the United States I was considered Puerto Rican. It was really confusing. And I'm an adult. I've thought about this and I can deal with it, but I think to myself: "a child cannot deal with this, it is an impossible burden."

CDH: Can you really deal with it?

ES: Well, I'm very clear about it. I came to the point where I said: "The people who think I'm not Puerto Rican, it's their problem, not mine, because I feel Puerto Rican and if they can't accept it, they're going to have to deal with it, to deal with the Puerto Rican that I am. If they don't like that Puerto Rican, they can go find somebody else to talk to because I'm not going to change."

CDH: I take it the title of your book is an ironic commentary on just that.

ES: You got it. There's a woman from Puerto Rico who was incensed about the title, even after I explained why I called it *When I Was Puerto Rican*: that it refers to my life as a Puerto Rican girl, when I had no idea that I would ever leave the island, that I would ever visit another culture, let alone live in it for ten or fifteen years. It really is a Puerto Rican life for most of the book. And then when I was in New York, a couple of days after I arrived, a little girl came up to me trying to make friends, and she asked: "*Tú eres hispana?*" And I said, "*No, yo soy puertorriqueña.*"[3] And she replied: "Oh, it's the same here." I go, "Really? In the United States we're not Puerto Ricans?" She said, "Oh, no, no, all the people from Spanish countries, we're all *hispanos* here." It was the sense—the minute you arrive—that you lose your culture because you're no longer from a specific place, you're now lumped into this morass of Spanish-speaking people. But it's really interesting that you get that sense that you are no longer from a country, that you are a part of a whole other community that stays in the United States. So that was a second reason for the title.

CDH: Was there a third?

ES: Yes, it's that when I came back to Puerto Rico, *los puertorriqueños mismos me negaron*[4] because I was so Americanized, so it is an ironic comment and it is a way of starting a discussion about what is Puerto Ricanism. These degrees of Puerto Ricanism have to be addressed. It is causing a lot of pain because it's so easy to go back and forth, from one place to the other. I think that's why so many of our children are so confused and have such low self-esteem. They don't have a sense of belonging to one or the other culture. You feel guilty for becoming Americanized, and you feel guilty because you're not Puerto Rican enough.

CDH: On the other hand, I find it fascinating that Puerto Ricans keep on feeling Puerto Rican even if they are second- or third-generation immigrants; even if they no longer live in the ghetto or in New York or among other Puerto Ricans. Why is that? Why is it that Puerto Ricanness does not become diluted into the general American culture?

ES: I think that it is because we make a conscious choice to be Puerto Rican. The Italians, the Germans, and all the other immigrants who came to the United States were anxious to learn English and to become American. But I don't know of any Puerto Rican who wants to be American. Every

Puerto Rican I know wants to be Puerto Rican. And even though we're American citizens, this has a different meaning to us than to Americans. I am technically, legally, American. I know that, but the only time I identified myself as American was when I traveled to Guatemala and they asked me what passport I had. I said, "American passport." Maybe it's that insular— island—mentality. Even though we're in the continent, we're still little islands within the continent.

CDH: Perhaps it's difficult to determine now what is *the* American culture that is the basis of the melting pot, with so many groups defining themselves as African Americans, Native Americans, Latinos, and so on, within the United States.

ES: Everyone is trying to hold on to the culture they had. Your culture is your identity. I don't think there is an American sense of identity, not in the urban areas. I think this kind of thing is a conscious choice. There is that attitude that you are going to hold on to what makes you different, what separates you rather than to what brings you together.

Besides, I think culture is something that you can often only define through contrast. We define it from a difference. The only way we can experience it is in relation to what we bring to it, so Americans find it a lot easier to know what Puerto Rican culture is than to know what American culture is.

CDH: So that would explain the rise of multiculturalism in the United States?

ES: I think multiculturalism is a defensive word. It's a way of covering your back. I go to a lot of lectures as part of multicultural awareness, but I have noticed that they only take place at certain, predetermined times of the year. If we are serious about multiculturalism, it shouldn't be for only one week or one month of the year, it should be part of our everyday lives.

CDH: That persistence in the identification of Puerto Ricans in the United States in relation to their particular culture is evident in the literature that they write. Even though, like yourself, they are not from the ghetto, nor from New York and they have other experiences, Puerto Rico seems to be always the preferred frame of reference.

ES: Yes, the identification is always Puerto Rican. I think I'll be writing of Puerto Rico and Puerto Rican women the rest of my life.

CDH: But you write about a different kind of Puerto Rican, who is not circumscribed to the ghetto or to New York.

ES: That's where I'm heading with the things I'm writing about. It's always about the Puerto Rican experience, but I don't have the same experience as Abraham Rodríguez, for example. That experience is so foreign to me that I couldn't even begin to invent what it would be like in a convincing way. But I know very intimately what it is like to be a suburban

Puerto Rican. I know all these rich people in suburbia. Even though I'm not rich, I've observed them in a way that's convincing. América González, the principal character in *América's Dream*, comes from Vieques[5] to work as a maid in a house in Bedford, New York, a place up in Westchester County, and she's isolated there. She's not in the middle of a Puerto Rican community; she gets to see what it is to be a Puerto Rican adrift.

I think that is interesting because people keep thinking of us as a group in the ghettos of New York or Chicago, yet we are all over. Hartford, for example, has a huge Puerto Rican community. Some of the people there have been in the States for two generations, but they seem to have come up from the Puerto Rican countryside just yesterday.

This novel has given me the opportunity to reflect on Puerto Rican culture and its difference from American culture. Our culture has a lot to do with why Puerto Ricans are not further ahead than other groups. There's something about the way that we are taught to behave that doesn't fit in with American culture. I'm not really sure exactly what that is, but, for example, in the case of América, the reason she can't get ahead is because she is very passive. That passivity was something I noticed immediately when I came to Puerto Rico in 1976. I noticed it because I wasn't that way. I was assertive and if you're assertive you're not feminine in Puerto Rico. American women got rid of that thirty years ago, but not Puerto Rican women.

People are taught to edit their thoughts, to censor them, so as not to be disrespectful. When you censor yourself you're not open to the world, to what is happening, and I think in a way to be successful you have to be disrespectful to a certain point, especially in the American community, where the symbols of respect are very, very different.

CDH: It seems as if we speak two entirely different cultural languages.

ES: Exactly. Our cultural language is different. In Spanish there is a greater distance between what is said and what is thought. The language doesn't permit the intimacy that English does.

CDH: Did you buy into the American Dream as a young woman living in the States?

ES: Yes, I bought into it in a way that my sisters and brothers didn't. My mother had made it very clear: she lined us up like a general getting her troops ready and said, "We're going to the United States and this is going to be your job: you're going to learn English, get a good education and you're going to get good jobs." It was very clear to us that this was what was going to happen. And I really just took off with it. I didn't let the other things that stopped my sisters and brothers stop me. And I think that I had to overcome a lot of fear: fear of New York, fear of being the object of prejudice and fear of being stereotyped, something that affects your self-esteem. You cannot perform well if you're constantly worried about how people are going to perceive you, and one of the first things that I did away with in my personality was to stop worrying about what other people were going to think: the Puerto Ricans in my neighborhood because I was leaving to study in Manhattan, my mother because I was becoming Americanized and doing things that she didn't particularly agree with but which I knew I had to do. A lot of us never really lost that fear about what people were going to think.

CDH: Maybe it's easier to lose that fear when you're in a big place like New York.

ES: I know. I have friends here in Puerto Rico, very talented friends, who tell me they have to leave because they can't deal with people constantly judging their private lives. Maybe that was what happened to me when I was here those four months. I didn't want to live in a context in which my work and what I was trying to do was secondary to everything else. I really came with a mission. I'm a very driven, goal-oriented person, and I couldn't perform because I was being stopped at every turn. In Puerto Rico there is always a sense that you're being evaluated, that you're being judged.

CDH: Did you ever get to work as an actress in New York?

ES: I did, briefly. I was a terrible actress. They taught method acting at Performing Arts High School, and one of the things I always say about that is that I wasn't really willing to give myself to the character because I was creating myself. I was already in character. I was already trying to create the person my mother said I had to be to succeed in the United States: a girl who spoke English, who had a good education, who had some culture, all those things she wanted me to do. So for me to get into character and play Emily in *Our Town* was practically impossible. I couldn't do it: I was already acting.

CDH: You did write screenplays, though. How does that compare with creative writing?

ES: I don't write for the screen any more; it was very frustrating. You have to write in shorthand, you can't develop the prose. And ultimately, it's not your vision; you're writing a blueprint for somebody else's vision. I couldn't handle that. I don't think I could write the screenplay for a film about my book.

CDH: But did your screen writing contribute to the way you see things and describe them in writing? I found *When I Was Puerto Rican* to be very visual, in a way.

ES: I probably see things when I write them. I'm clear about what I'm observing, and I probably use the same dramatic structure as I would in a film. But my background is in documentary film, so the details that I pick up on are not the dramatic details of a fiction filmmaker.

CDH: Well, *When I Was Puerto Rican* has a lot of document.

ES: That's really how I saw it; it was a documentary on paper. That's how I see my job as a Puerto Rican writer, to document Puerto Rican culture, to convey a sense of that culture and of the Puerto Rican experience in the United States from many different angles. My next book after the sequel to *When I Was Puerto Rican* is about a Puerto Rican who's never been to Puerto Rico, and how somebody with new eyes sees her culture. It's going to be interesting for me to become unfamiliar with what I see in order to be able to see it through new eyes.

CDH: Were you aware of the strong tradition of immigrant memoirs in the States?

ES: No, I wasn't. When I undertook to write my book, I went to one of my teachers because I had read a lot of biographies, but usually of dead people. So I asked her, "What is a memoir?" She gave me the definition. I thought that I should read some memoirs to get an idea of what the form is. And she told me to read *Remembrance of Things Past*. But when I began reading it, I was thinking, "I don't really want to write something like this. . . ." Then I read *The Lover* by Marguerite Duras, which I loved and I thought it was more in line with what I wanted to do. I think that the difference between a male writer and a female writer is the sensibility.

Another teacher said to me: the great thing about a memoir is that it's invented each time it's written. There isn't a form; whoever is writing is inventing it. So I said: "OK, I'm going to invent a Puerto Rican memoir."

Photograph of Piri Thomas supplied by the writer.

12

PIRI THOMAS

Piri Thomas breaks into poetry like birds break into song. At the slightest "provocation," his deep, beautiful voice begins a recitation and his fingers seem to acquire a life of their own, dancing in the air, conveying all the feelings that pour forth from his words. These mark the persistent beat of his rhythmic speech with the repetition of "love," "children," "mother" and "poetry."

Piri is a born actor, and when asked about his life, instead of talking about it, he "performs" for the benefit of the listener. It is a life that well bears performing. Born on September 30, 1928, he grew up in El Barrio (Spanish Harlem) in New York. He is the oldest of seven children, three of whom died very young. Although his parents tried to give their children a better life by moving to Long Island, the pull of the streets was too strong for the young Piri and he succumbed to it. In 1950 he was wounded in a shoot-out with the police during an armed robbery of a nightclub. He spent the next seven years in Sing Sing prison and Comstock, Great Meadows Correctional Institution. (He includes the time spent recovering from serious wounds in the prison ward at Bellevue Hospital as well as some nine months in the Manhattan Tombs, awaiting disposition of his case.)

Since his release, Thomas has dedicated a great deal of his time to work with street gangs and young junkies, to whom he talks about addiction and where it leads, using examples from his own experience. He has lived in Puerto Rico on three occasions, also working with drug addicts.

Piri Thomas's first book, *Down These Mean Streets* (New York: Knopf) was published in 1967. It is now considered a classic confessional autobiography in the best tradition of Eldridge Cleaver's *Soul on Ice* and *The Autobiography of Malcolm X*. It became a success and was hailed as "a linguistic event" in *The New York Times Book Review*.

Recently, *Down These Mean Streets* was among the top in a list drawn up of the ten best books that represented life in New York (*New York Times,* February 5, 1995).

His other books are *Savior, Savior, Hold My Hand* (New York: Doubleday, 1972), an autobiographical work; *Seven Long Times* (New York: Praeger Publishers, 1974), a prison memoir; and *Stories of El Barrio* (New York: Knopf, 1978). He is in the process of writing the sequel to *Down These Mean Streets* with the working title of *A Matter of Dignity.*

Thomas has written several plays, among them *Las calles de oro* ("The Golden Streets") in two acts. It was produced and performed in 1972 in New York by the Puerto Rican Traveling Theater, directed by Miriam Colón.

Thomas's articles have appeared in newspapers, magazines, and reviews such as the *Saturday Review of Literature, Crisis,* and *Social Justice.* His work has appeared in anthologies such as *Boricuas: Influential Puerto Rican Writings,* edited by Roberto Santiago (New York: Ballantine, 1995). He has lectured frequently in colleges and universities, among them Yale, Rutgers, Brown, Cornell, Syracuse, the University of Puerto Rico, and the University of Erlangen in Germany.

He moved to San Francisco in 1983 and has been working on tapes and CDs of what he calls "wordsongs"; these are recitations of his poetry against a background of Latin jazz played by an ensemble of musicians, among them Carlos "Patato" Valdez. He is currently working on a second CD entitled *No Mo' Barrio Blues,* with wordsongs and with Patato on the conga.

In 1964 a documentary film of his work with street gangs, *Petey and Johnny,* was produced by Time–Life Associates. It was awarded first prize in the Festivale dei Populi in Florence, Italy. Another documentary, *The World of Piri Thomas,* was directed by Gordon Parks, produced by National Educational Television, and written and narrated by Thomas. He has appeared on the "Today Show," and on numerous other TV and radio programs. He has also recorded his books to produce dramatic readings of his works. His musical recording director is Greg Landau.

Thomas is married to Suzanne Dod, an American who as one of four children of Christian missionary parents, spent her childhood in the mountains of rural Puerto Rico. She is Piri's business manager as well as executive producer on the CD projects. She is currently translating *Down These Mean Streets* into Spanish for Vintage Press. She is also on the editorial board of *Social Justice* as a founder and contributor. The journal publishes articles on crime, conflict, and the world order or the lack of it.

"IN PUERTO RICO THERE ARE THOSE WHO HAVE DENIED US OUR HERITAGE BECAUSE WE WERE BORN IN EL NORTE, WHERE WE ALSO HAVE BEEN DENIED"

CDH: I am curious about your name, John Peter Thomas. It's certainly not a Spanish name.

PT: I was born in Harlem Hospital on September 30, 1928. John Thomas, Jr., was the name on my birth certificate; Peter was added later. My father, Juan Tomás de Cruz, born in Cuba, in Oriente Province, in 1907, must have no doubt been convinced in Harlem Hospital that I might have a better chance of making it in America if my name in Spanish were translated into its Yankee Doodle version. After all, Europeans have been doing that for quite some time; but still, let's face it, a *borinqueño*[1] with a name like John Peter Thomas?

Some have remarked over the years, that how in the world could I have gone wrong as a youth, with the names of three such distinguished disciples. Search me, but I must say that the name I felt more at ease with was Thomas (Tomás) with a slight difference. Tomás doubted the appearance of Christ; I doubt injustice, which walks hand in hand with racism and greed.

Growing up, my father Juan called me Petey, my brothers and sister called me Pete, and Mami called me Piri (Pee-ree). It was not till many years later, when I was introduced to Professor Piri Fernández in Puerto Rico, by her husband, Dr. Robert Lewis, that I realized that Mami had either given me a woman's name or she had named me after the tiny Puerto Rican bird named *el pirri*,[2] who with long, sharp beak, strikes the enemy bird under the wing, thus crippling it. It is said that each hawk or eagle has its Pirri. Whatever Mami's intentions were, I wear the name with great honor, for I'm part of my mother's song.

My beautiful and most spiritual mother, Dolores Montañez, was born in 1909 in Puerto Rico, in Cerro Gordo, Bayamón, a town famous for *lechón asado* and *chicharrones*.[3]

CDH: When did your parents come to the United States?

PT: My father, Juan Tomás, left Cuba in 1923 at the age of 16 and worked his way to Puerto Rico on a small boat. Puerto Ricans had been made citizens of the United States with or without permission through the 1917 Act of Congress. Papi lived in Puerto Rico for a year, cutting sugar cane. He saved some money while he practiced his Puerto Rican accent, which is a bit different from a Cuban one.

My father to be left the port of San Juan, Puerto Rico, for Nueva York aboard the SS *Marine Tiger*, which had been used as an army transport ship during World War I. It was then being used to transport cheap island labor to the United States. My father made his way to East Harlem, Nueva York. He found a furnished room, got himself a job as a bus boy, and eventually upgraded himself to a two-room furnished apartment. He was a fine athlete who loved to play baseball and, being a likable person, had lots of friends. Among them was Catín Castro, who was the sister of Dolores Montañez, my Mami to be.

My mother to be had suffered quite a bit after her parents had died. She had been a *criada*, a servant. Some familes were kind, others were cruel. Mami emigrated to America in 1925 and came to live with Catín, her oldest sister.

Catín threw a party in honor of my mother to be and introduced Papi to Mami to be, and it was recorded that it was love at first sight. They were married in 1927. I was born nine months later on September 30, 1928, leaving nothing at all for barrio tongues to waggle about.

CDH: And you are, I believe, the eldest of seven children?

PT: Yes, I also count those who died during childbirth, because they remained in spirit and can feel what I say. Those of us who have survived, and are still alive, are Lillian, Ramón, Efraín, and myself.

CDH: You grew up in those streets of *El Barrio*,[4] the same ones you wrote about in *Down These Mean Streets*?

PT: Yes, and among the first things I remember as I came into my age of awareness were the fires that kept breaking out in the ghettos. The tenements were fire-traps. The brutalities suffered by the people of the Barrio led us to believe that what we needed, instead of police protection, was protection from the police. I believe the same is still felt in the ghettos of today.

I lived in the world of the streets and in the world of home. True, we lived in a ghetto, but when you went into our home it was so clean you could eat off the floor. In those days everybody did his part. We cleaned the walls and my father cooked. My mother was at the vanguard of women's rights. No man is 100 percent man. No woman is 100 percent woman. I have learned most of my wisdom from women, beginning with my mother. Somehow, in a woman's arms you listen. Men don't admit that. A poem: *A man's gotta learn to respect a woman's dreams. / A man's gotta learn what love really means. / A man's gotta learn that it's in the whisper of love. / A man's gotta learn that it's not the angry shout. / A man's gotta learn that love is born of tender times. / Hey, a man's gotta learn just like a woman, too.*

CDH: I didn't know you wrote poetry.

PT: Of course I'm a poet—I believe every child is born a poet and every poet is the child. I've never published a volume of poetry, although there is poetry in my books. I have an audio, *Sounds of the Street*, a compact disc where I read poetry with a background of music. I actually don't read the poetry, I flow it. It's an art form of speaking. My Aunt Angelita—who was a Pentecostal—took me to church with her. I really liked that church because I could jump around and express myself. Years later I got the idea to blend poetry and music. I had a group of three or four boys and girls who grew into a thirty-voice choir. About 1959, I wrote a poem called *Heaven Bound*, which is now on the CD, *Sounds of the Streets.*

CDH: Was your family Pentecostal?

PT: My beautiful mother, Dolores Montañez, was a Seventh Day Adventist, which was the closest you could get to Jews. We didn't cook when the sun went down on Friday until the sun went down on Saturday. We didn't eat pork, and we ate very healthy food. My father was a deathbed Catholic; the only time he went to see the priest was when he was ready to kick the bucket. But I liked my Tía Angelita's Pentecostal church best, because I could jump and dance in the spirit, shout *¡Aleluya y gloria a Dios!*.[5] In Mami and Papi's churches I had to sit very quietly, with my ass getting cold.

CDH: What language did you use when you were growing up?

PT: Spanish. I began to forget it because at school they only allowed English. I could speak both, one not as well as the other because the assimilation was greater in school. I remember one or two times that I was speaking Spanish in my class, and my teacher came at me, hollering: "Stop talking that!" And I said: "But that's my mother 's language," and she said, "Well, you are in America now, you speak English. How in the world do you think you can become president of the United States if you don't speak English?" And I tell you, I looked at that teacher and I think my eyes must have said, "Well Ma'am, you have more faith than I." That was the 1930s; they were still lynching blacks and browns, yellows and reds. But something the system never took away from us was our faith and our ability to laugh in spite of everything. Unfortunately, many of us fell into depression, apathy, disappointment, despair. And since there are many ways of committing suicide, some went into drugs, like me; others began to drink, others took out their frustrations on their families and beat their wives, and still many others remained decent people.

But my parents gave me good advice. My mother, Doña Lola, she was the word of God. When she spoke, God was speaking. When we left to go to the streets, my mother would give us *la bendición*:[6] "May God go with you, everything good come your way," because who knew if she would see us alive again. There was a lot of violence in the streets because of racism. The Italians and the Irish hated us with a vengeance. When we had to go to the store, we had to go with convoys of *la ganguita*[7] for protection. And if there was a fight, the police came out on the side of the Italians and of the Irish and attacked us, who were still boys. The first thing that impressed me was death; the second thing that made an impact on me was racism. The child knows how to read people like people read books. Children are born with instinct; they acquire reason. I could walk into a place and the hair on the back of my neck would stand on end: Warning, warning, warning, danger, danger, danger!

CDH: Where did you go to school?

PT: I went to the public schools near my home, in East Harlem.

CDH: Did you like to read as a child?

PT: Yes, I've read books. I've stepped into books and absorbed all the experiences and feelings that were put there by the writer's flow. I was getting an education. How life was here, how life was there . . . I read Jack London's *Sea Wolf*, I read *For Whom the Bell Tolls*. I remember joining the 110th street library. I was given two books to take out, but they were not enough for me. I read them fast. The next time I went to the library, besides my two legal ones, I put three extra books under my jacket. I came to the library pregnant and left it pregnant (with books). Years later, when my book *Down These Mean Streets* became a success, I was invited to a conference in Connecticut on censorship because they were censoring my book along with others. I heard someone call me "Mr. Thomas," and I readily recognized her as the librarian that had let me get away. And she said, "I was the librarian and I knew that you were taking those books and I was so glad because you were reading, I was glad you brought them all back too."

You know what finally cured me of my identity problems? A philosopher, whose name is Popeye, the sailor man. He said: "I am what I am and that's what I am." I thought: "*Vaya*, that's good enough for me."

CDH: When did you begin to write?

PT: I was 13 when I began to write. I used to write little stories. But it wasn't until we moved from El Barrio to Long Island that I started to flower. I fell in love with Mrs. Wright, my English teacher. She was very kind to me, and like most children I respond to kindness. There were teachers who were only interested in their paychecks, and not in nonwhite kids. Some even told us who we were and what we were. For years America has used the color of our skin as a measuring stick of our intelligence. How can anyone say that a child, because of a lovely coloring, is considered a minority? God is the smile on the face of a child that is not being wasted, and that includes children like me. No matter what lovely colors children are, none should be considered a minority, which means *less than*. Minorities is another way of calling humans niggers and spics.

CDH: Did she encourage you to write?

PT: *Sí*[8]—she asked the class to write a composition on whatever subject we chose. I wrote two and a half pages of how much I loved her in my best *barrio*[9] way. How I loved her beautiful, curly, auburn hair, those hazel eyes! And I really loved it when she came and leaned over my shoulder to look at my work, because I could inhale her perfume. However, I wrote, "I don't particularly care for your adjectives, your pronouns and your verbs 'cause I really don't know what the hell you're talking about."

When the paper came back, there was a postscript in red letters. It said: "Son, your grammar is lousy, your punctuation is nonexistent; however, if you wish to be a writer, someday you will be. P.S. We both love my wife. Signed: Her Husband." The teacher had shown the paper to her husband. That day I learned two things: that someone had recognized that I had the talent to be a writer someday. The other thing I learned was never to write a love letter to another man's wife. I might not be so lucky next time.

CDH: Why did you want to become a writer?

PT: I chose writing because I like words and putting them together into a story. I was a self-proclaimed poet laureate of the Barrio in the 1930s and 1940s and 1950s. We used to play a game called "The Dozens"—*la docena*—where you insult each other, as well as your families, in perfect rhyme. I was very good at it, so I was always getting into fights. I thought there must be an easier way to use poetry other than for getting into fights.

CDH: Did you draw on your personal experience from your very beginning as a writer?

PT: Of course, I've always been a storyteller; most children are. But it wasn't until I went to prison that I began to get all my thoughts together. I lived in such a rage that I hardly spoke, unless it was through poetry. In prison I began to think and meditate, going back into time and checking out where I went wrong. Of course, I knew where I started to go wrong: the very moment I forgot my mother's wisdom, the wisdom of the *viejos* and of the *abuelos*.[10] It took centuries to gain these wisdoms, but the conquerors, the first thing they do is to destroy your wisdom and your cultures and plunge you into a chasm of darkness. No one can escape because the conquerors don't want to just conquer you physically, they want to conquer you commercially and exploitatively, they want to conquer your spirit too. It's the same kind of insatiable lust for gold that people have for power. It's an addiction. Life is all about addictions. We have to make a choice about which one you're gonna get hooked up to.

CDH: Did you write in prison?

PT: Yes, of course. About the constants of tensions . . . and the hope of survival. I wanted so much to say, "Burn, *guerra!*"[11] Instead, the poet said: "Learn, don't burn," so that when you have to burn you know what to burn. For how can you blame all whites for what white racists are doing?

CDH: Was *Down These Mean Streets* written entirely in prison?

PT: I started what was to be known as *Down These Mean Streets* and gave it a somewhat corny title: *Home Sweet Harlem*. It got its definitive title because somebody read my manuscript and sent it back with a note quoting

Raymond Chandler: "Keep writing: a man who himself is not mean, can walk down these mean streets." That's the only book that I did not give a title to on my own. But after all, like countless others, I come from those mean streets.

When I came out of prison, I eventually went to work in an organization called YDI, Youth Development Incorporated. It was in New York. I worked with gang kids telling them about my experiences. They were Puerto Ricans, blacks, *cubanitos*,[12] Italians, human children. I worked with all the colors. When the gangs were warring I was there. Many times I was in great danger because when a bullet comes it doesn't care what your name is. I said to those kids, "Look, you don't know what it's like in prison, it's hard in there, brothers. Go to school; don't throw away your life. I'm one of the miracles who came out from there. There are many who are never going to get out and others who are so programmed, they think that they are better off inside than out. Somebody said to me once: "I have everything here; three meals a day, my own room, I don't have to pay rent or income tax and when I want sex, I grab me—a young punk." Abnormal? Not to him.

At that time I was writing *Down These Mean Streets*, I was working in a bakery, I was writing in the basement of my aunt's church. I needed a halfway house. I needed to be away from the pull of the streets.

CDH: Was there one particular stimulus that prompted you to write that particular book?

PT: One day in prison a friend of mine (I had very few tight friends in prison. You don't trust too much) knocked on the wall of my prison cell. He was locked in the next cell. He said to me: "Tommy (everybody called me that because of the Thomas), read this. They wrote a book named after me." His nickname was Youngblood, and the book's title was *Youngblood*, written by John Oliver Killens.[13] It had been read so much that its pages seemed like onion skin. A couple of days afterward, Youngblood asked me: "What do you think of the book?" And I said, "Strong," and then added, "You know something, Youngblood? I can write too." Youngblood answered quietly, "Sure, Tommy, I bet you can."

Creativity: it's the strength, the power; it's healing. Creativity was my salvation in prison because it kept me from becoming a vegetable or a psychopath. It opened worlds up to me where I could time travel. Through reading—I eased off the anguish of wanting to be free. One time they gave me a canary as a present, and I had it for two or three days. Me in that cell and the canary in its cell and I got up and took the canary out of its cage and the windows across from the bars were open a little bit and I told him, "Listen, I don't see the logic in this. I am here doing time, and I got you doing time with me when all you want is to be free, to fly, to use those little wings of yours." The bird flew to the ledge of the window and looked back. I don't know if the little canary was looking behind to see if there was any danger or if he was looking back at me. I chose to think that he looked back to say "bye, bye" to me. And then he flew off. The next day the one who gave me the canary asked me "How's the canary doing?" So I told him I just couldn't feel right—me doing time and making him do time. The brother looked at me and said, "Wow, man don't you know you sentenced him to death? He won't be able to survive all the wild birds that are out there." I smiled at him, "At least he'll die free and not locked up in a birdcage like me." I thought: "They only got my body, not my mind."

I promised myself not to serve time, but rather make time serve me. I'll educate my mind, not eradicate it. I, Piri, Thomas, will be born anew at each A.M. I changed my name from Pete to Piri, like my mother used to call me. I took a piece of paper and said, "Paper, I'm going to tell you a story, so that whoever reads it will walk in it, hear it and feel it." I began to tell the paper a story, and in the process I could feel memories being drawn out of me. I could feel the conversations of long ago, but instead of hearing them, I was feeling them over again. I learned to transpose those feelings into words. I had halfway failed English and my spelling was pretty lousy, but I just kept on going. If I could not spell the words, I would write them phonetically! At least I knew what the words meant and later on I could check Webster's Dictionary, but at the moment never stop the flow! Write till the feelings pour out all and then make all the corrections that are needed.

CDH: It's a real achievement for a first book to come out so well-rounded, with such command over the language, the action, the sense of rhythm, the way you put in all the background.

PT: I had two fine editors: Angus Cameron, senior editor, and Joseph Alvarez, working editor, as well as my own natural talents. I believe every child is born a poet as every poet should be the child.

CDH: How did Knopf become interested in the book?

PT: A film company wanted to make a documentary about the work of YDI and the work with gangs and my role as peacemaker among all the violence and whatever. The film was called *Petey and Johnny*. One of the filmmakers was Richard Leacock. I talked to him about my experiences and he says, "Hey, I bet you got a book there; let me talk to my friend Angus Cameron." Leacock made an appointment for me to go to see Angus. I went home looking for the manuscript I had written in prison. I couldn't find it. So I asked and was told, "Well, the kids were playing with it and I thought it was garbage so I threw it into the incinerator." I remember going into the bedroom and sitting on the bed, feeling my hot tears leaping from my eyes. We lived in one of the projects on the fourteenth floor. I stared out the window and thought to myself, "Wait a minute, you did it once, you can do it again." Thus, *Down These Mean Streets* was born. I had almost said, "Fuck it, the hell with it," but I didn't. I rewrote it and much better. I would not leave a chapter until I finished it, even though it took me hours, ten hours, two days, three days. I would work on that chapter until I was finished. I thought that if I left off I might not be in the same mood when I picked up on it again. The anger at times was so great that I punched walls, kitchen cabinets, and closet doors. Then I found out that I was writing too angrily. So I began to add humor. Writing is like weaving a tapestry; you add to it in layers and blend. So I did my best to blend the terror and violence with warmth and gentleness and humor, things that hopefully people could relate to.

CDH: So, the first feelings were in anger, then you blended it with humor?

PT: Yes, humor has always been important for me. If I could laugh, the demons would go away. So I added a little humor and then things became a little better. But getting that out of me was a catharsis. I had taken the demons and put them on paper. I was writing prose, I was writing my feelings and my feelings danced like musical notes. What a lot of people don't understand is how in writing *Down These Mean Streets*, I would feel the psychological pain of opening up Pandora's Box once again and bringing back to mind my past.

CDH: What about the language, that wonderful language that's street language but it's also poetic and everybody can understand it?

PT: My idea was clarity without restraint. I am a medium in the sense that I pass words on that hopefully communicate.

CDH: You use Spanish in a very effective way in that book.

PT: Yes, like art work. You know why? They said, "You can't do that," and I said, "What do you mean you can't do that? When you open up a book, there are French terms and German terms: *Bon soir, ma cherie*, and all that, so why can't I put in *adiós, corazón*?"[14] Everyone knows *adiós*, and surely everyone knows *corazón*. I love to feel I am a universal human.

CDH: Did you have a model for this book?

PT: My own life on the mean streets was more than enough. By the way, my editor, Angus Cameron, said I had created a new genre in writing where everybody speaks like themselves. Somehow I knew that if I wrote everything from my point of view, then it would be a one-man description. But I wanted the perspective of other living characters, and so I remembered them all as I wrote.

CDH: You were one of the first Puerto Ricans in the United States to write about life in the streets, you gave an impulse to ghetto literature.

PT: There were others like Pedro Juan Soto, Pura Belpré, Jesús Colón. But my book became better known in the United States, as well as in

England and Canada, and now there is interest in Italy. *Down These Mean Streets* is being translated into Spanish by my wife Suzanne Dod Thomas, for Vintage Español. I'd rather be with the children. That's why some people have not heard of me—or even have forgotten me—but when I'm asked: "What have you been doing all those years?" I say, "Ask the communities, the schools, the universities and colleges."

I won't use my writing to sell people out. They were interested in me doing some writing for a series about Latinos. Hollywood sends the producer and gets together all the Latinos, brothers and sisters, writers of the barrios, and I say to them before we go into the meeting: "We have to be united among us." So we went in, and this producer is telling us the negative things he wants us to write about, it's a slap in the face. I told him, "What you need is writers who will write about people with their sense of dignity and, as for humor, the laughter would be real. You don't have to demean people just to get a cheap fucking laugh out of it." He looked at me in arrogance, and said, "What we need is writers who will write what we tell them to write." I looked at him in quiet anger and said, "Fuck you," and walked out. I had ten cents in my pocket. I was expecting some brother and sister writers to walk out with me but not one followed me out. They were so hungry to make it that they were ready to sell their sense of dignity, and Mami always told me that nobody can take away your dignity, only you can give it away or sell it. I wasn't about to give mine away or sell it—*punto*!!15

CDH: Puerto Ricans in the United States are forging a very energetic way of writing which is hardly known in Puerto Rico. Your book is among what is best known.

PT: When *Down These Mean Streets* came out, I was invited to speak at San Germán, a university in Puerto Rico. I looked to the wall and saw photos of Spanish writers. I looked and looked because I knew we had writers from the barrios of Nueva York like Bimbo, Jesús Colón, Pedro Pietri, Miguel Algarín, Mickey Piñero, Sandra Esteves, and Nancy Mercado among others. So I said, " I don't see any of the writers from los barrios here." Someone said, "It's because you don't write in Spanish." And I said, "Really? And what about those Puerto Ricans who write in other languages, French and Italian?" We have them, we have great intellectuals on that little island.

CDH: The problem is that those who write in English are not generally accepted as real Puerto Rican writers. It's a very tragic circumstance: they are rejected in the States for being Puerto Rican and they're rejected in Puerto Rico for being American.

PT: That's why I wrote "We've hung up in the middle, with no place to go." They tolerate us here in the land of the Yankees, and in Puerto Rico they deny us our heritage. This has been very bitter for me. They have forced me to be universal, a citizen of the world; wherever my feet stand, that's my turf. I found out I am a majority of one, not a minority, for that means less than. I know that I'm not just a geographic location, color, or sex. I am an earthling, born of Earth and the Universe; we all are.

Years ago, I spent hours practicing the Puerto Rican-born way of speaking. I wanted with all my heart to be accepted, and when I felt the rejection, my heart got heavy with hurt. How dare you deny me my inheritance? I did not survive the Yankees only to be hurt so by you! I know that some of us born in the United States can be arrogant. But arrogance is found everywhere. When I talked like that in San Germán, my brothers and sisters were truly sorry because they realized that we were fighting to regain our Mother Tongue after being trained for so long to forget it. My heart is pouring out to you, *negrita*.[16] I've wanted for a long time to talk like this to someone from the island.

CDH: Well, I think the U.S.-Puerto Rican writers could bring a breath of fresh air to island literature.

PT: That's nice to know. Puerto Rico could be a trap for the arts because you can get laid back and there's only so far you can go creatively in Puerto Rico. The only way you can really start to get it is to get out of Puerto Rico and come over here and spend the energy, or spend some time in Europe. That allows you to grow because the island can have a greenhouse effect. After a while you get into the same *vaina*,[17] and then what you are writing is fluff. You're not writing about life, and life, if you please, is all about feelings, good, bad, or indifferent. If you haven't got the feelings, then you are torpid. You have to keep creatively charging yourself as part of Earth with the energy of the rest of the world.

I have to tell you there are people in Puerto Rico who love me as I love them; I need the drive that I was breast-fed on. I need the tempo of the barrios of New York. But I must return to Puerto Rico from time to time to recharge myself. *El Norte*[18] drains me at times.

CDH: Do you relate to these other Puerto Rican writers in the United States who have also written about the ghetto?

PT: Of course, I've met a lot of the brothers and sisters; I know most of their work and hold them in my heart.

CDH: Has it been easy for you to publish after *Down These Mean Streets'* success?

PT: Yes, pretty much so. The ones who are having trouble are young writers. For years they've been told, "Piri Thomas wrote *Down These Mean Streets* so what you got is old hat." Don't take that. They write all kinds of books on Tarzan and the Apes, not to leave out Lone Ranger and Tonto. There are a million stories in the barrios, if not more. The system tries to behavior-modify us into making us feel less than. I am proud being *un puertorriqueño*[19] in Nueva York as I am of being one in Puerto Rico.

CDH: Do you plan a sequel to *Down These Mean Streets?*

PT: Sí. The sequel is to be called *A Matter of Dignity*. I'm working on it, I have notes and feelings and chapters. What I need to do is finish some CDs of poetry and music and then find a place to go in order to write. Sometimes I slip into Puerto Rico quietly, into places like Patillas, Rincón, or Boquerón, *callaíto*.[20]

In the book I will go to a beginning that I did not include in *Down These Mean Streets*. *A Matter of Dignity* is the one book I must finish so that the readers know what happened to young Piri in *Down These Mean Streets*. Did he curl up and die? No, *más nunca*[21]—in the struggle for justice I will never stop.

CDH: Since when are you setting your poetry to music on cassettes and CDs?

PT: Oh, it's been years. I've been one of the vanguard in experiments in creativity, or poetry and music I call "wordsongs." I always thought to myself, "Why is that only lyrics can be married to music? Why not the poetry of the spoken word?" So in the 1960s and 1970s here and there, I would get together with various brothers and sisters of the music world to play and extend poetry's flow. There was a flow going at that time called "Da, Da," which means free flows. Creations without hesitations. I would do poetry as the musicians listened to me. My words became musical notes to them. Humans are also musical instruments. We talk, we sing, we flow. My talented musical director, Greg Landau, creates the music. I'm woven into the music. It's a beautiful blend of poetry and music.

As a child, I listened to the songs of our singers. We grew up with that powerful energy. And now finally, two CDs are done, the third on the way.

CDH: What kind of music is it?

PT: It's the blending of drums from Africa and bongos, guitars, and our aguinaldos.[22] All these conglomerations and manifestations coming out in the form of what we are as *puertorriqueños*, "cause that is what we are from the first."

I got together with Greg Landau, a musician as well as an anthropologist. He's a professor who loves music. Landau became my music producer in San Francisco. I said: "I want to do blues rhythm, I want to do jazz, I want to do African beats, and I want to do the salsa[23] of the ghettos, of Llorens Torres."[24]

Give me the first note and that is my beat. Give me something like BAM, BAM, BAM, BAM, BAM, [he marks a rhythm with the words], and I begin: *Bullets flying, children dying, mommies crying, papis crying too. . . .*

We meet, we talk, and the atmosphere gets charged. I recite the poetry, the musicians listen to it and begin with their music. It's a creation without hesitation. Our first CD is called *Sounds of the Streets*—with salsa. The second—*Barrio Blues*—has New Age music. The third CD is called *Creations Without Hesitations* and it's back to salsa, Afro-Cuban flows.

CDH: Who produced those CDs?

PT: We have a company called Cheverote Productions. My wife is vice president and I am president. The word "chévere" is an African word that means "great" or good. And if "chévere" means great, then cheverote and cheverota mean the greatest.

CDH: When did you move over here to San Francisco?

PT: 1983.

CDH: Because of the music?

PT: No, I had to get out of New York for personal reasons. When my first book came out, many in Puerto Rico didn't like it. One time, the wife of a very important man from the Puerto Rican government came up and said: "Oh, Piri, why did you write *Down These Mean Streets*? It makes us look bad." And I said: "I'm not presenting you, I'm presenting us, who live here in the belly of the shark. We're out here fighting our hearts out, and you, instead of looking at us as brave warriors, you look at us with contempt. We went through the most brutal assimilation process of the spirit and the mind, and we rose above it."

When *Down These Mean Streets* came out, it was a new genre. Then it rose to be a classic in my own time. Puerto Rico never truly opened its arms to it.

CDH: I understand you have also worked in films.

PT: I've worked in two films. The first one was when I was working with the gangs. It was called *Petey and Johnny*. Johnny was Juan Maldonado, a Puerto Rican kid. And then we worked on one called *The World of Piri Thomas*. I did narrations on other films. After I learned enough about filming I went and filmed the riots, the Harlem riots, but they gave me no credit. We are currently working on a documentary called *Oye, familia!: A Dialogue with Society*.

CDH: Where is it being filmed?

PT: Most of it is being filmed in the barrios where I grew up during the thirties. I did my poetry from the rooftops, from the backyards, and from the street corners. Some of the work is also being filmed in San Francisco.

CDH: Who's directing *Oye, familia*?

PT: Jonathan Robinson is the director. He's a young filmmaker. Most of the people I'm working with are young people. I am also working with Pete Resto on a screenplay. He's a young Puerto Rican born in los barrios de Nueva York.

CDH: You wrote a play once, right?

PT: I've written a few—but only *Las calles de oro* ("The Golden Streets") was produced and directed by Miriam Colón, founder of the Puerto Rican Traveling Theater.

CDH: Your writing seems to be mainly autobiographical.

PT: Sure, *¿por qué no?*[25] I can only write about what I have lived. I can write fiction too. After all, words are words, are words.

CDH: How did you feel when your books, especially *Down These Mean Streets*, became such a tremendous success? It was a first for a Puerto Rican writer within the American literary mainstream.

PT: The first thing I did was remember what my mother's spirit said to me. "You accept the accolades, the honors, the recognition, you accept it in the name of the children." It's very hard for those who had nothing to all of a sudden get something. And many go mad. They think: "I am so much better than everybody else." Never forget where your *ombligo*[26] comes from. I never have. *Yo soy del Barrio.*[27] What I am I owe to my mother. When I was in prison, I made a promise to her spirit. I promised: "Everything you wanted me to be, Mami, I'm going to be with the help of God."

Viva Puerto Rico libre![28]

Photograph of Edwin Torres taken by Miguel Trelles.

13

EDWIN TORRES

Judge Edwin Torres of the New York Supreme Court is a sharp, forceful man. Presiding over a murder case, he exhibits a direct, confrontational style of questioning that is strongly reminiscent of the swift dialogue of his three novels. He leans forward in his chair, listening intently, occasionally pressing a point, admitting or overruling objections with a sonorous voice. He is at all times very much in charge of the proceedings.

When he speaks of Puerto Rico, however, his tone softens. There is even a certain nostalgia in his voice, despite the fact that he was born in the States of Puerto Rican parents. When he talks about literature, he waxes enthusiastic. Very well read in both English and Spanish, the judge is a writer conscious of a strong literary tradition in both languages.

A successful, self-made man who has risen to the top of his profession, Judge Torres has received some of his greater accolades for his writing career. He is the author of three of the most widely read detective or gangster novels of any Latino in the United States: *Carlito's Way* (New York: Dutton Books, 1975) became a major motion picture in 1993, directed by Brian de Palma and starring Al Pacino and Sean Penn. It incorporated material from *After Hours*, another Torres novel, written in 1979 (New York: Dial Press). *Q & A* (New York: Dial, 1977), dealing more with police corruption, was made into a film in 1990, directed by Sidney Lumet and starring Nick Nolte, Timothy Hutton, and Armand Assante.

Judge Torres's work has been included in the anthology *Boricuas: Influential Puerto Rican Writings,* edited by Roberto Santiago (New York: Ballantine Books, 1995).

"NO ONE KNOWS WE'RE HERE; NO ONE IS WRITING THIS"

CDH: Are you from Puerto Rico?

ET: No, I was born in Harlem, in the Barrio, on 115th Street and Lenox Avenue on January 7, 1931. I was raised on 107th Street and Madison, also in El Barrio. I went to school there.

CDH: Do you define yourself essentially as a Puerto Rican?

ET: When I was raised in the Barrio, it was like a pocket of Puerto Rico. You could spend twenty years there and not hear a word of English. Now, of course, it's changed. There are projects and there are different groups, not like in the thirties and forties when I was growing up in the Barrio. The Barrio was all *boricua*.[1] There were no Dominicans or Cubans in those days. The Mexicans hadn't arrived; it was an extension of the island. Many of my friends are still there. I am a product of that extension of the island. I go there every chance I get.

CDH: When you were growing up, did you feel different because you were Puerto Rican?

ET: The distinctions were quite stark at that time. There were boundaries, literally, it was a *ghetto* in the classic sense. We could not, for example, go east of Park Avenue because of the Italian gangs, and then we couldn't go west of Fifth Avenue because of the black gangs. So we were boarded in like a frontier settlement.

CDH: Was your writing in any way a product of that difference, of your feeling as a Puerto Rican? Did you want to have other people experience those same feelings?

ET: No, I think my writing is an offshoot of many things. But one of them is the fact that I lived a very tumultuous, extraordinary era, as my father would point out, because my father was a frustrated novelist. It was a tumultuous time, the things that were happening in the Barrio in the thirties—the Depression—and then in the forties with the war and then in the late forties and early fifties, the advent of drugs. These were extraordinary events. And as my father used to say, "No one knows we're here, no one is writing this." So I ended up writing them, by default, since no one else did.

CDH: Did your father write?

ET: He once wrote a novel, believe it or not. But we don't know where it ended up. It was never published.

CDH: Is he still living?

ET: He's dead and buried in Jayuya, where he was born. My mother lives in Villa Carolina. They went back to Puerto Rico and were there for about twenty years before he died five years ago. They always wanted to go back, especially my father. He always knew he would return, despite the fact that they were here for fifty years, fifty winters. They had come over in the late twenties.

CDH: Were both parents from Jayuya?

ET: My mother is from "el viejo San Juan,"[2] right next to *El parque de las palomas.*[3] That house overlooking the park, that's where she grew up. She is 81 now, so a few years have gone by. But my father was born and raised in Jayuya. My uncle, his brother, Adrián Torres Torres, was mayor of Jayuya for many years, and then he was a senator for the District of Arecibo. He stayed in Puerto Rico, but my old man went into the Army when he was a teenager and after going to Panama ended up here, during the twenties. I was born in 1931.

CDH: Were they looking for the so-called American Dream?

ET: In 1929 the dream was very opaque, very bleak. But they were dreamers, you know. All they ran into, however, was a Depression in Harlem. It was a very bad time, very bad, very bad: chronic unemployment and all that. My father was out of work for years. It was a drastic time. Not having two cents for the *Daily News.* Not having a nickel for the subway.

CDH: How did you get out of the Barrio?

ET: Well, that's another novel. I attribute it mainly to my father's efforts. My father spent eleven years in the Army. He was very disciplined, very strong, and he was on top of me constantly. Because when I was a kid I was on the streets and there was a lot going on, believe me. But my father was always on my case. He was a very strong man, very domineering. And it was he who led me out. If it hadn't been for my father, I probably would have lost my way like so many others.

CDH: Did you resent his being so domineering?

ET: Of course, but eventually he prevailed, because I followed his path. I never aspired to be a lawyer or anything like that; those were his ideas. I don't know what I aspired to in life; I had no ambition. Those were his ambitions. He was a very community-conscious man, he was an activist in the Barrio. He would go to court although he was not a lawyer and had not attended law school, but as he spoke good English for his stint in the Army, he was always helping people. He was into politics and into the Puerto Rican community and its problems. At that time he was a fairly well-known figure, even legendary you might say. His name was Edelmiro Torres. And of course, my mother also was always there for me because my sister was born when I was already 10 years old. That was important. I had a lot of attention; my mother didn't work, that was not allowed at that time. It reflected badly on the husband. My mother was always there and since she was only 17 when I was born, we sort of grew up together. I had that attention from both parents at home, and they set a good example. Nothing of that "Do as I say and not as I do" stuff. It's very important to have a father figure and a mother figure, but I think a father figure with a boy. That seems to be a constant with lots of people that go astray: the absence of the father.

CDH: Where did you study law?

ET: I went to City College as an undergraduate and then to Brooklyn Law School.

CDH: Could you tell me about your career in the law?

ET: First I was an assistant district attorney. I was the first Puerto Rican assistant district attorney in New York County, that's Manhattan. That was in about 1958. And then I was in private practice from about 1961 to about 1977. I was a defense attorney in criminal law. In 1977 I was put on the criminal court bench; I was appointed by the mayor. Then in 1980 I was elected to the Supreme Court of New York and I've been here ever since.

CDH: Are you the first Puerto Rican Supreme Court justice of the State of New York?

ET: No, there have been others before, not as many as one wishes, but there have been some. There are some very fine judges from Puerto Rico. There's Ramírez in Brooklyn, for example.

CDH: Is your novel, *Carlito's Way*, autobiographical in any sense?

ET: *Carlito's Way* is autobiographical in large measure, especially "la paliza"[4] at the beginning and the chases.

CDH: It seems to me that you are attempting in that work to give a mirror image of society with its power struggles; that it is an attempt to show the "wrong" side of society?

ET: In a sense. I perceive of it like *El Lazarillo de Tormes*, you know, the picaresque novel. It's a picaresque novel: the misadventures of a *pícaro*,[5] which is Carlito Brigante. In Spanish literature, *Lazarillo* is a seminal work. It always stuck in my mind.

And I've had people say, "Well, why don't you write about positive characters, such as yourself?" That's been proposed many times, how I clawed my way out of the *ghetto* to the Supreme Court. But I find that very boring. Myself, personally. That's not the type of literature that I would be interested in, and I don't think anybody else would be reading. Unfortunately, these *pícaros* have a certain fascination because they live close to the edge. And it may be commendable that someone gets up and goes to work from nine to five every day and goes home and does what he has to, but how interesting is that as a subject for literature? I don't know.

CDH: Your case would certainly be interesting.

ET: Yes, it would. But let somebody else write that.

CDH: You mentioned *El Lazarillo de Tormes*. Are you conversant in Spanish literature?

ET: I'm very steeped in that. I'm a devotee, I read all the Spanish authors: García Márquez, Vargas Llosa, Cortazar, you name it. Anybody. I read everything in Spanish. I took a lot of Spanish literature courses in college. Of course, I've read all the English classics too. But *Lazarillo de Tormes* has always fascinated me because here's a work written in, I think 1453, author unknown, and yet it's hilarious, humorous, and it talks about a scamp, a pícaro. I think that was unique at that time because people used to read about the adventures of Amadís de Gaula and other legendary heroes. So *Lazarillo* was a kind of an ice-breaker. I see Carlito as a kind of *pícaro,* a Candide, sort of.

CDH: You also have the tone, that philosophical, slightly disenchanted tone of the picaresque novel.

ET: The thing that I figure is Carlito's saving grace, which I'm shooting for throughout, is the humor. This basic sense of humor is very important to literature because you cannot write on one note or one dimension. This becomes flat and boring, so I've always striven, in all my writing, even in *Q & A,* in *Carlito's Way,* in all my novels, to have humor. People tell me they read them out loud and they laugh at some of these things. I find that to be flattering. That's what I like to read. Because that's what life is about. I didn't want to write a novel where he bewailed his fate at every turn, "Poor me, I'm in the middle of Harlem, I don't have this, I don't have that . . . " because a real tough guy—the kind that I knew, and I knew plenty, believe me—they don't bewail or whine about their fate, you know what I mean? Like he says, he was "happy as a pig in shit" in the Barrio, he didn't know he was in the ghetto. And neither did I, for that matter. I thought it was the greatest place in the world.

CDH: The monologue at the end seems to sum up everything.

ET: Oh, you mean when he was dying. The publishers always said to me that we can still revive him in another sequel because I don't pronounce him dead. So we can have some drastic surgery and revive him.

CDH: Are you happy with the picture made from your novel?.

ET: Yes, who would not be? I liked *Q & A,* the other film. It was very good also, with Nick Nolte, Armand Assante, and Timothy Hutton. *Carlito's Way* was a superproduction, with Al Pacino, Sean Penn. . . . Those people spent $45 million; it was a big film.

CDH: How come you didn't end up in Hollywood?

ET: Well, this is what I do, I'm a judge. The writing is like a hobby-time thing. I don't consider myself a writer per se.

CDH: But you are.

ET: That's very kind of you to say, but I didn't write a word until 1974. I was 45 or 46 years old. I had never written anything. I never took a writing course. I'm not a writer per se, but it's something I had to do. I had a story to tell, so to speak. I don't want to sound arrogant, but I had a unique experience and a unique exposure and a unique perspective, because not only was I there throughout these decades, I merged and then I went to the other side of the law, so to speak. I was exposed to that. And I was in that unique position of being able to assess the situation. I was on both sides. And I also served as a criminal defense lawyer for eighteen years. That's another perspective, because I've been a prosecutor, I've been a defense attorney, and I've been a judge. And I still am. So I had a peculiar exposure to all of that. And I don't know of anyone—certainly not on the bench—who came through the Barrio, a writer, and had the experiences that I did in large measure. So that was a tremendous wealth on which to draw. And what I've lived on the bench here . . . I could write a novel every year, for that matter.

CDH: Are you going to do that?

ET: No, I've been in the throes of writer's block since I got on the bench, literally. Because I came on the bench in 1977, and that was when I wrote the last novel. I wrote three novels in three years. But since then I have been unable to write any more novels because the work I do is so consuming, mentally. You carry it around at night.

CDH: Maybe the bench is making us miss out on a great Puerto Rican writer.

ET: I don't think it's missing much, but put it this way: I would like to, some day, get back to writing something more serious. To write a novel. I've seen a lot of things here, but the work is very painstaking, and in the evening, when I'm home, it's very difficult for me to be in a state of repose which writing would entail. Look at the case I'm on now, it's four murders. If you came every day to hear what goes on in court, your hair would stand on end. These people's throats were cut, their heads were almost severed. This case in particular is quite serious. It's very difficult for me to deal with this by day and to go and create fiction by night. Perhaps some day, when I retire.

CDH: Do you consider your writing as an advocacy for Puerto Ricans in the United States?

ET: No, it's somewhat difficult to explain . . . because I came so late to writing. I wrote my novels because it's something I know, the street. And I had been critical of books that I read and pictures I have seen pertaining to the street. It was my wife's challenge, in effect. She felt that if I could write at all, why not write it myself? I could do it better. So I said I'll show you. And that's how I came to write *Carlito's Way*. I felt I had what I consider to be a clearer, more authentic picture of what the street is about. I felt I knew it.

After Hours is a sequel to *Carlito's Way*. And *Q & A* was more geared to my experiences as a district attorney because Al Reilly in the novel is, of course, an assistant DA and I was an assistant DA in the homicide bureau in New York County. So *Q & A* was more of a sequential novel. It had a beginning, middle, and end, and it is written in the third person. So that was a more deliberate attempt to write a novel per se. *Carlito's Way* was written more in the first person; it's more in the stream of consciousness mode of a street guy, whereas *Q & A* is a more conventionally structured novel, which I wanted to try my hand at. And then also it has what I felt to be the essence of it, which I'm not sure it came across in the film: it was more a love story, an interracial love story. That's what I sought to do, the cross-cultural aspect of it. I wrote *Carlito's Way, Q & A* and then I wrote *After Hours.*

CDH: Have you written anything else?

ET: I have written a screenplay within the last few months. It's not a novel. I'm not sure if I want to turn it into a novel because writing a novel is an imposing prospect, and I don't have the time as I am going from one case to the other. But I'm compromising and wrote a screenplay. It's about East Harlem, Italians, and Puerto Ricans, and I am exploring various avenues of production. Maybe I'll produce it myself, something else that I've contemplated. It'll not be on the astronomical budget of the Hollywood productions, but maybe I can produce it on a smaller, more intimate scale.

CDH: Do you feel related in any way to the Puerto Rican literary tradition in the States that began with Piri Thomas and his *Down These Mean Streets*?

ET: No, none whatever. As far as I'm concerned it's nonexistent.

CDH: Do you relate to any individual Puerto Rican artist or writer in the States?

ET: Mikey Piñero was a friend of mine. Every time he was arrested he would call me up and ask me to get him out of trouble. I would tell him, "Listen, I'm a Supreme Court judge, I can't be mixed up in this."

Once I had a meeting with an English film producer, Barry Hansen, who was originally interested in *Carlito's Way.* He came from England; he was the one who discovered Bob Hoskins, that great actor. We went to see one of Piñero's plays in the Village, *Midnight Moon at the Greasy Spoon.* When Mikey saw me, he fell all over me, and I had to take him with me to dinner with the producer. We went to a very fancy restaurant, and he began with his maneuvers, his thing, he was really crazy. And that Englishman, who was so proper, was there. I had a terrible time. But it didn't stop there. Piñero wanted to go on to the Lower East Side, which was really wild at that time, much worse than now and I told him I was not going. The Englishman, with the true heart of a tourist, insisted on going. Mikey said he would show him what street life was really about. I told Hansen—he has told this story all over Europe—not to go with Piñero. "No, no, no," he said, "I want to go." "OK," I said, "go."

Next day, at around eleven or twelve noon, he called me from the hotel and told me what had happened, where Mikey had taken him, because back then all that Lower East Side (the Puerto Ricans called it *Loisaida*), all that was like the catacombs. He can write a book on all that he saw and what happened to him that night. And he couldn't leave, because Mikey kept telling him that he wouldn't reach the corner alive. Mikey took him up and down and all around, and the man was half dead by the time he reached his hotel. He honestly believed he would die that night. I said, "I warned you."

I loved Mikey, he was a great talent. I remember I went to see *Short Eyes*, and he came out and we became friends. He was a big fan of my novels, saying he should play the screen role of "Carlito." But he was a man who, in spite of his talent, of his genius, had a self-destructive streak in his character. I don't know where that came from. And it wasn't only the drugs, because that wasn't so bad. The thing is he challenged people in the streets, everywhere he went he challenged and provoked constantly. I don't know how he lived as long as he lived. He lived on the edge. Like a rage to die.

CDH: Do you feel the literature of Puerto Ricans and of Latinos in general is getting more attention now in the United States?

ET: I think a sort of impetus, a sort of momentum has evolved, and I like to think that the transformation of my properties into film may provide a kind of push and encouragement. There's so much talent out there, there's so much writing talent, I'm sure, that has not been given the proper exposure.

We lost major talent in the passing away of José Ferrer and Raúl Juliá. Juliá was a phenomenal loss; I admired his work immensely. He cared for his people. He was an inspiration. He was able to transcend in so many ways those limits that we tend to find in our past; he went beyond them.

CDH: You've entered the American mainstream with your novels. Right now I think you're the only Puerto Rican writer to have a major motion picture made out of one of his novels. Abraham Rodríguez, Jr., may have one made soon out of *Spidertown*, but that's in the future.

ET: Two films: *Carlito's Way* and *Q & A*.

CDH: That may make Puerto Rican literature in the States more visible.

ET: I'm happy to have contributed to that stream, to that force.

CDH: By the way, let me compliment you on your excellent Spanish.

ET: My father was very "borinqueño,"[6] he felt a lot for the island. And at home everybody was always talking about the island and its culture, and its literature and music. This was very strong. That's why I never lost the language. Many of my contemporaries lost it but not me. Listen, when I went to school, in 1935, a school that was on First Avenue and 100th Street, they assigned me an interpreter. I didn't speak English; only Spanish was spoken at home.

CDH: Have you thought about writing in Spanish?

ET: I could write in Spanish, and I will someday. I'm very proud of my knowledge of Spanish. But I don't feel I master it to the point I would like to, since my education was in English. I practice my Spanish constantly. I think Spanish writers are the greatest in the world. I don't think even Kundera in Europe—or any of the writers here—can stand up to Vargas Llosa and García Márquez and all those people. I don't think they have equals in this hemisphere.

CDH: Do you go back to Puerto Rico often?

ET: I go every chance I get because my mother's there. I try to go every year. I'd go twice a year if I could. I love Puerto Rico. Both my parents are from there; my sister's there. My uncles, aunts, nephew, nieces, they are all in Jayuya mostly.

CDH: Would you like to go back to live in Puerto Rico someday?

ET: Well, that's a fantasy we all live, because I find the island, the climate, the physical beauty, the scenic aspects of it so compelling. And I'm a man who has been around. I've lived in Africa, I've been to Russia, I've been to Spain, to the Greek islands. . . . I've been all over Western Europe and North Africa. I've spent a lot of time there. But I find Puerto Rico . . . to me it's the singularly most beautiful spot that I know of.

Photograph of Ed Vega, *El Nuevo Día* newspaper.

14

ED VEGA

Ed Vega's full name is Edgardo Vega Yunqué. A patient, meticulous, thoughtful man, he is precise in his speech and prolific in his work, having one of the most extensive literary *oeuvre* (including both published and unpublished texts) among the Puerto Rican writers who live in the United States. He is also an excellent promoter for this literature and for Latino art.

Vega was born in 1936 in Ponce, Puerto Rico, but raised in Cidra, a small town on the northern part of the island. He and his family moved to the United States in 1949. He was in the Air Force from 1954 to 1958. He holds a Bachelor of Arts degree from New York University, which he received in 1969. Ed Vega has taught at Hostos University, Hunter College, and the State University of New York in Old Westbury. He has also worked in community projects such as Addiction Service Agency and Aspira.

Since 1972 Vega has dedicated himself almost exclusively to writing, although he also holds creative writing workshops at the Institute for Latin American Writers and at the New School for Social Research. Currently, he is the director of the Clemente Soto Vélez Cultural and Educational Center in New York City.

He has published one novel, *The Comeback* (Houston: Arte Público Press, 1985) and two books of short stories, both with Arte Público: *Mendoza's Dreams* (1987) and *Casualty Reports* (1991). His work has also appeared in anthologies such as *Puerto Rican Writers at Home in the USA*, edited by Faythe Turner (Seattle: Open Hand Publishing Inc, 1991); *Iguana Dreams*, edited by Delia Poey and Virgil Suárez (New York: Harper, 1992); *Short Fiction by Hispanic Writers of the United States*, edited by Nicolás Kanellos (Houston: Arte Público Press, 1993); and *Currents from the Dancing River*, edited by Ray González (New York: Harcourt Brace, 1994).

"IN THE PLACE WHERE I WAS BORN, WHICH I LOVE
AND GIVE MY HEART TO, NOBODY KNOWS MY WORK"

CDH: When did you come to the United States?

EV: I came here in 1949, a month before my thirteenth birthday; I came from Cidra, Puerto Rico.

CDH: You were born in Cidra?

EV: I was born in Ponce in 1936, but my father was a Baptist minister and he was relocated to the town of Cidra when I was 1 year old, so that I consider myself as being from Cidra.

My parents organized theater performances and poetry readings for the church. My father was a very artistic and studious man. He brought the first rabbits to Puerto Rico, those white ones, the ones you eat; he sent for them to Australia. He raised carrier pigeons and that way communicated with seven or eight ministers, friends of his. He did experiments with different kinds of plants, of flowers, and he would make passionfruit juice when nobody drank that yet. That was after the war, in 1946 or 1947. Once, in our yard, he had a hole made and filled it with water. And when my little sister and I came home from school one day, we found a bird swimming around in there. She recognized it at once: it was a swan. There was a swan there, in Cidra, in the yard of the Baptist minister.

Abelardo Díaz Alfaro[1] came often to our house. His father was Don Abelardo Díaz, Baptist minister of Caguas, my father's colleague. And Abelardo Díaz Alfaro was a social worker in one of Cidra's barrios; from there he got the stories of *La Cuchilla, Don Peyo*, and all of that. I didn't know then that he was a writer.

My father wouldn't let us go to the movies, it was forbidden. We couldn't play cards or anything of that sort. Coincidentally, Cidra's casino was very near the church, and I was very much in love with the girls whom I saw there. I completely forgot about religion.

CDH: You rebelled against religion?

EV: Totally. At 16 I was already an atheist. I resented the church's restrictions, I was adventurous in matters of women, and that made me retire from the church. Summers, my sister and I went to a Baptist camp, and we, the minister's children, were the most rebellious there. She continued in the church, but I didn't.

CDH: Before you went to live in the United States, had you had any first-hand contact with North Americans?

EV: Being the son of a Baptist minister in Puerto Rico, I had a lot of contact because, as in every colonialist system, the ones in authority were the Americans. I had a friend called James, who was the son of the Baptist ministers' supervisor. Boxes of clothes would arrive at my house, sent by the good Christian Baptists to the poor Puerto Ricans. They would send jigsaw puzzles, those that have landscapes on them. My sister and I would spend hours doing them. And strange shoes would arrive, that my mother once forced me to put on. We were aware that there was a place where all that came from.

CDH: Why did your parents migrate to the United States?

EV: I never knew why my father came. I have a feeling it was because he was looking for freedom of speech and better opportunities for his children. He died young, at 55. What he left me was the ability to think, to invent.

CDH: Tell me about your first years here.

EV: My father established himself in a Protestant church that had been of a Lutheran-German congregation. It was an immense building, with a choir and an organ, and there were stained-glass windows; one had the Good Shepherd. There were eight windows in each side of the church. It was like a cathedral. I was brought up in a very large house, very pretty. When my father arrived, the congregation was already Latino. The Germans had dispersed after the war. There had also been Irish in the community, but they had sold their property and left. In my first book, *The Comeback*, I wrote about that.

CDH: Did you feel that you fit in?

EV: I fit in for the simple reason that I was pretty big and athletic, and could play football, baseball, hockey, and everything. I was a little stupid then. Once a friend of mine, who knew that I liked his little sister and that she liked me, said: "It's a shame that you'll never be able to marry my sister." "Why?" I asked, naively. "Because you're a nigger," he answered. It was a totally innocent thing that his parents had taught him. He said it sadly, not as if he were insulting me; he said it sadly: "What a shame that you can't marry my sister because you're black. . . . " He wanted us to be family. We were 14.

CDH: Is there a difference between racism in Puerto Rico and in the United States?

EV: In Puerto Rico it does exist and people feel it. My father was a good-looking man, in a certain way, but already marked by the inferiority of being mulatto. He was sentenced to that inferiority. I remember that when he took the bus to go home and blacks came in, he'd say, "It's getting dark."

And yet, before coming to the United States, one of my fondest memories is going to my father's aunt's restaurant in Cayey, a mountain town. Titi Clemen was the mother of Pedro Montañez, the boxer. She was a black woman, but there I felt as if I were in heaven: she spoiled me, she loved me a lot because I was Alberto's first son. It was such a pure love that I felt good. I have never been able to make distinctions between my white mother and grandmother and my aunt Clemen. They were night and day as far as skin is concerned, but equals when it came to loving. I've always kept as my role models my maternal grandmother, Suncha, and Titi Clemen, my father's aunt.

In the United States it is different. Here they say "half-black," "one-quarter black," "one-eighth black."

CDH: Did you have to face further prejudice for being Latino?

EV: First for being Latino, then for not being able to speak the language correctly when we came here; there was prejudice. Both blacks and whites attacked us. When I began speaking English better, skin became the issue.

When I joined the Air Force, I went to Washington to take a train for Mississippi. I made friends with a guy who was going to the same place, a blonde guy, and when I got on the train with him, the conductor told me: "not that way, you have to go over there." "But I have a first-class ticket," I told him. "No, you go over there." And when it was getting dark I wanted to go to the dining car, but when I got there they told me it was closed. A white couple that came behind me went into the restaurant. It was then that I realized why they hadn't let me in.

CDH: Did your father notice the prejudices against you?

EV: I criticized him a lot during a certain period of time, because in my opinion he was too condescending with people's attitudes towards us. He identified a lot with the United States. We spoke in Spanish, and they spoke in English. They would speak English among themselves to practice.

They always pretended. They would always talk about Our Lord Jesus Christ and his trials. They took shelter in religion.

CDH: What are your feelings regarding Puerto Rico?

EV: Sentimentally, I feel toward it like a child who loves his parents totally, without reserve. I don't go to Puerto Rico very often because the reality corrupts the vision I have of Puerto Rico. Sometimes I get sick when I go. Sometimes I see a brook and it is all filled with garbage; the brooks of my childhood weren't that way. You could see the "buruquenas," the shrimp at the bottom.

I'm planning on going more often now. I am going to buy some land in Aguas Buenas.

CDH: When did you decide that you wanted to be a writer?

EV: I was in the Army in Greece, I was 20 or 21 years old, and I read a lot. A curious thing happened: I was in love with my little sister's friend, and when I was on leave she had gotten a job cleaning houses in upstate New York. It was an estate with several houses. They asked the owners' permission for me to go there and mow the lawn and cut the shrubbery. They said yes. One day I was helping to clean up the guest house, and I found a collection of about a thousand pocket books. I picked out about one hundred of them by looking at their covers and put them in my bag. Curiously enough, I had taken William Faulkner's entire works, and those of Ernest Hemingway. . . . I didn't know about them because I still hadn't gone to the university. There were also books by John Steinbeck, Scott Fitzgerald, and James M. Cain, although Cain is not very well known. I started reading, and I noticed that some books were like cutting butter with a warm knife; they were empty, easy. But Hemingway's stories, the things that happened to those characters were serious, dramatic. And Steinbeck would eat my soul away with pity. I sometimes had to read a paragraph by Faulkner two or three times in order to understand what he had wanted to say. But Faulkner was the one who totally fascinated me. At 22 I had already read all of Faulkner.

On another occasion, while I was in the Air Force my father sent me a book, *Cuentos puertorriqueños de hoy*,[2] that had stories by Díaz Valcárcel and other writers. It had, for example, José Luis González's *En el fondo del caño hay un negrito* ("There is a little nigger at the bottom of the river"). That became part of my literary formation, those writers from the fifties. I started to see myself, to see my memories in what these authors had written, and I began to realize at 19 or 20 years of age, that I wanted to continue this tradition and write short stories. I wrote my first story when I was 21, in English. It's title was *A Grain of Sand*. I was reading a lot of existentialist literature, especially Camus. I had just finished reading *The Stranger*, and I wrote a story about a guy who commits suicide by swallowing grains of sand.

CDH: Did anybody in your family write?

EV: My aunt, Filí Yunqué, Josefa Filomena Yunqué Martínez, was a great poet. She studied in the University of Puerto Rico in the 1940s and later went on to get her Master's degree in Columbia University. She worked in the Department of Romance Languages at Queens College. And although she never published, she had a poet's soul. Also my great-grandfather Francisco Yunqué López de Victoria, a bohemian from Yauco, was a journalist and a poet.

CDH: Did you, at some point in your career, study literature?

EV: When I came out of the Army I started studying, first in the University of California, and then I transferred to New York University. I decided to study Spanish-American literature, history, and languages. I met Francisco Ayala, a Spanish professor who had been to Puerto Rico. I wrote my papers but never said anything in class. He called me to his office one day and said to me, "Vega, why don't you participate in class?" "I am very ashamed of the way in which I speak Spanish because the professors here want me to speak with Z's and I don't know why. I just speak like I do," I answered. He told me, "Stop that nonsense, Spanish from Puerto Rico is Andalusian." He was Andalusian and asked me, "Haven't you heard me speak?" "Yes, but you are the professor," I replied. "No, you have to stop that nonsense. I want you to participate in class because I want the other students to hear what you have got to say. You should be a writer," he told me.

Some of my professors were excellent. They inspired me a lot; they also helped me because there were people who would make fun of me when I showed them the stories I wrote. My next-door neighbor, a journalist from *The Village Voice*, once asked me, "What are you going to do with your life?" When I told her that I wanted to be a writer, she said: "Come on, you can't be a writer." That's why I respect anyone who tells me that they want to be a writer, especially if they are young.

CDH: What happened after NYU?

EV: I wanted to do a Ph.D. and applied for the Woodrow Wilson scholarship and another grant. When I was in my senior year at the University, I was called to the dean's office, and he told me, "I understand you want to pursue an academic career, that you want to get a doctorate. You have been accepted at the University of Wisconsin and at the University of California. But you ought to think of your community, you ought to teach at the public schools to help your people." I got very haughty and told him to go to hell. After what my father had gone through, I wasn't going to do the same. Because of that, and because of economic concerns—I already had children—I didn't graduate.

Afterward I started working on weekends at Sargent Shriver's office. There I met Bobby, Jackie, and all of the Kennedys. I happened to have worked in a community project with a man who was married to Viviana Muñoz Mendoza. They lived in El Barrio. There I also met Melo.[3] By 1971 or 1972 I decided to drop everything and dedicate myself to writing. When I told my wife—she said, "I've been waiting five years for you to take that decision."

CDH: Who supported the family?

EV: She did. That went well with her character, because she liked doing business and being out of the house. I became one of the first "housefathers" or "househusbands." I would take care of the kids, cook, clean, do the laundry, and all of that. I taught my wife Puerto Rican cooking.

CDH: When did you start to publish?

EV: I lost ten or twelve years of my literary career when I came here. I am of Wico's and Ana Lydia's generation,[4] the 1970s generation. But I couldn't write in Spanish. It took me twelve more years to have the necessary impulse to begin my literary career. I had to switch languages.

I first published a story in 1977, in a review called *Nuestro*. It was titled *Wild Horses*; it's in *Casualty Report*. It's about a mother who gives her children dog food. I got paid $400 for that story. They continued publishing my stories, and in 1985 I published a book with Arte Público Press, a Texas publishing house directed by Nicolás Kanellos, that publishes in Spanish and English. They also published *Mendoza's Dreams* and *Casualty Report*.

Now I have an agent who sends my work to the interested publishing houses, about fifteen or sixteen. She does an auction among them. It is a very complicated industry. But my work is getting to be known in Europe.

CDH: How is that?

EV: Since the Europeans have this penchant for criticizing the United States and since the work of Afro-Americans, Chicanos, and Puerto Ricans has this aggressiveness toward the United States, well, they love it. They study the Nuyorican question a lot. Many of my stories have been translated to Dutch. I was in Holland two years ago in a conference about Third World writers with authors from Senegal, India, and several other countries.

CDH: Have you had a similar experience in Spanish-speaking countries?

EV: No. At this moment Professor Ramón Luis Acevedo, from the University of Puerto Rico, is translating one of my stories. It is important to me that my story be published in Puerto Rico, not out of resentment, but because I know that in the place I was born, the place I love, the one I give my heart to, there my work is not known.

CDH: What, in your opinion, is the reason for that?

EV: The fact is that my work is an enormous challenge to Puerto Rican literature, particularly to that of the men over there. The writers doing the most significant work in Puerto Rico are women, except, of course, for Luis Rafael Sánchez. I hope that my writing will challenge male writers to tell the truth about what they see; they tell a story, but they don't tell the whole picture. However, I admire the women writers. *Felices días Tío Sergio* is a fabulous book, and I love Ana Lydia Vega. I met her over here, at a conference. I respect Wico [Luis Rafael Sánchez] a lot, but in order to understand Wico's work you have to swallow the official Spanish-language dictionary. What we do over here is more feminine. Our literature, no matter how close it is to the heart of the people, is more accessible. And without meaning any disrespect toward Wico or Rodríguez Juliá, to do what they do is like taking off your underwear and parading around in the Plaza de Colón. It is shameless. How can I, at this point in time, start writing like that?

There is something that prevents the contemporary Puerto Rican novel from being known. Novelists are very used to minimalism and the minimalist novel makes no sense to me, unless you are a genius, like Hemingway, who could write *The Old Man and the Sea* in a hundred and some pages and make a monument out of them. But our models are Cortázar, García Márquez, Vargas Llosa, Carlos Fuentes . . . they are expansive, eloquent writers. They pick a topic and give you a whole forest of knowledge. Puerto Ricans haven't published books like that, or at least I haven't seen them. What I have seen from Puerto Rico—maybe the colonial situation makes paper scarce, so you can only make editions of 100 pages—is that no one can give himself the luxury of writing a 400-page book. But I also don't see that they have profited from the resources available in the United States, being, as there is, so much contact between the two. I mean, if there is a person over there who has a 600-page manuscript and can't get it published, have it sent to the States. Some publishing houses publish in Spanish as well.

CDH: The fact that many Puerto Rican writers are obscure in their writings might be related to the fact that the insular writers are almost all university professors.

EV: They all want to outdo one another. Writing novels in Puerto Rico seems to be a manly game to see who can be more obscure, who has the biggest verb. . . . But nobody is going to take from them the fact that they know the language very well. The thing is that in any hierarchy those who are on top are going to go on acquiring power in order to despise and devalue those who are below. And what better way than to dictate from a podium, to have a stage from which to inferiorize everyone else, instead of being a platform, which is how it should be. Professors are the pyramid's base; it is students who form the apex. In my case, I treat every young Puerto Rican writer as if he or she were a newborn.

CDH: So you perceive a definite division or difference between Puerto Rican writers on the island and those on the mainland?

EV: There is a difference. Puerto Rico, because of its colonial status, because of its position in the hemisphere as the "little sister" of the other Latin American countries, and also because it is a country with such an incredible culture, it has, for better or for worse, a kind of inflated view of itself. It believes that this place, which measures 100 miles by 35 miles, is the center of the universe. It certainly has its charm, but at the same time, we have to realize what place it occupies.

I notice that when a book sells 1,500 copies in Puerto Rico, there's a big celebration, as if it were a success, whereas in the United States a book that sells only 35,000 copies is considered a failure. There is a tendency to make things go out of proportion, there is a myopic point of view.

The only place where I don't see that happening is in the music. The music being produced in Puerto Rico is international and has been for a long time.

CDH: Do you think the political situation in Puerto Rico has something to do with that way of thinking?

EV: Puerto Rico is a country that has not had any wars; sometimes we get criticized, and they tell us that we should just commit suicide. The Taínos already did that.

I have some resentment for the 1970s generation, which made fun of the jíbaro.[5] But the truth is that our conscience is of *jaibería,*[6] that's the wisdom of the *jíbaro.* We have to get our autonomy with cunning, not making the people bleed. Puerto Rico can, in the future, have the opportunity of deciding its status, and frankly, I would like to see a free Puerto Rico, but it's not going to be at the cost of making some other Puerto Rican's life miserable because he's pro-statehood. Life is miserable enough already.

I think that the only way that Puerto Rico will be independent is through a Caribbean federation. All of those territories—with the Virgin Islands and Jamaica—could become a "common market." They would have economic power, and you wouldn't have to go around torturing people with worn-out ideologies. There is a new sociopolitical panorama now.

CDH: How much do Puerto Rican politics weigh on the writing by Puerto Ricans in the United States?

EV: There is a strong political consciousness, but propaganda is terrible. It doesn't work, neither in capitalist nor in socialist societies. You can't condone it. I myself, in *Mendoza's Dreams*, deal with the topic of politics through a kind of self-satire, because sometimes there is so much rage that there's no other way for it to be expressed.

CDH: There seems to be a lot of interest in the literature produced by Hispanics in the United States.

EV: Carlos Fuentes said it. They asked him which was the most valuable literature in the world at this moment, and he replied that it was the one written by Caribbeans in the United States. I'd like to live a hundred years longer, because I know that someday even the policemen are going to speak Spanish. It's inevitable. Our culture, Hispanic culture, it's such a powerful thing that everywhere it's been, it has transformed its surroundings. And more and more Latinos are coming all the time.

CDH: Nevertheless, it is still difficult for Latinos to get into the U.S. literary mainstream.

EV: There's a tradition of immigrant writing in the United States. Every immigrant group has had its authors. For Puerto Ricans, Piri Thomas was a groundbreaker. But after the first works describing the immigrant experience, the next generation is supposed to go on to a more profound way of writing.

The definitive novel about the Latin American experience in the United States has still not been written. *The Mambo Kings Play Songs of Love*, by

Oscar Hijuelos, was a promising development and helped our literature by winning the Pulitzer Prize. It created a small boom for Latino writers. Sandra Cisneros has just obtained the MacArthur fellowship, and that has also helped.

But there's still a stigma attached to being Latino in the U.S. It's still an exotic part of America because of the mixture of races, I think. All that marginalizes Latino literature. The United States can't get past the idea that something that's produced in the U.S. by Latin Americans is not good. It accepts what comes out of Latin America itself—García Márquez, for example—but not what's produced here.

CDH: Would you say ghetto literature is the truest expression of Latino or Puerto Rican literature in the United States?

EV: I am not drawn in by ghetto literature. That is the manner in which the United States—and not only the United States, which is a large and benevolent country, a huge animal that bites if you tease it, but if you don't, you can enjoy yourself tremendously with it, but also the literary institutions—creates a myth, the myth of the ghetto, in order to keep the Puerto Rican, the Afro-American, whoever, separated from society's material benefits. That ghetto literature has been an obstacle throughout the years. And that is why—and this is not in the spirit of criticism, because he's a pioneer—the work of Piri Thomas marked the parameters of our Puerto Rican literature. The publishers only want that type of thing. When Abraham Rodríguez, Jr., published *Spidertown*, everyone said, "This is the best in Puerto Rican literature since Piri Thomas," because it's that kind of thing. That is to say that what Jack Agüeros publishes, what Judith Ortíz Cofer publishes, doesn't have any merit. What Ed Vega has done has no merit. They don't want short stories like mine, satirizing ghetto literature. Up until now we have been stereotyped, and we are not recognized when we step out of the designated stereotype. In movies, as in literature, our stereotype is that of the killer, the shantytown, the prostitute.

I don't like to get pigeonholed as a minority. When you get labeled like that, you belong to a group whose mediocre works get published and whose outstanding works are read as part of that spectacle. They get read as sociology or the exotic literature of a "boricua." Sometimes, in this respect, I think that there isn't any difference between a white and a black American. When you reach a certain point, they both have that arrogance, that North American rudeness. I have to face the fact that people are going to say, "Ah, he doesn't want to admit his African blood." It isn't that. I am very proud of my African forefathers, but also of the Europeans and the Indians. I don't want anybody to tell me that I have to go by what they decide that I am. They, the North Americans, don't have the faintest idea of what dialectic reasoning is. This is a country that is in constant change, in flux. Even language changes constantly.

CDH: Can you expand a little on what dialectic reasoning is?

EV: That's how the world works; Marx and Hegel were right. When you reach a synthesis, it is something that looks like it is something else, but it is in reality a mixture of thesis and antithesis. But here, there's a rock and roll mind: either this or that but not a synthesis.

CDH: Well, your literature is certainly not ghetto literature. Your characters are generally common folk who happen to be Puerto Rican or, better yet, common Puerto Rican folk.

EV: I think of literature as something that produces thoughts and ideas. It is an expression of ideas which forces the reader to rethink and re-view reality. And another element is the language. I try to use language as a way to convey ideas and that can be done from any kind of place, from any scenario. I write about the middle class; it is closer to the experience I had, to my aspirations and those of my family. I have a great need to see my work accepted on a literary level, so I made a conscious decision to use language to convey ideas.

CDH: The fact that you satirize ghetto literature in *Mendoza's Dreams* speaks of the growing complexity and sophistication of Latino literature.

EV: My point is that rather than have people criticize us from outside, I would rather criticize from inside. Besides, people from outside have a very condescending attitude. They will not say what they think; they will not criticize our literature, they will not say this is a clown show. They think, "let them play their little games." But if I say it, it's another story, it's as if somebody inside recognizes what it is. I'm a step ahead of criticism. It's a way to protect our integrity.

CDH: Another element of your writing that I find indicates a development in Latino literature is your humor, which is particularly evident in *The Comeback* and in *Mendoza's Dreams*.

EV: I don't know where the humor comes from, I just know that humor is sometimes the only way to deal with grief. I wrote *Mendoza's Dreams* under extremely difficult circumstances.

On a more profound literary level, one of my greatest influences as a writer was John Steinbeck. He dealt very well with humor in books like *Tortilla Flat,* which is often overlooked. Structurally, I modeled myself after Steinbeck, even though linguistically I modeled myself after Faulkner.

CDH: Have you ever thought about writing in Spanish?

EV: I've written in Spanish, or rather, in Puerto Rican. I am using the slang from over here, the mixed idiom we use, with a grammar that follows phonetics in *Los dinosaurios de Perico Colón*, a story I am working on: a narrative with dialogue mixed in. The dialogues are "cantos."

When I write in Spanish, I sign my full name. In English it's Ed Vega, but in Spanish Edgardo Vega Yunqué. I would have liked having used that name from the start, but they would have called me Mr. Yunqué. Yunqué had more impact, because there's about fifty Ed Vega's around. There are lawyers, doctors, everything. There's one called Nelson Eddy Vega, and he's an advocate of independence for the island.

CDH: How do you conceptualize Nuyorican literature, which is caught between two languages?

EV: I don't like it when people talk to me about Nuyorican literature. I don't like the word for the simple reason that the first thing that got here was pure "show," that is to say, the Nuyorican poets. So that all that has interested people is "show" and not narrative. For that reason I have tried to convince my colleagues over there, on the island, that there is a Puerto Rican literature and that because of the island's sociopolitical situation, it is in two languages. For me there isn't such a big divide between the literature from over there and the literature here. The division is already big enough without adding on to it.

CDH: What do you feel are the main differences between Puerto Ricans in the States and those on the island, not only the writers, but the people themselves?

EV: The thing that is missing in the United States is *el trato*, the way people deal with each other courteously on the island. There's a patina of it among Puerto Ricans in the States, but you see it much better in Puerto Rico. You can really appreciate how different classes treat each other with respect. It is something which I saw in my family and which I rejected as superficial, as too stifling and conventional, but now I really miss it. I broke with those familial ways of respect, and yet now I find they make social life easier.

Part of the situation may be due to the fact that many of the Puerto Ricans in New York belong to the working class or descend from the *jíbaros*, and there's a set of manners among them that's more complex because any breach to the code, any breach of conventions and respect to dignity could bring violence and misunderstanding. The *jíbaros* will take out their *machetes* right away to avenge an offense. North Americans do not understand that code.

CDH: Besides narration, do you work in other genres?

EV: I have some essays, but I still haven't achieved in them the ease I feel in fiction narrative. For me, the scale of difficulty ranges from story to novel to essay to theater and poetry. The challenge I have in front of me is the essay form.

CDH: Apart from Puerto Ricans, do you have contact with other Hispanic groups?

EV: I am director of the Clemente Soto Vélez Cultural and Educational Center in the Lower East Side. (Every time I say this to an American they think it's about Roberto Clemente; Clemente Soto Vélez was a Puerto Rican poet who lived many years in New York. He had been imprisoned for being a Nationalist.) There we have studios for sculptors and painters, many of them Latin American, but there are also Europeans. We have a 150-seat theater, La Tea, where we stage modern Latin American plays, mostly experimental works. There's also a rehearsal studio and a forty-seat puppet theater. The first floor is a jazz club during the night. We want to make this into a true center for Latin culture in New York City.

Regarding Chicanos I have to say that, contrary to them, we Puerto Ricans have had so much contact with Afro-Americans that we have caught their rhythms, that come from "American English," which is a big advantage. "American English" is really "Southern English." The rhythms of speech and things like jazz and blues are the most authentic contribution to the culture of this country. And we Puerto Ricans have a lot of that. I was in the Nuyorican Poets Café one day when there was a jazz band playing. I read a poem from Miguel Piñero, really long, which I had never read. I started reading it during the band's first set, and I told the bass player to accompany me. The whole quartet—piano, battery, sax, and bass—started playing behind me, and I, using the Afro-American rhythms, read the poem. It was perfect. Miguel Piñero had a magnificent ear. You couldn't read that in Puerto Rican; you had to read it as Afro-American or in Afro-Caribbean English. It was a mixture of our stuff and Afro-American. And that's why our stuff is much more adaptable than thc Chicanos.'

CDH: Why do you think that Puerto Ricans in the United States have kept a definite Latino identity, despite the fact that the Great Migration of islanders to this country is already more than half a century old? Why haven't they melted in the famous melting pot?

EV: It is something unusual, because almost all groups that come to the United States—especially European immigrants—lose their identity in one generation. But for the same reason that there is a strong racial consciousness in the United States, a separation of whites and blacks, the "mestizo" (or racially mixed) individual is called upon to declare him or herself white, which is sheer madness, or to declare him or herself black, and in so doing to invite marginalization. I think that in the case of Puerto Ricans, since we do not have so many racial hang-ups, we have chosen a very astute way of not having to make that decision: we maintain our Puerto Rican identity.

That is my opinion after analyzing my feelings and talking with other people, and reading and observing what goes on around me. I have to admit, however, that the analysis fails when you look at the case of Puerto Rico, which, after so many years maintains itself—at least culturally—faithful to its heritage instead of totally capitulating to North American culture. That is to say, it may also be that we have the ability of maintaining our culture alive; that it does not have so much to do with being in the United States. But there is no doubt that it gets much stronger in the United States.

CDH: So the American experience strengthens the Puerto Ricans' national identity?

EV: That has been very evident in these last few years, in which I have seen the care taken in maintaining what is ours. Puerto Rican identity in New York is very well known. It is not always positive, but we know we are here to stay, living in this country, in this geographical region, and that we are what we are for good or for bad.

CDH: Do you think Puerto Ricans—or Latinos in general—have made any important contribution to United States culture?

EV: To grow up Latino in the United States is a powerful experience, and that is what we bring to literature and to the arts. Somewhere down the line people are going to realize what a great contribution Latinos have made in that sense to the culture of the United States.

NOTES

INTRODUCTION

1. Puerto Ricans have been migrating to the United States ever since the early 1800s, mostly in connection with the rum, molasses, and tobacco trade. A Puerto Rican and Cuban Benevolent Merchants Association was established in New York early in that century. In the 1890s the New York-based Puerto Rico Section of the Cuban Revolutionary party attracted many illustrious political refugees and emigrés.

After the Spanish-American War and particularly after American citizenship was granted to Puerto Ricans by the Jones Act in 1917, migration to the mainland increased. In 1940 there were about 70,000 Puerto Ricans living in the States. From 1940 to 1950 the numbers went up to more than 300,000 and reached nearly a million and a half in 1970. Today there are more than 2.7 million Puerto Ricans in the United States, according to the 1990 Census.

2. It was not only the post–World War II expansion of industries in the States that favored this migratory trend, but also the establishment of a new political formula in Puerto Rico, called a Commonwealth. Inaugurated in 1952 according to Law 600, approved by Congress in 1950, the policies of the ruling Popular Democratic party, which had devised the new political status, called for the industrialization of a traditionally agricultural economy, thus displacing a large number of farm workers from the lands they had either owned or helped to cultivate. They migrated from the countryside to San Juan (where many settled in slums) or directly to the States.

3. Arturo Alfonso Schomburg (1874–1938) was a black Puerto Rican who went to New York in 1891 and there became a member of the Cuban Revolutionary Party's Puerto Rico Section. He started to publish a steady stream of articles and essays on Caribbean and North American black culture. In 1911, together with

John E. Bruce, David Fulton, W. Wesley Weeks, and William E. Braxton, he founded the Negro Society for Historical Research in order to further the study of black history and to collect books, photographs, letters, and works of art dealing with African-American culture. His collection of black literature and art, donated in 1926 to the New York Public Library, became the basis for the Schomburg Center for Research in Black Culture, now located in Harlem.

4. Colón (1901–1974), another black Puerto Rican, migrated to the States in 1918. His experiences in New York, where he encountered not only the diversity and challenge of the big city but also its prejudices, are recorded in his collection of stories, *A Puerto Rican in New York and Other Sketches* (published in 1961), which appears to be the first full-fledged book by a Puerto Rican in the United States to have been written and published in English.

5. Bernardo Vega (1885–1965) was a Puerto Rican tobacco worker who migrated to New York in 1916 as a young man. He wrote a memoir about his life within the Puerto Rican community in the States, which was published posthumously in Puerto Rico in 1977, as edited by César Andreu Iglesias. In it he traces the history of the Puerto Rican community in New York from the late nineteenth century to the 1940s.

6. Clemente Soto Vélez (1905–1993), who wrote vanguardist poetry in Puerto Rico during the twenties, was imprisoned in the States for taking part in Nationalist meetings and activities in Puerto Rico in 1935. After his release from prison in 1942, he stayed in New York, returning for brief periods to Puerto Rico from the mid-eighties until his death.

7. Daniel Stern, in a review for *The New York Times Book Review*, wondered at "the pervasiveness of the Hispanic cultural and social legacy" in the streets of Harlem (May 21, 1967, p. 44).

8. Piri Thomas, *Down These Mean Streets*, (New York: Vintage, 1991), p. 106.

9. The exaggerated esteem for what are considered overtly male traits, such as physical courage, dominance over the female, and sexual aggressiveness.

10. The *autos sacramentales* were medieval morality plays and others with ecclesiastical themes—especially the seven sacraments—further developed by playwright Calderón de la Barca in Spain in the seventeenth century.

11. See Luce López Baralt, *San Juan de la Cruz y el Islam* (Colegio de México 1985) and also her edition of Miguel Asín Palacios, *Sadilíes y alumbrados* (Madrid: Hiperión, 1990).

12. There were serious manifestations on campus in Columbia University in 1968, and in June 1969 the famous Stonewall Rebellion, which launched the gay rights movement, erupted in a bar in Greenwich Village. That decade was also marked in New York by racial disturbances such as those that took place in the UN building in 1961 and in Harlem in 1963. There were also riots in nearby Newark in 1967.

13. Ann Charters, ed., *The Portable Beat Reader* (New York: Penguin Books, 1992), p. XVII.

14. On November 16, 1952, an article by Holmes in the Sunday Magazine of *The New York Times* described the group as a culturally disaffiliated one that could not identify with the moral values of a country entering the Cold War. In 1957 Allen Ginsberg's book *Howl and Other Poems* brought the writers to national attention through a censorship trial in San Francisco, while Jack Kerouac's novel, *On the Road,* attracted much attention and became, with *Howl,* the hallmark of the Beat Generation.

15. This was the way Miguel Algarín identified the group of poets and play-wrights who were Puerto Rican in origin but who lived in New York and wrote either in English or in mixed English and Spanish. He used it in the title of the anthology he edited together with Miguel Piñero, *Nuyorican Poetry: An Anthology of Puerto Rican Words and Feelings* (New York: William Morrow, 1975).

16. For a history of the Nuyorican Poets Café, see Akira Nogami, "Fervent Wind from the Poets Café in Miguel Algarin's *Time's Now/ Ya es tiempo*" (Tokyo, 1992).

17. Frances Aparicio explains this very clearly in her essay "La vida es un Spanglish disparatero: Bilingualism in Nuyorican Poetry," which appears in *European Perspectives on Hispanic Literature of the United States*, edited by Genvieve Fabre (Houston: Arte Público Press, 1988), pp. 147–160.

Code-switching is the term given to the practice of going back and forth continuously between two or more languages, either in speech or writing. It also refers to the cultural assumptions inherent in the culture represented by each language. Here it is used to signify the going to and from English to Spanish and vice versa.

Code-switching, of course, is not unique to Puerto Rican writers. It has also been used by other Latino groups and their writers, especially Chicanos (Mexican Americans). It was in the Southwest, in fact, that code-switching was first used in folksongs during the late nineteenth century. Alurista, a Chicano writer who took active part in the literary and political awakening of that ethnic group during the 1960s (in which poets undertook affirmative actions, reading their verses at meetings, strikes, and marches), is credited with being one of the first to use bilingualism with a literary intent in his poetry.

18. *Nuyorican Poetry: An Anthology of Puerto Rican Words and Feelings*, p. 9.

19. Michel Foucault, "What Is an Author?" in *The Foucault Reader,* ed. by Paul Rabinow (New York: Penguin, 1984), p. 102

20. Luce López Baralt, "Al-Andalus," in *The Cambridge History of Arabic Literature,* to be published by Cambridge University Press.

21. Cuban poet Nicolás Guillén (1902–1989) may be the most widely known of the Afro-Antillean poets who flourished during the twenties and thirties. Others were the Cuban Emilio Ballagas, the Dominican Manuel del Cabral, and the Puerto Rican Luis Pales Matos.

22. Négritude was a term coined in France during the thirties by Martinican poet Aimé Césaire, then a student in Paris. He sought to signify a supranational black cultural and artistic identity and a pride in African heritage. It also became a

springboard for political action. Among those writers who became identified with Négritude were Léopold Sedar Senghor of Senegal and Léon Damas of Guyana.

23. The presence of Spanish-speaking radio in the States dates back to the 1920s. Spanish-language programs and then stations began in California and Texas and later were established in New York.

24. See Ruth Glasser, *My Music Is My Flag: Puerto Rican Musicians and Their New York Communities 1917–1940* (Los Angeles: University of California Press, 1995).

25. These songs, composed in the poetic form of the *décima* or ten-verse stanza, have only recently begun to be collected in written works. See Santiago Díaz Orlando, *Decimario Nacional* (Santo Domingo: Comité Amigos del Autor Puertorriqueño, 1994).

26. The states with the biggest Puerto Rican populations are, in that order, New York, New Jersey, Florida, Massachusetts, Pennsylvania, Connecticut, Illinois, California, Ohio, and Texas. See Francisco Rivera-Batiz and Carlos Santiago, *Puerto Ricans in the United States: A Changing Reality,* (Washington, D.C. The National Puerto Rican Coalition, 1994).

27. A discussion of such relations can be found in Immanuel Wallerstein, *Geopolitics and Geoculture,* (Cambridge: Cambridge University Press, 1991).

28. A condition that usually refers to the mixing of races through intermarriage but that can also be applied to cultural matters in the sense that different traditions can merge and develop into a "new" cultural product.

29. Homi K. Bhabha, *The Location of Culture* (New York: Routledge, 1994), p. 172.

30. During the 1970s there was a reversal of the migratory trend from the island to the States. See Juan Hernández Cruz, *Migratory Trends in Puerto Rico* (San Germán: Universidad Interamericana, 1994).

31. This was the name given to the sudden burst of Latin American narrative writing which took the Americas and Europe by surprise in the sixties and seventies. The phenomenon was attributed to several causes, among them the increase of a reading public in Latin America; a new interest by Spanish publishing houses in the literature of that continent; and also the new perspectives developed by the writers themselves from the vantage point of Europe.

32. Nancy Morris, *Puerto Rico: Culture, Politics, and Identity* (Westport, Conn.: Praeger, 1995), p. 153.

33. In 1991 the Commonwealth government, then ruled by the Popular Democratic party, passed a law making Spanish the only official language in Puerto Rico. The next year the island received a prestigious award, Premio Rey de España, from Spain for this action. The law was later repealed by an administration dominated by the New Progressive party, which favors statehood.

34. Bhabha, *The Location of Culture*, p. 9.

35. Edward Said, *Representations of the Intellectual* (New York: Pantheon Books, 1994), p. 39.

36. A comprehensive view of this literature in relation to island literature can be found in Frances R. Aparicio's "From Ethnicity to Multiculturalism: An His-

torical Overview of Puerto Rican Literature in the United States," in *Handbook of Hispanic Cultures in the United States: Literature and Art,* ed. by Francisco Lomelí (Houston: Arte Público Press and Instituto de Cooperación Iberoamericana, 1993), pp. 19–39.

1. JACK AGÜEROS

1. A specific neighborhood within a town, usually of rural or semirural character.

2. See note 3 to the Introduction.

3. The Great Migration refers to the wave of poor Puerto Rican immigrants who entered the States during the forties. In that decade, the number of Puerto Ricans living in the States (most of them in New York) increased from 70,000 to more than 300,000, according to Census Bureau statistics. This migration seems to be directly linked to the economic policies of the newly founded Commonwealth of Puerto Rico, which stressed the industrialization of the island and left many farm workers unable to integrate themselves into the new economic structures. Rapid population growth was another factor because the Puerto Rican government used migration as a safety valve for the problem.

4. A typical Puerto Rican expression that means something like *Goodness me!*

5. An agricultural tool with a long, slightly curved blade used to cut sugar cane; it can also be used as a weapon.

6. A term generally applied to the country people who practiced subsistence farming in mountainous center of the island). The figure of the *jíbaro* has become a quintessential symbol of traditional Puerto Rican values associated with a patriarchal, agriculture-based society.

7. A small theater *cum* cafe and nightclub, established by Miguel Algarín in the seventies to provide a forum for *Nuyorican* (New York–Puerto Rican) poets. It is now located at 236 East 3rd. Street.

8. See note 10 to the Introduction.

9. A beautiful flowering tree that is common in the Antilles. It grows fiery-red blossoms in the summer.

10. Small, carved wooden figures depicting saints from the Catholic Church and even different scenes and mysteries. They were very popular in Puerto Rico's religious milieu from the nineteenth century and are now studied and analyzed as representative of one of the best expressions of popular art.

11. Julia de Burgos (1914–1953) is a well-known Puerto Rican poet who lived in New York from 1942 until her death in 1953.

2. MIGUEL ALGARÍN

1. A very famous radio program of the forties and fifties in Puerto Rico where amateurs went to sing. Some later became well-known entertainers.

2. The Nuyorican Poets Café.

3. Miguel Piñero (1946–1988) was a Puerto Rican poet and playwright who wrote *Short Eyes*, a well-known play that dealt with life in prison, based on his own experiences.

4. "Lucky" Cienfuegos was part of the Nuyorican Poetry movement.

5. Jorge Brandon died at the beginning of 1995, after this interview was conducted.

6. The first part of this interview was held in the home of Carmen Ana Figueras, Algarín's aunt, who lives near Trujillo Alto, in Puerto Rico.

7. Algarín is referring to the plebiscite on the political status of Puerto Rico held in November 1993.

3. SANDRA MARÍA ESTEVES

1. Tía means aunt.

2. Typical Puerto Rican dishes.

3 "To Julia and Me."

4. Airplane ticket.

5 Something very country-like.

6. Typical.

7. Cousin.

8. A derogatory term for foreigner, in this case North American.

9. I am not a gringa.

10. You are going to disgrace the name of the family; you cannot come back at this hour, it is outrageous. I don't know how things are in New York, but here things are different.

11. An anthology of Puerto Rican poetry written in New York, in both Spanish and in English. The book was edited by Pedro López Adorno and published by the University of Puerto Rico Press in 1991.

12. "Hey, Mami, come with me."

13. The *bomba* is a folkloric song/dance combination associated with black culture in Puerto Rico. It involves a dialogue that is often a battle of wits between two groups of people, usually men and women. The *plena* is a popular musical form that originated in Ponce, the second largest city in Puerto Rico. It has a lively rhythm and is often accompanied by lyrics that chronicle an event.

14. María Christina became a poetic *persona* who has appeared in several of Sandra María Esteves's poems, embodying the traditional virtues of Puerto Rican womanhood. In assuming them consciously, however, she is set free.

15. Very popular dances from the Caribbean. The *merengue* has its origins in the Dominican Republic, and the *cha cha cha* is Cuban.

16. A word play on Table of Contents; *contentos* in Spanish means happy.

17. *Hear me, your spirit is speaking.*

18. The Taínos were the peace-loving Indians who inhabited Puerto Rico in pre-Columbian times.

19. Pedro López Adorno, a Puerto Rican professor at Hunter College who is also a poet and writes in Spanish, edited the anthology of Puerto Rican poetry written in New York, *Papiros de Babel.* He also is the editor of a review, *Tercer Milenio,* that attempts to bring together Puerto Rican writers on the island and in the United States.

4. VICTOR HERNÁNDEZ CRUZ

1. See note 18, chapter 3.
2. See note 2 to the Introduction.
3. One of contemporary Puerto Rico's best known writers.
4. Soursop, a sweet, white-fleshed tropical fruit with dark green, spiked skin.
5. A traditional Spanish verse form consisting of stanzas of ten eight-syllable verses that often rhyme alternately. It is recited and sung by country poets in Puerto Rico who not only touch on the ever-present themes of love and death but also comment on current events and refer to particular people. Sometimes the words are improvised as the singer goes along, accompanied by a guitar.
6. *El brindis del bohemio,* a very melodramatic poem dealing with a drunken man's declaration that a mother's love is sacred. It is widely recited at midnight on New Year's Eve.
7. There was a significant migration of Puerto Ricans to Hawaii at the turn of the century. They went as laborers to cut cane under contract to American landowners or sugar cane companies. Their descendants have retained some characteristics of Puerto Rican culture.
8. A long cotton shirt widely used by men in the Caribbean. It is worn without tucking into the pants and has four pockets and several tucks in front.
9. Traditional Puerto Rican Christmas carols.
10. Juan Antonio Corretjer (1908–1984), a Puerto Rican poet who passionately defended independence for the island and was jailed in a federal prison for his activities in the Nationalist party.
11. Country folk.
12. A somewhat derogatory term used to name the way Hispanics—especially New York Puerto Ricans—combine Spanish and English in their speech and writings.
13. Mayagüez is Puerto Rico's third largest city, an important seaport on the western side of the island.

5. TATO LAVIERA

1. *Cangrejos,* which literally means "crabs," was the name originally given to the Santurce area (San Mateo de Cangrejos), which was outside the walled city, to the east. It was settled mostly by freed slaves, runaways from non-Hispanic islands of the Caribbean who found their freedom in Puerto Rico, and by poor people. It later became the prosperous, "new" part of San Juan and is now in decay.

2. Operation Bootstrap, referring to the effort made by a person to pull him or herself up by the bootstraps, was the name given to the industrialization program set in motion by Luis Muñoz Marín and his Popular Democratic party after establishing the Commonwealth formula.

3. Rafael Cortijo (1928–1982) was a percussionist, composer, and founder of a popular musical group, *Cortijo y su combo*, which cut numerous records. They played Afro-Antillean rhythms and became the symbol of an indigenous sort of music as opposed, in the sixties, to the "foreign" influences of rock music coming from the States. He is considered a precursor of "salsa" music, the contemporary manner of making Afro-Caribbean music. Ismael Rivera (1931–1987) was an immensely popular singer for Cortijo's group. He was an extraordinary innovator in terms of popular song.

4. Celia Cruz, born in Cuba during the twenties, went into exile during the sixties and has lived since then mostly in New York. She is a very popular singer of the Cuban "son," the seminal rhythm of Cuban music, from where salsa sprung up. She is universally revered by Spanish-speaking audiences.

5. Cantera is a working-class section of Santurce, the part of San Juan that developed during this century.

6. "We're going to the airport, little black one."

7. The Skull and Bones gang.

8. Canóvanas is a town in the northeastern part of Puerto Rico.

9. Juan Boria was a well-known reciter of "black" or Afro-Antillean poetry.

10. Luis Palés Matos (1898–1959) is one of Puerto Rico's best-known poets. He was the first to write Afro-Antillean verse, even though he didn't publish his book *Tuntún de pasa y grifería* until 1937.

11. *Tertulias* are group conversations on different topics, generally held in cafés, which were part of the social scene in all Spanish-speaking countries until recently. In some instances, they became literary institutions because prominent writers took part in them.

12. Lips.

13. "Don't consort with dark-skinned fellows, little black one."

14. The Puerto Rican Nationalist party was founded in the early twenties with a platform that sought independence from the United States. When Pedro Albizu Campos joined shortly afterward, he turned increasingly to violence. He was incarcerated for preaching armed resistance to the U.S. government but was released. Things came to a head in 1950, when the Nationalists staged an armed uprising that was quickly quelled. Albizu Campos was jailed.

15. Code-switching is a term applied to the practice of going from one language to the other (from Spanish to English or vice versa) within a text. It refers not only to the use of two distinct languages but also to the use of two different cultural outlooks that take into consideration accepted social norms, values, and prejudices and addresses them directly.

16. A person who recites poetry in public for the enjoyment of others.

17. Jorge Brandon (1905–1995) was a Puerto Rican street poet, considered by many as the father of Nuyorican poetry.

18. The Popular Democratic party was founded by Luis Muñoz Marín after he broke away from the Liberal party in 1937. It was continuously in power in Puerto Rico from 1944 to 1968, and in 1948 its founder became the first elected Puerto Rican governor in history. It brought about a deep transformation that affected all aspects of Puerto Rican society, setting in motion a vast industrialization plan and defining a new form of relationship with the United States which came to be known in Spanish as Estado Libre Asociado (or ELA: it literally means Free Associated State) and in English as a Commonwealth. Its industrialization program had a deep effect on agriculture. The *jíbaro,* or peasant, became uprooted from the land and in many cases migrated either to the cities on the island or to the States.

19. René Marqués (1919–1979) was one of the foremost Puerto Rican literary figures during the fifties and sixties. A fiction writer, poet, and playwright, he saw the Puerto Rican question in terms of a clash between two sets of values: those of the land, attached to the old patriarchal culture and those that came with the North American "invaders" and which depend above all on money and power.

20. *La Carreta* is a three-act play originally published in *Asomante* review in 1951–1952. It was staged in New York in 1953; in San Juan in 1954; and in Madrid in 1957. It was also published in Prague, in a Czech translation, in 1964. It revolves around a Puerto Rican family that migrates from the country (where the first act is set) to the slums of San Juan (second act), to New York (third act). As the family moves, it also loses its values and becomes morally dissolute.

21. *A pava* is a typical wide-brimmed straw hat used by peasants in Puerto Rico; it was used as a symbol of the Popular Democratic Party.

22. Ana Lydia Vega (1946–) has integrated popular forms of language and culture in her short stories and essays. She is the author of, among other books, *Pasión de historia* (1987), *Falsas crónicas del sur* (1992), and *Esperando a Loló* (1994).

23. A Puerto Rican stew with all kinds of ingredients.

6. NICHOLASA MOHR

1. From Ponce, Puerto Rico's second largest city.

2. A typical Puerto Rican food that consists of plantain dough formed in a rectangular shape with meat in the middle. It is eaten at Christmas.

3. Rice and pigeon peas, another typical dish.

4. Gringo is a derogatory term for a stranger. In Puerto Rico it is used in relation to Americans.

5. Howard Fast is an American novelist born in New York City in 1914. During the forties and fifties, his historical novels became very popular. They revealed a sense of class consciousness and his leftist convictions.

6. Spiritualism is the belief that humans can communicate with each other through a medium even after death.

7. A *coquí* is a tiny singing frog that is unique to Puerto Rico.

8. It is the only book by Nicholasa Mohr up to the present that deals with a Caribbean reality that is not Puerto Rico. The story is about a boy from the Dominican Republic whose family moves to the United States.

9. El Yunque is one of Puerto Rico's highest mountains, and its slopes are covered with a tropical rain forest.

10. See note 17 to the Introduction.

11. This essay appeared in *Barrios and Borderlands: Cultures of Latinos and Latinas in the United States,* edited by Denis Lynn Daly Heyck (New York: Routledge, 1994).

7. JUDITH ORTIZ COFER

1. The coffee plantation.
2. Stories.
3. "I'll toss you a story," that's what my grandmother used to say.
4. "When I was at home we did this and that . . . "
5. Home, mother, the island.
6. Death.
7. Death came into this house.
8. Evil.
9. Forgetfulness.
10. Belonging to the pro-statehood party, or a nationalist with a pro-independence position in relation to the political status of Puerto Rico.
11. Generally used to signify Spanish Harlem but in a wider sense it refers, as used here, to any ghetto-like slum.
12. An influential 1966 book by an American sociologist who studied the culture of poverty in the slums of Puerto Rico.
13. *The Wedding March.*

8. PEDRO PIETRI

1. The *guayabera* is a typical cotton dress shirt used by men in the tropics.
2. Radio soap operas.
3. A very well-known Puerto Rican radio, TV, and movie comedian whose real name was Ramón Ortiz del Rivero. He lived from 1909 to 1956.
4. Jorge Brandon died after this interview was conducted.
5. The anthology edited by Miguel Algarín and Bob Holman and published by Henry Holt and Co. in 1994.
6. The Trío Los Panchos was a very popular Mexican ensemble of three guitarists who sang romantic ballads; the lead singer at one time was Puerto Rican. They were widely known in Latin America during the forties and fifties. For décimes, see note 5 to chapter 4.
7. The name of an old prison in San Juan which was used during the Spanish colonial period.

8. Spiritualist.

9. Iván Silén and Che Meléndez are Puerto Rican poets. Alfredo Matilla is a critic and professor who has studied Puerto Rican literature in the States extensively. He is translating some of Pedro Pietri's work into Spanish.

10. "Look, if I don't speak Spanish well, it's because I was not born in Spain; if I don't speak English well, it's because I'm not an S.O.B."

11. The Young Lords was a radical group of young Puerto Ricans formed in the 1960s after the advent of the civil rights movement. It was similar in intent and tactics to the Black Panthers, seeking to right the wrongs of the Puerto Rican community through radical politics and protests.

12. The Movement for Independence: another radical group espousing more explicitly political aims, namely, independence for Puerto Rico by any means, including violence. It had contacts with Castro's Cuba.

13. A ceremony to exorcise evil spirits practiced in the African-based Caribbean religions of *santería*.

14. A poetry slam is a competition held regularly at the Nuyorican Poets Café in which poets stand up and recite and a master of ceremonies picks ten people in the public to be the judges. They have to rate the poems on a scale of 1 to 10.

9. LOUIS REYES RIVERA

1. Ramón Emeterio Betances and Segundo Ruiz Belvis, two Puerto Rican patriots, were exiled from the island by Governor Marchesi in 1867 for their supposed involvement in the uprising of some Spanish artillery soldiers stationed in San Juan. They were to present themselves before the Madrid government but chose instead to flee to New York via the Dominican Republic. There they established contact with the Republican Society of Cuba and Puerto Rio, whose secretary was the Puerto Rican José Francisco Basora.

The *Grito de Lares* (September 1868) was a failed uprising against Spain that took place in the mountains of Puerto Rico. El Grito de Yara (October 1868) was a similar uprising that took place in Oriente Province in Cuba.

2. The Ten Years' War was a long revolt against Spain that took place in Cuba from 1868 to 1878 and ended in a truce, *el Pacto del Zanjon,* with Spain promising reforms and a greater autonomy.

3. José Martí is the Cuban poet and patriot who organized resistance to Spain from New York. He is the best-known hero of that country's War of Independence, in which he died. Eugenio María de Hostos is a Puerto Rican patriot who was also active in the organization of the resistance to Spain. He was a staunch defender of union between the Antilles.

4. Flor Baerga was a member of the Artisans League in New York and one of the founders of *Los Independientes* club, one of the many organizations formed to promote the struggle for Cuban and Puerto Rican independence from Spain.

5. The "Little War" was waged in Cuba against Spain from 1879 to 1880.

6. Because of the intellectual sophistication they gained by being read to (newspapers were also read in the factories), cigar makers were at the vanguard of workers' rights. In June 1919, as tobacco worker Bernardo Vega recounts in his memoirs (*Memorias de Bernardo Vega*, ed. by César Andreu Iglesias, Huracán, 1988, 4th ed.), a strike paralyzed cigar factories in New York and spread to all the States. As a result of that strike, several unions recognized the importance of Puerto Rican workers in the industry. Puerto Ricans in other industries also started to organize themselves.

7. See note 3 to the Introduction.

8. Antonio S. Pedreira (1899–1939) was an important Puerto Rican scholar who, in a seminal 1934 book, *Insularismo*, attempted to define the Puerto Rican personality and Puerto Rican culture.

9. "Spoiling or improving the race." It is a way of speaking in Puerto Rico that refers directly to racial questions. It is said that someone "spoils" the race when he or she marries a person who is darker, and, conversely, they "improve" the race when they marry someone lighter.

10. See note 6 to Chapter 1.

11. Peasant.

12. Rural district.

13. Pedro López Adorno, a Puerto Rican poet, anthologist, and professor at Hunter College.

14. A Puerto Rican poet who lives in New York.

15. A town in the southwest coast of Puerto Rico. It used to be famous for being the center of coffee-growing activities.

16. Making fun of her.

17. See notes 4 and 5 to the Introduction

18. Cayey is a town nestled in the mountains of central Puerto Rico.

19. People from Galicia, Spain, who migrated in great numbers to Cuba.

20. See note 22 to the Introduction.

21. All these isms, and also *Atalaya de los Dioses*, refer to experimental poetic movements that flourished in Puerto Rico during the 1920s and 1930s.

22. Felipe Luciano is a Puerto Rican journalist and TV personality who was well-known during the seventies, when he was also a member of the Young Lords. (See note 23.)

23. The Young Lords was a radical group of young Puerto Ricans who established themselves first in Chicago and then in New York City during the sixties. Like the Black Panthers, they adopted a quasimilitary style and advocated both political revolution and self-help programs for the Puerto Rican poor.

24. Palés Matos is Puerto Rican; Ballagas and Guillén are Cubans. The three poets wrote in the so-called Afro-Cuban style.

25. Langston Hughes was an American poet, playwright, and novelist generally considered the poet laureate of Harlem. He lived for some time in Cuba, where he came into contact with Afro-Caribbean poetry and poets.

10. ABRAHAM RODRÍGUEZ, JR.

1. René Marqués (1919–1979) is a Puerto Rican playwright whose play, *La Carreta* (the Ox-cart, 1951), was widely represented. See note 20 to Chapter 5.
2. He is referring to *Spidertown*, his 1993 novel (New York: Hyperion).
3. I don't like it.
4. Lolita Lebrón is a Puerto Rican Nationalist who took part in the attack against Congress on March 1, 1954. On that date, three Puerto Rican Nationalists, Lebrón, Andrés Figueroa Cordero, and Oscar Collazo, opened fire on the assembly of congressmen from the visitors' gallery of the House of Representatives. They fired thirty shots, wounding five people, two seriously.
5. Pedro Albizu Campos (1891–1965) was elected president of the Puerto Rican Nationalist party in 1930. A Harvard-educated lawyer who had served in the U.S. Army, in 1950 he organized an armed revolt to proclaim Puerto Rican independence.
6. People.
7. Luxury and jewelry.
8. Dominicans and Cubans.
9. New York: Plus Ultra Educational Publisher, 1971.
10. Luis Muñoz Marín (1898–1980) was the first Puerto Rican to be elected governor of the island. He governed from 1948 to 1960. He is the architect of Puerto Rico's present political status, a Commonwealth with a degree of internal autonomy but subject to the federal laws and regulations of the United States.
11. Pablo Neruda (1904–1973), Chilean poet who won the Nobel Prize for Literature in 1971.

11. ESMERALDA SANTIAGO

1. A nineteenth-century literary movement in Spanish-speaking countries which emphasized the detailed description of the habits and daily lives of common, ordinary people, especially the regional idiosyncrasies. It is an offshoot of realism.
2. Soap operas.
3. "Are you Hispanic?" "No, I am Puerto Rican."
4. Puerto Ricans themselves rejected me.
5. Vieques is a small offshore island lying to the northeast of Puerto Rico; it is a municipality within the administrative structure of Puerto Rico.

12. PIRI THOMAS

1. Familiar name for *Puerto Rican.*
2. It is really the *pitirre*, or small sparrow, that is capable of fighting against the *guaraguao*, a much bigger bird.

3. Roast pork and fried pork rinds—two delicacies of the Puerto Rican cuisine.

4. El Barrio is used here to signify Spanish Harlem.

5. "Hallelujah, glory be to God!"

6. A blessing. It's a long-established custom of rural Puerto Rico for parents to bless their children when they greet them and when they say goodbye.

7. A little gang.

8. Yes.

9. A rural neighborhood or a neighborhood in a big city; usually a slum.

10. The elders and the grandparents.

11. War!

12. Little Cubans.

13. John Oliver Killens (1916–1987) was an African-American writer, born in Georgia, who wrote several novels. He was also a playwright and a screenwriter.

14. Good-bye, my heart.

15. Period!

16. My little black one. *Negrito* and *negrita* are endearing terms in Puerto Rico.

17. The same old stuff.

18. The North: that's the way many Latin Americans refer to the United States.

19. A Puerto Rican.

20. Quietly; Patillas, Rincón, and Boquerón are small island towns.

21. Never.

22. Puerto Rican country music, often sung by rustic troubadours during Christmas time.

23. A Caribbean musical form that is enormously popular worldwide. It combines jazz rhythms with Latin beats.

24. Llorens Torres is the biggest housing project in Puerto Rico. The government built it in the fifties to house families from slum areas.

25. Why not?

26. Belly-button.

27. I am from the Barrio.

28. Long live a free Puerto Rico!

13. EDWIN TORRES

1. Another word for "Puerto Rican" that alludes to the Indian name for the island.

2. Old San Juan.

3. The Park of the Pigeons.

4. The beating.

5. A rogue or scoundrel, a type of character around whom a whole narrative genre sprang up in Spain during the fifteenth, sixteenth, and seventeenth centuries.

6. Puerto Rican, a familiar term.

14. ED VEGA

1. Abelardo Díaz Alfaro (1919–) is a short story and radio script writer who has also worked as a journalist and who is well-known for his nativist themes and style, especially for his book *Terrazo* (1947), where he emphasizes traditional Puerto Rican country values.

2. *Cuentos puertorriqueños de hoy*, René Marqués, ed. (San Juan: Editorial Cultural, 1959).

3. Viviana and Victoria Muñoz Mendoza are the daughters of Luis Muñoz Marín, Puerto Rico's first elected governor. Victoria (Melo) was a candidate for governor during the island's 1992 elections.

4. Luis Rafael Sánchez (Wico) and Ana Lydia Vega are two of the best-known contemporary Puerto Rican writers. They are often referred to as members of a group who started to publish during the seventies.

5. See note 6 to Chapter 1.

6. A very idiomatic word meaning an astute cunning that masquerades as ignorance or innocence.

CHRONOLOGY

A comparative chronology of important dates for the writers interviewed and of selected events in Puerto Rican, Latino, and mainstream writing in the United States.

	Writers Interviewed	**Other Writers and Events**
1922		—Claude McKay's *Harlem Shadows* (poetry) signals start of Harlem Renaissance.
1928	—Piri Thomas born in El Barrio (Spanish Harlem), New York City.	
1930		—Sinclair Lewis is the first U.S. writer to win the Nobel Prize for Literature.
1934	—Jack Agüeros born in El Barrio, New York City.	—Antonio S. Pedreira's essay identifying Puerto Rican culture with mainstream culture from Spain is published in Puerto Rico.
1935	—Nicholasa Mohr born in New York City.	
1936	—Ed Vega born in Ponce, Puerto Rico, moves with his family to New York in 1949.	

Writers Interviewed	Other Writers and Events
1937	—Luis Palés Matos's *Tuntún de pasa y grifería* (black poetry) is published in Puerto Rico.
1938	—Pearl S. Buck wins Nobel Prize for Literature.
1940	—Richard Wright's novel of African-American life in Chicago's South Side, *Native Son* was the first novel by an African American to become a Book of the Month Club Selection.
	—José I. de Diego Padró's novel *En Babia,* a lengthy, original work with many different styles and themes, is published in Puerto Rico. Its main story line deals with life in New York among Latinos.
1941	—Miguel Algarín born in Santurce, Puerto Rico, moves to New York in 1950.
1942	—Mexican-born María Christina Mena Chambers publishes one of the first "Chicano" novels: *The Water Carrier's Secret.*
1943	—Pedro Pietri born in Ponce, Puerto Rico, moves to New York in 1947.
1945	—Louis Reyes Rivera born in New York City.
	—Chilean poet Gabriela Mistral wins Nobel Prize for Literature.
	—Josephine Niggli's novel *Mexican Village* is a precursor of the new

Writers Interviewed	**Other Writers and Events**
	Chicano narrative. It includes folklore and legend while combining Spanish with English.
1947	—Luis Pérez's picaresque novel in English, *El Coyote,* about a deserter from the Mexican Revolution is published.
1948 —Sandra María Esteves born in the Bronx, New York.	—U.S.-born expatriate poet and essayist, T.S. Eliot, wins Nobel Prize for Literature.
—Esmeralda Santiago born in Santurce, Puerto Rico, moves to New York in 1961.	
1949 —Victor Hernández Cruz born in Aguas Buenas, Puerto Rico, moves to New York City in 1954.	—Southern novelist, William Faulkner, wins Nobel Prize for Literature.
1951 —Tato Laviera born in Santurce, Puerto Rico, moves to New York in 1960.	—J. D. Salinger's *The Catcher in the Rye* is published.
	—Guillermo Cotto Thorner's novel *Trópico en Manhattan* is published in Puerto Rico.
1952 —Judith Ortiz Cofer born in Hormigueros, Puerto Rico, moves to New Jersey in 1955.	—Ralph Ellison's novel, *Invisible Man*, wins National Book Award.
	—Ernest Hemingway's *The Old Man and the Sea* is published.
1953	—James Baldwin's *Go Tell It on the Mountain* is published.
	—Puerto Rican playwright René Marqués's drama, *The Ox-Cart,* about a migrant island family, is presented in New York and has a lasting impact.

Writers Interviewed	Other Writers and Events
1954	—U.S. novelist and short story writer, Ernest Hemingway, wins the Nobel Prize for Literature.
	—John Oliver Killens's *Youngblood* (novel) is published.
1955	—Cleofas M. Jaramillo establishes the New Mexican Folkloric Society.
1956	—Spanish poet Juan Ramón Jiménez, a resident of Puerto Rico, wins Nobel Prize for Literature.
	—Allen Ginsberg's *Howl and Other Poems* is published.
1957	—Jack Kerouac's *On the Road* (novel) is published.
	—*West Side Story,* a Leonard Bernstein/Steven Sondheim musical, opens on Broadway.
1958	—Final (fifth) volume of William Carlos Williams's long epic poem, *Paterson,* appears.
1959	—William Burroughs's *The Naked Lunch* is published.
	—José Antonio Villarreal publishes *Pocho,* considered the starting point of contemporary Chicano literature. It deals with the exodus to the United States after the Mexican Revolution.
1961	—Jesús Colón's *A Puerto Rican in New York and Other Sketches* is published in New York.	—Allen Ginsberg's *Kaddish and Other Poems* is published.
	—Abraham Rodríguez, Jr., born in the South Bronx.	—The film version of *West Side Story* (directed by

Writers Interviewed	**Other Writers and Events**
	Jerome Robbins and Robert Wise) wins an Oscar for Best Picture. Rita Moreno, a Puerto Rican, wins an Oscar for Best Supporting Actress.
	—Pedro Juan Soto, a Puerto Rican novelist who lived for a time in the United States, publishes *Ardiente suelo, fría estación* in Puerto Rico.
1962	—U.S. novelist John Steinbeck wins Nobel Prize for Literature.
	—*Guajana,* a highly politicized review of poetry associated with independence-minded and socialist students of the University of Puerto Rico, begins publication.
1964	—Amiri Baraka establishes Black Arts Repertory Theater School, which revolutionized black theater. It was an important starting point for the Black Arts movement.
	—Joseph Papp begins producing Shakespeare in Spanish.
1965	—*The Autobiography of Malcolm X as Told to Alex Haley* is published.
	—Claude Brown's *Manchild in a Promised Land* (novel) is published.
1966	—Victor Hernández Cruz's *Papo Got His Gun* (poetry).
	—Luis Rafael Sánchez's innovative collection of stories, *En cuerpo de camisa,* is published,

Writers Interviewed	Other Writers and Events
	inaugurating a new manner of using literary language in Puerto Rico.
1967 —Piri Thomas's *Down These Mean Streets*, a novelized memoir, is published in New York.	—Miguel Angel Asturias, from Guatemala, wins Nobel Prize for Literature.
	—Movement Poetry, a Chicano poetry movement with critical overtones and confrontational strategies which both affirms Latino identity and denounces discrimination, begins.
	—Miriam Colón establishes Puerto Rican Traveling Theater in New York City.
1968	—Eldridge Cleaver's *Soul on Ice* (novel) is published.
	—Puerto Rican singer José Feliciano's album *Feliciano!* reaches second place in the charts.
1969 —Victor Hernández Cruz's *Snaps* (poetry).	—Philip Roth's *Portnoy's Complaint* (novel) is published.
	—Raymond Barrio's novel *The Plum Plum Pickers,* described as the "Chicano *Grapes of Wrath*," is published.
	—Museo del Barrio is founded in East Harlem.
1970 —*Stuff: A Collection of Poems, Visions and Imaginative Happenings for Young Writers in Schools* edited by Victor Hernández Cruz (with Herbert Kohl).	
1971	—Chilean Pablo Neruda wins Nobel Prize for Literature.

Writers Interviewed	Other Writers and Events
	—Chicano Renaissance begins. The phrase is coined by Philip D. Ortego and applied to the new creative spirit that appeared in the sixties.
	—Alurista's *Floricanto en Aztlán* (poetry) is published. He incorporates an Aztec (Mexican) sensibility with Spanish and North American resonances, creating a mythic Southwest homeland called *Aztlán* and combining Spanish with English.
	—Rudolfo A. Anaya's *Bless Me, Ultima* (novel) is published.
1972 —Piri Thomas's *Savior, Savior, Hold My Hand* (autobiography).	
1973 —Victor Hernández Cruz's *Mainland* (poetry).	—*Revista Chicano-Riqueña* is founded. It is still published with the name *The Americas Review.*
—Nicholasa Mohr's *Nilda* (novel).	
—Pedro Pietri's *Puerto Rican Obituary* (poetry).	
1974 —Piri Thomas's *Seven Long Times* (a prison memoir).	—Puerto Rican Miguel Piñero's play, *Short Eyes,* is presented Off-Broadway. The prison drama wins an Obie Award, the New York Drama Critics Circle Award, and the Drama Desk Award.
1975 —Nicholasa Mohr's *El Bronx Remembered* (stories).	
—Edwin Torres's *Carlito's Way* (novel).	

Writers Interviewed	Other Writers and Events
—Miguel Algarín edited (with Miguel Piñero) *Nuyorican Poetry: An Anthology of Puerto Rican Words and Feelings.*	
—Nuyorican Poets Café first established by Miguel Algarín at East 6th St.	

1976	—Museo del Barrio (1976–1986) directed by Jack Agüeros.	—U.S. writer Saul Bellow wins Nobel Prize for Literature.
	—Miguel Algarín's translation of *Canción de Gesta,* a book of poetry by Pablo Neruda, as *Song of Protest.*	—Isabelle Ríos's (pseudonym for Diana López) *Victuum* is published. It is an innovative Chicano novel with a feminine perspective and incorporates elements of science fiction, *bildungsroman,* and psychology.
	—The anthology *Poets in Motion* edited by Louis Reyes Rivera.	
	—Victor Hernández Cruz's *"Tropicalization"* (poetry).	—Luis Rafael Sánchez's groundbreaking novel, *La Guaracha del Macho Camacho,* is published in Puerto Rico.
1977	—Nicholasa Mohr's *In Nueva York* (stories).	—Spanish poet Vicente Aleixandre wins Nobel Prize for Literature.
	—Louis Reyes Rivera's *Who Pays the Cost* (poetry).	
	—*Love, A Collection of Young Songs* edited by Louis Reyes Rivera.	
	—Edwin Torres's *Q & A* (novel) is published.	
	—*Memorias de Bernardo Vega* published in Puerto Rico. They are the memoirs of a Puerto Rican cigar factory worker who migrated to New York in 1918. It	

Writers Interviewed	Other Writers and Events

is subtitled "A Contribution to the Study of the New York Puerto Rican Community."

1978 —Miguel Algarín's *Mongo Affair* (poetry).

—U.S. writer Isaac B. Singer wins Nobel Prize for Literature.

—Piri Thomas's *Stories of El Barrio* (stories).

—Alex Haley's *Roots* becomes the basis for a TV mini series: *Roots: The Next Generation.*

—*Womanrise (6 Women Poets)* edited by Louis Reyes Rivera.

—Puerto Rican novelist Emilio Díaz Valcárcel publishes *Harlem todos los días* in Puerto Rico.

1979 —Nicholasa Mohr's *Felita* (novel) is published.

—Jimmy Santiago Baca, a Chicano poet, publishes *Immigrants in Our Own Land.*

—Edwin Torres's *After Hours* (novel) is published.

—Ana Castillo, a Chicana poet, publishes *The Invitation.*

—Tato Laviera's *La Carreta Made a U-Turn* (poetry) is published.

1980 —Miguel Algarín's *On Call* (poetry) is published.

—José Luis González publishes a controversial essay on Puerto Rican culture, *El país de cuatro pisos,* where he highlights the role of blacks in the country's development. He develops the thesis that blacks were the first to feel truly Puerto Rican.

—Judith Ortiz Cofer's *Latin Women Pray* (poetry) is published.

1981 —Sandra María Esteves's *Yerba Buena* (poetry) is published.

—Lorna Dee Cervantes's publishes *Emplumada,* (new Chicano poetry).

Writers Interviewed	Other Writers and Events
—Judith Ortiz Cofer's *Among the Ancestors* and *The Native Dancer* (poetry) is published.	—Ana Lydia Vega and Carmen Lugo Filippi publish "*Vírgenes y mártires*" (stories), initiating a "boom" in Puerto Rican women's writing.
—Pedro Pietri's *Lost in the Museum of Natural History* (narrative) is published.	
—Tato Laviera's *Enclave* (poetry) is published.	

1982 —Victor Hernández Cruz's *By Lingual Wholes* (poetry) is published.

—Miguel Algarín's *Body Bee Calling from the XXI Century* (poetry) is published.

—Colombian novelist Gabriel García Márquez wins Nobel Prize for Literature.

—Richard Rodríguez's *Hunger of Memory: The Education of Richard Rodríguez; An Autobiography* proves controversial because of his position on acculturation: to be Mexican in private and American in public.

1983 —Pedro Pietri's *Traffic Violations* (poetry) is published.

—Louis Reyes Rivera's *This One For You* (poetry) is published.

—Alice Walker wins Pulitzer Prize for *The Color Purple*.

—Ana Lydia Vega publishes *Encancaranublado,* a book of stories, in Puerto Rico.

1984 —Miguel Algarín's *Time's Now/ Ya es tiempo* (poetry) is published.

—Sandra María Esteves's *Tropical Rains: A Bilingual Downpour* (poetry) is published.

—Pedro Pietri's *The Masses Are Asses* (plays) is published.

—*Portraits of the Puerto Rican Experience* edited by Louis Reyes Rivera is published.

1985 —Nicholasa Mohr's *Rituals of Survival: A Woman's Portfolio* (stories) is published.

—Sandra Cisneros publishes *The House on Mango Street* (novel).

Writers Interviewed	Other Writers and Events
—Ed Vega's *The Comeback* (novel) is published.	
—Tato Laviera's *AmeRícan* (poetry) is published.	
1986 —Nicholasa Mohr's *Going Home* (novel) is published.	—Ana Castillo's *The Mixquiahuala Letters* wins Before Columbus Foundation American Book Award for Fiction.
—Judith Ortiz Cofer's *Peregrina* (poetry) is published.	—Rosario Ferré publishes *Maldito amor* (novel) in Puerto Rico.
	—Rosario Morales and Aurora Levins Morales published *Getting Home Alive* (narrative).
	—Magali García Ramis' publishes *Felices días, Tio Sergio* (novel) in Puerto Rico.
1987 —Judith Ortiz Cofer's *Reaching for the Mainland* and *Terms of Survival* (poetry) is published.	
—Ed Vega's *Mendoza's Dreams* (stories) is published.	
1988	—Cuban-American writer Oscar Hijuelos wins Pulitzer Prize for Fiction for *The Mambo Kings Play Songs of Love*.
1989 —Judith Ortiz Cofer's *The Line of the Sun* (novel) is published.	—Spanish novelist Camilo José Cela wins Nobel Prize for Literature.
—Victor Hernández Cruz's *Rhythm, Content and Flavor* (poetry) is published.	—Chicano poet Jimmy Santiago Baca publishes *Black Mesa Poems*.
—Victor Hernández Cruz's return to Puerto Rico.	—Puerto Rican Luz María Umpierre's *The Margarita Poems* are among the first Latino writings with a lesbian theme.

Writers Interviewed	Other Writers and Events
—Tato Laviera's *Mainstream Ethics* (poetry) is published.	
1990 —Sandra María Esteves's *Bluestown Mockingbird Mambo* (poetry) is published.	—Mexican poet and essayist Octavio Paz wins Nobel Prize for Literature.
—Judith Ortiz Cofer's *Silent Dancing: A Partial Remembrance of a Puerto Rican Childhood* (essays and poems) is published.	—Derek Walcott, a poet from the island of St. Lucia, in the Caribbean, publishes *Omeros* (epic poem).
	—Cuban-American Virgil Suárez publishes semiautobiographical novel, *The Cutter.*
1991 —Victor Hernández Cruz's *Red Beans* (poetry) is published.	—Dominican writer Julia Alvarez publishes *How the García Girls Lost Their Accents*.
—Jack Agüeros' *Correspondence Between the Stonehaulers* (poetry) is published.	
—Ed Vega's *Casualty Report* (stories) is published.	
1992 —Pedro Pietri's *Illusions of a Revolving Door* (plays) is published.	—Derek Walcott wins Nobel Prize for Literature.
—Abraham Rodríguez's *The Boy Without a Flag: Tales of the South Bronx* (stories) is published.	—Cuban-American writer Christina Garcia's *Dreaming in Cuban* (novel) is published.
1993 —Jack Agüeros' *Dominoes and Other Stories* (stories) is published.	—Toni Morrison wins Nobel Prize for Literature.
—Nicholasa Mohr's *All for the Better: A Story of El Barrio* (biography) is published.	
—Judith Ortíz Cofer's *The Latin Deli* (prose and poetry) is published.	
—Abraham Rodríguez's *Spidertown* (novel) is published.	

Writers Interviewed	Other Writers and Events
—Esmeralda Santiago's *When I Was Puerto Rican* (memoir) is published.	
1994 —Nicholasa Mohr's *In My Own Words: Growing Up Inside the Sanctuary of My Imagination* (autobiography) is published.	
—*Aloud: Voices from the Nuyorican Poets Café* (anthology) edited by Miguel Algarín with Bob Holman is published.	
1995 —Nicholasa Mohr's *The Magic Shell* (children's story) is published.	—Puerto Rican Rosario Ferré's novel, *The House on the Lagoon,* published in English in the United States, is finalist for the National Book Award.
—Nicholasa Mohr's *The Song of El Coquí* (children's story) is published simultaneously in Spanish and English editions.	
—Judith Ortiz Cofer's *An Island Like You: Stories of the Barrio* (stories) is published.	
1996 —Louis Reyes Rivera's *Scattered Scripture* (poetry) is published.	—Jamaica Kincaid publishes *Autobiography of My Mother.*
—Esmeralda Santiago's *America's Dream* (novel) is published.	
—*Paper Dance: 55 Latino Poets* edited by Victor Hernández Cruz with Virgil Suárez and Leroy Quintana is published.	
—Nicholasa Mohr's *Old Letivia and the Mountain of Sorrows* is published simultaneously in English and in Spanish as *La vieja Letivia y el Monte de los pesares.*	

ADDITIONAL BIBLIOGRAPHY

Each writer's bibliography is found in the introduction to his or her interview. Besides the books and articles mentioned throughout the text and in the notes, the following have proved useful.

Acosta-Belen, Edna. "The Literature of the Puerto Rican Minority in the United States." *The Bilingual Review/ La Revista Bilingue* 5, No. 1–2 (1978): 107–116.

Alegria, Fernando, and Jorge Ruffinelli, eds. *Paradise Lost or Gained: The Literature of Hispanic Exile*. Houston: Arte Público Press, 1990.

Ashcroft, Bill, et al., eds. *The Empire Writes Back: Theory and Practice in Post-Colonial Literatures*. New York: Routledge, 1989.

Barradas, Efraín. "De lejos en sueños verla . . . Visión mítica de Puerto Rico en la poesía neorrican." *Revista Chicano-Riquena* 7, No. 4 (1979): 45–56.

Cortina, Rodolfo J., and Alberto Moncada, eds. *Hispanos en los Estados Unidos*. Madrid: Ediciones de Cultura Hispánica, 1988.

Diaz Quiñones, Arcadio. *La memoria rota*. San Juan: Ediciones Huracán, 1993.

Diaz-Stevens, Ana María. *Oxcart Catholicism on Fifth Ave: The Impact of the Puerto Rican Migration upon the Archdiocese of New York*. South Bend, Ind.: University of Notre Dame Press, 1993.

Fabre, Genvieve, ed. *European Perspectives on Hispanic Literature of the United States*. Houston: Arte Público Press, 1988.

Fernandez Olmos, Margarite. *Sobre la literatura puertorriqueña de aquí y de allá. Aproximaciones feministas*. Author's edition: printed in the Dominican Republic, 1989.

Fitzpatrick, Joseph P. *Puerto Rican Americans: The Meaning of Migration to the Mainland.* 2nd ed. Englewood Cliffs, N.J.: Prentice-Hall, 1971.

Flores, Juan. *Divided Borders: Essays on Puerto Rican Identity.* Houston: Arte Público Press, 1993.

Fox, Geoffrey. *Hispanic Nation: Culture, Politics and the Construction of Identity.* Secaucus, N.J.: Birch Lane Press, 1996.

Horno-Delgado, Asuncion, et al., eds. *Breaking Boundaries. Latina Writings and Critical Readings.* Amherst: University of Massachusetts Press, 1989.

Jackson, Kenneth T., ed. *The Encyclopedia of New York City.* New Haven, Conn.: Yale University Press, 1995.

Kanellos, Nicolás. *The Hispanic Almanac: From Columbus to Corporate America.* Detroit: Visible Ink Press, 1994.

Kanellos, Nicolás, and Claudio Esteva-Fabregat, general eds. *Handbook of Hispanic Cultures in the United States.* I. Anthropology; II History; III Literature and Art; IV Sociology. Houston: Arte Público Press and Instituto de Cooperación Iberoamericana, 1994.

Mohr, Eugene. *The Nuyorican Experience: Literature of the Puerto Rican Minority.* Westport, Conn.: Greenwood Press, 1982.

Negron-Muntaner, Frances, ed. *Shouting in a Whisper/ Los limites del silencio. Latino Poetry in Philadelphia. An Anthology/ Poesía latina en Filadelfia. Una antología.* Santiago de Chile: Asterion, 1994.

Novas, Himilce. *The Hispanic 100.* New York: Citadel Press, 1995.

Rodríguez, Camille, and Ramón Bosque-Pérez, eds. *Puerto Ricans and Higher Education Policies. Vol. I. Issues of Scholarship, Fiscal Policies and Admissions.* New York: Centro de Estudios Puertorriqueños, Hunter College, 1994.

Rodríguez, Clara E. *Puerto Ricans Born in the U.S.A.* Boulder, Col.: Westview Press, 1991.

Rodríguez de Laguna, Asela, ed. *Images and Identities. The Puerto Rican in Two World Contexts.* New Brunswick, NJ.: Transaction Books, 1987.

Said, Edward. *Culture and Imperialism.* New York: Alfred A. Knopf, 1993.

Sanchez Korrol, Virginia E. *From Colonia to Community; The History of Puerto Ricans in New York City.* Berkeley: University of California Press, 1983.

Seidel, Michael. *Exile and the Narrative Imagination.* New Haven, Conn.: Yale University Press, 1986.

Smith, Sidonie, and Julie Watson, eds. *De/Colonizing the Subject: The Politics of Gender in Women's Autobiography.* Minneapolis: University of Minnesota Press, 1992.

Sowell, Thomas. *Migrations and Cultures: A World View.* New York: HarperCollins, 1996.

Stavans, Ilan. *The Hispanic Condition: Reflections on Culture and Identity in America.* New York: HarperCollins, 1995.

Torre, Carlos Antonio, ed. *The Commuter Nation.* Rio Piedras: University of Puerto Rico Press, 1994.

Villanueva, Tino, ed. *Chicanos: Antología histórica y literaria.* México: Fondo de Cultura Económica, 1980.

Wagenheim, Kal, and Olga Jiménez de Wagenheim, eds. *The Puerto Ricans: A Documentary History.* Princeton, n.g.: Markus Wiener Publishers, 1994.

Williams, Eric. *From Columbus to Castro: The History of the Caribbean.* New York: Vintage, 1984.

INDEX

Interviews of featured writers designated by boldfaced page numbers.

About the Author

CARMEN DOLORES HERNÁNDEZ is a literary critic for *El Nuevo Día*, San Juan's largest newspaper. She earned a Ph.D. in Spanish Literature from the University of Puerto Rico, where she has taught. She is author of two books in Spanish.